The New Oxford Picture Dictionary contextually illustrates over 2,400 words. The book is a unique language learning tool for students of English. It provides students with a glance at American lifestyle, as well as a compendium of useful vocabulary.

The *Dictionary* is organised thematically, beginning with topics that are most useful for the "survival" needs of students in an English-speaking country. However, pages may be used at random, depending on the students' particular needs. The book need not be taught in order.

The New Oxford Picture Dictionary contextualizes vocabulary whenever possible. Verbs have been included on separate pages, but within a topic area where they are most likely to occur. However, this does not imply that these verbs only appear within these contexts.

Articles are shown only with irregular nouns. Regional variations of the primary translation are listed following a slash (/). A complete index with pronunciation guide in English is in the Appendix.

For further ideas on using *The New Oxford Picture Dictionary,* see the *Listening and Speaking Activity Book,* the *Teacher's Guide* and the two workbooks: *Beginner's* and *Intermediate* levels. Also available in the program are a complete set of *Cassettes,* offering a reading of all of the words in the *Dictionary,* and sets of *Wall Charts,* available in one complete package or in three smaller packages. All of these items are available in English only.

Этот Новый Оксфордский иллюстрированный словарь контекстуально иллюстрирует более 2400 слов. Книга является уникальным учебником для студентов, изучающих английский язык, и предоставляет возможность студентам познакомиться с американским стилем жизни и в то же время дает краткий словарь широко употребляемых слов.

Словарь разделен на темы, начиная со слов наиболее необходимых для повседневной жизни в стране английского языка. Темы становятся более обобщенными по своему содержанию и могут быть использованы в школах Соединенных Штатов. Студенты могут не следовать данному в книге порядку, а избирать темы в зависимости от индивидуальных потребностей.

Слова, данные в этом учебнике, наиболее необходимы для студентов, нуждающихся в изучении основы английского языка. Наиболее распространенные названия предметов в этой книге были избраны по их простоте в употреблении. Различные местные вариации слов приведены в учебном справочнике для этой определенной страницы.

Этот Новый Оксфордский иллюстрированный словарь поясняет слова, где только возможно, рисунками, таким образом облегчает процесс изучения языка. Глаголы, приведенные на страницах, разбиты по темам, где они могут встретиться чаще всего. Однако, это не значит, что эти глаголы применяются только в данных ситуациях.

Полный индекс с указанием произношения слов приведен в приложении. Для дальнейшего пользования Новым Оксфордским иллюстрированным словарем смотрите Учебник-путеводитель или два других учебника для начального и среднего уровней.

Также в этой программе имеется полная коллекция магнитофонных кассет, предлагающая слушателям произношение слов, включенных в этот словарь, и картотека из 40 слов и соответствующих иллюстраций на 80 карточках с инструкцией и идеями для многочисленных игр, а также коллекция плакатов с соответствующими рисунками из этой книги. Эту коллекцию можно приобрести в одном пакете или в трех меньшего размера.

Contents
Оглавление

	Page
People and Relationships Человек и семейные отношения	2
The Family Семья	3
The Human Body Человеческое тело	4–5
Vegetables Овощи	6–7
Fruits Фрукты	8–9
Meat, Poultry, and Seafood Мясо, домашняя птица и морские продукты	10–11
Containers, Quantities, and Money Упаковки, количества и деньги	12–13
The Supermarket Гастроном	14–15
Family Restaurant and Cocktail Lounge Ресторан и бар	16
Restaurant Verbs Глаголы, употребляемые в ресторане	17
Common Prepared Foods Основные готовые продукты	18
Outdoor Clothes Зимняя одежда	19
Everyday Clothes Одежда	20–21
Underwear and Sleepwear Нижнее белье	22
Jewelry and Cosmetics Ювелирные изделия и косметика	23
Describing Clothes Описание одежды	24
Describing the Weather Прилагательные, описывающие погоду	25
Seasonal Verbs Глаголы, употребляемые в соответствии с временем года	26
Houses Частные дома	27
The Living Room Гостиная	28
The Dining Room Столовая	29
The Kitchen Кухня	30
Kitchen Verbs Глаголы, употребляемые в кухне	31
The Bedroom Спальня	32
The Baby's Room Детская комната	33
The Bathroom Ванная	34
The Utility Room Подсобное помещение	35
A Workshop Мастерская	36–37
Housework and Repair Verbs Глаголы, относящиеся к домашней работе и к ремонту	38
Medical and Dental Care Медицинское и зубоврачебное обслуживание	39
Ailments and Injuries Болезни и (телесные) повреждения	40
Treatments and Remedies Лечения и лекарства	41
Firefighting and Rescue Пожар и спасение при пожаре	42
Crime and Punishment Преступность и наказание	43
The City Город	44–45
The U.S. Postal System Почта Соединенных Штатов	46
The Public Library Библиотека	47
The Armed Forces Вооруженные силы	48
Trucks Грузовики	49
Cars Автомобили	50–51
Bikes Велосипеды	52
Highway Travel На шоссе	53
Public Transportation Городской транспорт	54–55
Air Travel Воздушный транспорт	56
Aircraft Самолеты	57

Оглавление

	Page
In Port В порту	58
Pleasure Boating Лодочный спорт	59
Plants and Trees Растения и деревья	60–61
Simple Animals Простые животные	62
Insects Насекомые	63
Birds Птицы	64
Fish and Reptiles Рыбы и пресмыкающиеся	65
Mammals I Млекопитающие 1	66–67
Mammals II Млекопитающие 2	68–69
Map of the World Карта мира	70–71
The United States of America Соединенные Штаты Америки	72–73
The Universe Вселенная	74
The Space Program Открытие Космоса	75
A Classroom В классе	76
School Verbs Глаголы, употребляемые в школе	77
A Science Lab Научная Лаборатория	78
Math Математика	79
Energy Энергия	80
Farming and Ranching Сельское хозяйство	81
Construction Строительство	82
An Office Контора	83
Occupations I: Main Street USA Городские профессии 1	84
Occupations II Профессии 2	85
Occupations III Профессии 3	86
Neighborhood Parks Городские парки	87
Outdoor Activities Отдых на открытом воздухе	88–89
At the Beach На пляже	90–91
Team Sports Спортивные соревнования между командами	92
Ballfields Спортивные поля	93
Individual Sports Индивидуальные спортивные игры	94
Fields and Courses Поля и площадки	95
Sports Verbs Глаголы, относящиеся к спорту	96–97
Musical Instruments Музыкальные инструменты	98
Music, Dance, and Theater Музыка, балет и театр	99
Electronics and Photography Электроника и фотография	100
Handicrafts Ремесла	101
Prepositions of Description Предлоги описания	102
Prepositions of Motion Предлоги движения	103
Appendix Приложение	104
Index Индекс	105

Человек и семейные отношения

женщина	**1.** woman
мужчина	**2.** man
муж	**3.** husband
жена	**4.** wife
ребенок, младенец	**5.** baby
родители	**6.** parents
дети	**7.** children
мальчик	**8.** boy
девочка	**9.** girl
дедушка и бабушка	**10.** grandparents
внучка	**11.** granddaughter
внук	**12.** grandson

Семья Мэри Смит	**Mary Smith's Family**
бабушка	**1.** grandmother
дедушка	**2.** grandfather
дядя	**3.** uncle
мать	**4.** mother
отец	**5.** father
тетя	**6.** aunt
воюродн(-ая) сестра, (-ый) брат	**7.** cousin
невестка	**8.** sister-in-law
брат	**9.** brother
сестра	**10.** sister
зять	**11.** brother-in-law
муж	**12.** husband
племянник	**13.** nephew
племянница	**14.** niece
дочь	**15.** daughter
сын	**16.** son

The Human Body

Человеческое тело

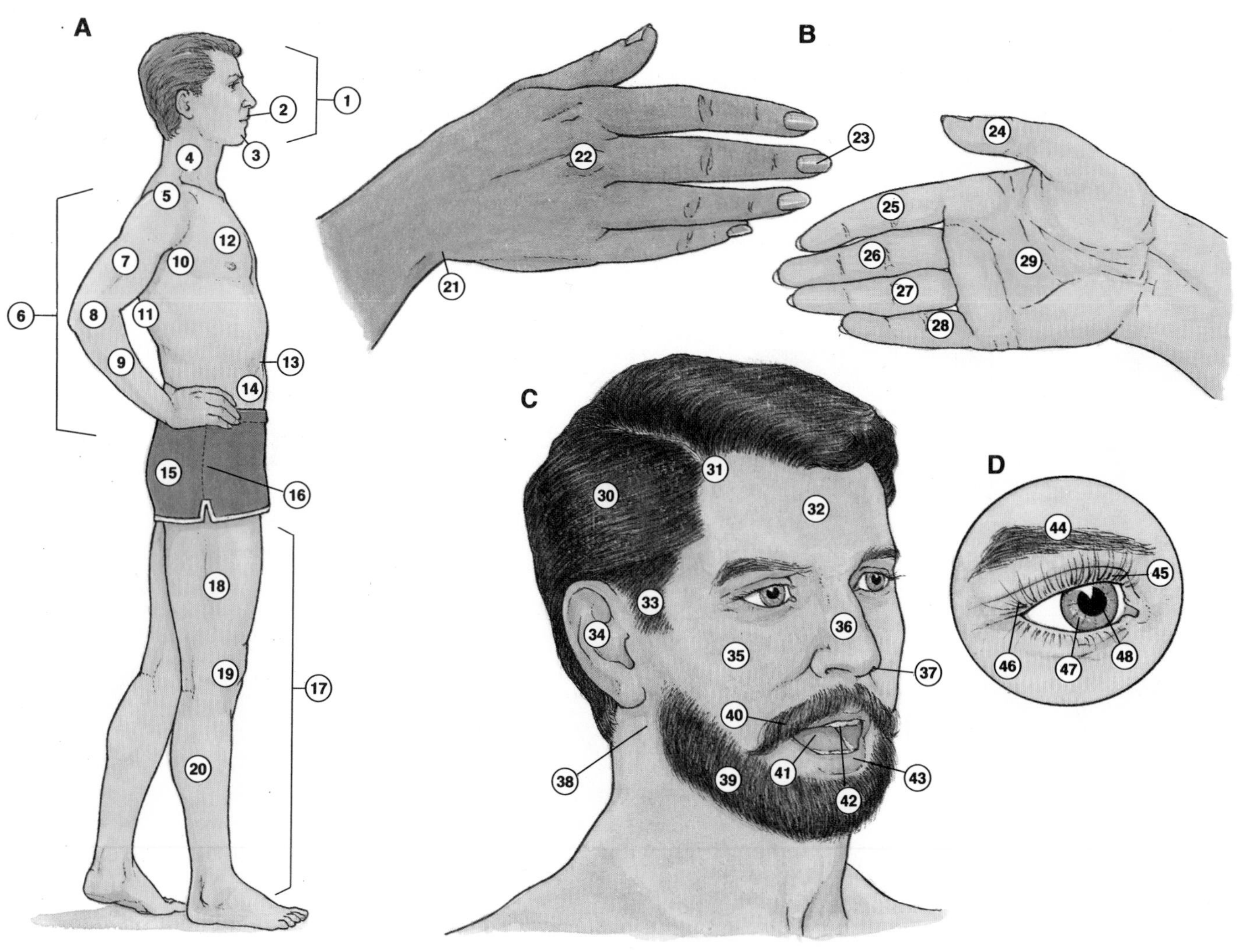

Тело	**A. The Body**
лицо	**1.** face
рот	**2.** mouth
подбородок	**3.** chin
шея	**4.** neck
плечо	**5.** shoulder
рука	**6.** arm
верхняя часть руки	**7.** upper arm
локоть	**8.** elbow
предплечье	**9.** forearm
подмышка	**10.** armpit
спина	**11.** back
грудь	**12.** chest
талия	**13.** waist
брюшная полость, живот	**14.** abdomen
ягодицы	**15.** buttocks
бедро	**16.** hip
нога	**17.** leg
бедро, ляжка	**18.** thigh
колено	**19.** knee
икра	**20.** calf

Рука	**B. The Hand**
запястье	**21.** wrist
сустав пальца	**22.** knuckle
ноготь	**23.** fingernail
большой палец	**24.** thumb
указательный палец	**25.** (index) finger
средний палец	**26.** middle finger
безымянный палец	**27.** ring finger
мизинец	**28.** little finger
ладонь	**29.** palm

Голова	**C. The Head**
волосы	**30.** hair
пробор	**31.** part
лоб	**32.** forehead
бакенбарды	**33.** sideburn
ухо	**34.** ear
щека	**35.** cheek
нос	**36.** nose
ноздря	**37.** nostril
челюсть	**38.** jaw
борода	**39.** beard
усы	**40.** mustache
язык	**41.** tongue
зуб	**42.** tooth
губа	**43.** lip

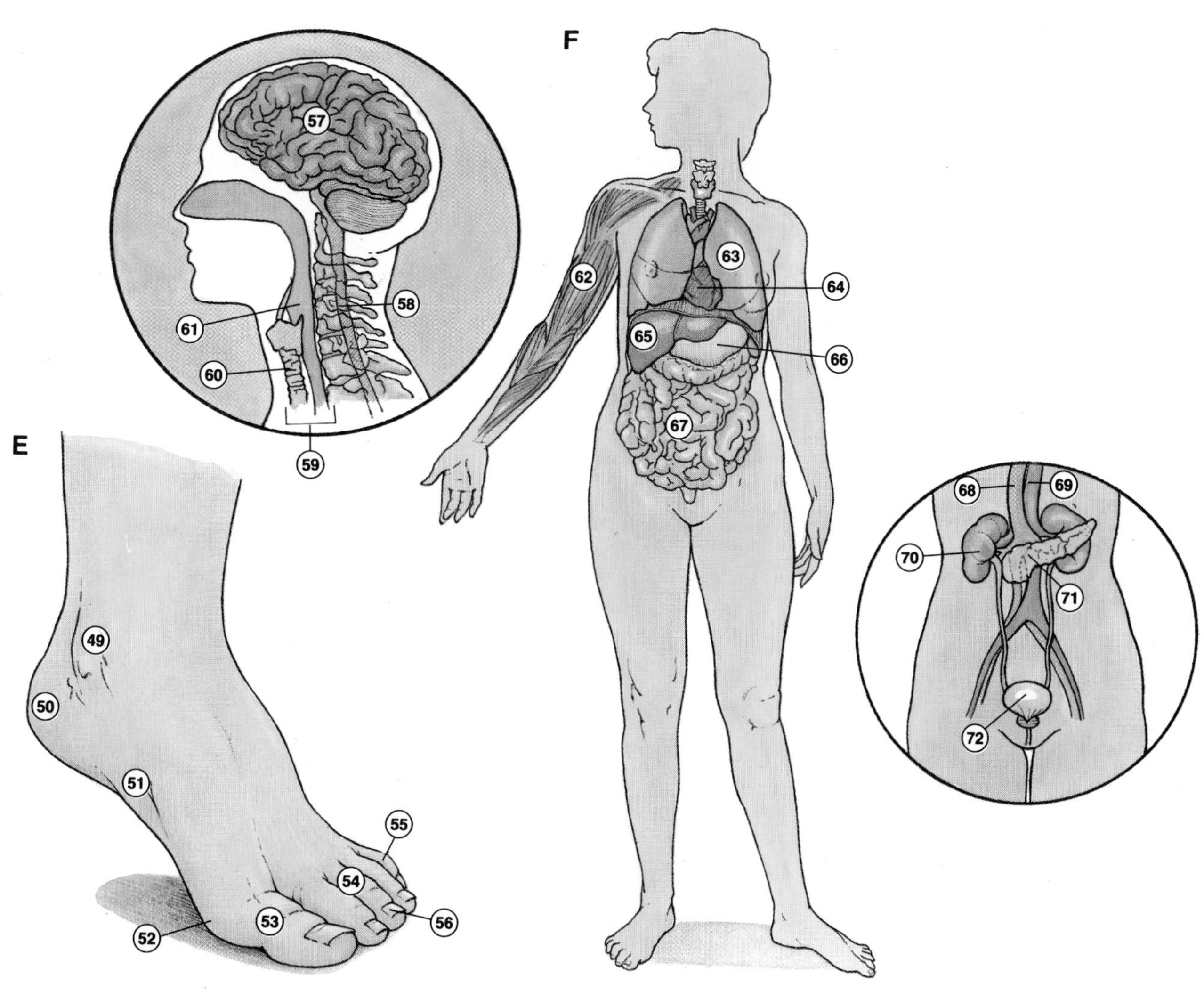

Глаз	D.	The Eye
бровь	44.	eyebrow
веко	45.	eyelid
ресницы	46.	eyelashes
радужная оболочка	47.	iris
зрачок	48.	pupil

Нога	E.	The Foot
лодыжка	49.	ankle
пятка	50.	heel
подьем	51.	instep
подушечка	52.	ball
большой палец	53.	big toe
палец	54.	toe
мизинец	55.	little toe
ноготь	56.	toenail

Внутренние органы	F.	The Internal Organs
мозг	57.	brain
спинной мозг	58.	spinal cord
горло	59.	throat
дыхательная трахея	60.	windpipe
пищевод	61.	esophagus
мускул	62.	muscle
легкое	63.	lung
сердце	64.	heart
печень	65.	liver
желудок	66.	stomach
кишечник	67.	intestines
вена	68.	vein
артерия	69..	artery
почка	70.	kidney
поджелудочная железа	71.	pancreas
мочевой пузырь	72.	bladder

Vegetables

Овощи

(кочан) цветной капусты	**1.** (head of) cauliflower
брокколи	**2.** broccoli
капуста	**3.** cabbage
брюссельская капуста	**4.** brussels sprouts
крес водяной (жеруха)	**5.** watercress
салат, латук	**6.** lettuce
зскароль (салат)	**7.** escarole
шпинат	**8.** spinach
травы (кулинарные)	**9.** herb(s)
сельдерей	**10.** celery
артишо́к	**11.** artichoke
початок кукурузы	**12.** (ear of) corn
кочерыжка кукурузного початка	**a.** cob
фасоль обыкновенная	**13.** kidney bean(s)
черные бобы	**14.** black bean(s)
стручковая фасоль	**15.** string bean(s)
лимская фасоль	**16.** lima bean(s)
горох	**17.** pea(s)
стручок	**a.** pod
спаржа	**18.** asparagus

помидор(-ы)	**19.** tomato(es)	кабачок «цуккини»	**27.** zucchini
огурец	**20.** cucumber(s)	желудевая тыква	**28.** acorn squash
баклажан	**21.** eggplant	редиска	**29.** radish(es)
перец	**22.** pepper(s)	грибы	**30.** mushroom(s)
картофель	**23.** potato(es)	лук	**31.** onion(s)
ямс, батат	**24.** yam	морковь	**32.** carrot(s)
чеснок	**25.** garlic	свекла	**33.** beet(s)
зубок чесночной головки	**a.** clove	репа	**34.** turnip
тыква	**26.** pumpkin		

Fruits

Фрукты

кисть винограда	**1.** (a bunch of) grapes
яблоко	**2.** apple
черешок	**a.** stem
сердцевина	**b.** core
кокосовый орех	**3.** coconut
ананас	**4.** pineapple
манго	**5.** mango
папая	**6.** papaya
Цитрусовые фрукты	**Citrus Fruits**
грейпфрут	**7.** grapefruit
апельсин	**8.** orange
долька	**a.** section
кожура	**b.** rind
зернышко	**c.** seed
лимон	**9.** lemon
лайм	**10.** lime
Ягоды	**Berries**
крыжовник	**11.** gooseberries
ежевика	**12.** blackberries
клюква	**13.** cranberries
черника	**14.** blueberries
клубника	**15.** strawberry
малина	**16.** raspberries
нектарин	**17.** nectarine
груша	**18.** pear

вишня **19.** cherries
кисть бананов **20.** (a bunch of) bananas
кожура **a.** peel

Сушеные фрукты **Dried Fruits**
инжир **21.** fig
чернослив **22.** prune
финик **23.** date
изюм **24.** raisin(s)

абрикос **25.** apricot
арбуз **26.** watermelon

Орехи **Nuts**
орех кешью **27.** cashew(s)
арахис **28.** peanut(s)
грецкий(-е) орех(-и) **29.** walnut(s)
лесной орех **30.** hazelnut(s)
миндаль **31.** almond(s)
каштан **32.** chestnut(s)

авокадо **33.** avocado
слива **34.** plum
дыня **35.** honeydew melon
дыня **36.** cantaloupe
персик **37.** peach
кожура, кожица **a.** pit
косточка **b.** skin

Мясо, домашняя птица и морские продукты

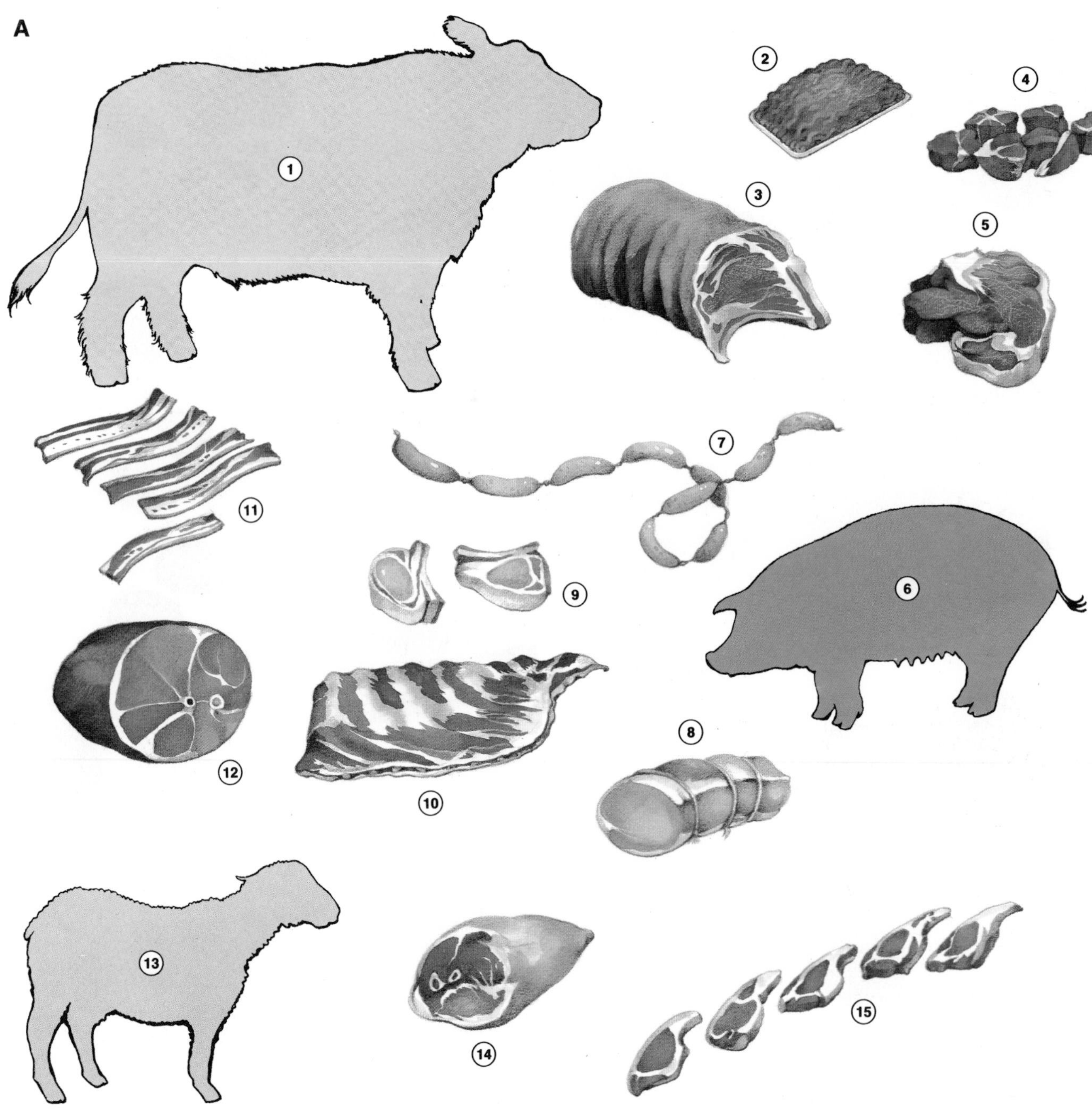

Мясо	**A. Meat**	кусок свинины для жаренья	**8.** roast
говядина	**1.** beef	свиные отбивные	**9.** chops
фарш говяжий	**2.** ground beef	ребра	**10.** spare ribs
кусок говядины для жаренья	**3.** roast	бекон, грудинка	**11.** bacon
мясо для тушения	**4.** stewing meat	ветчина	**12.** ham
кусок мяса для жаренья	**5.** steak	баранина	**13.** lamb
свинина	**6.** pork	нога баранья	**14.** leg
колбаса	**7.** sausage	бараньи отбивные	**15.** chops

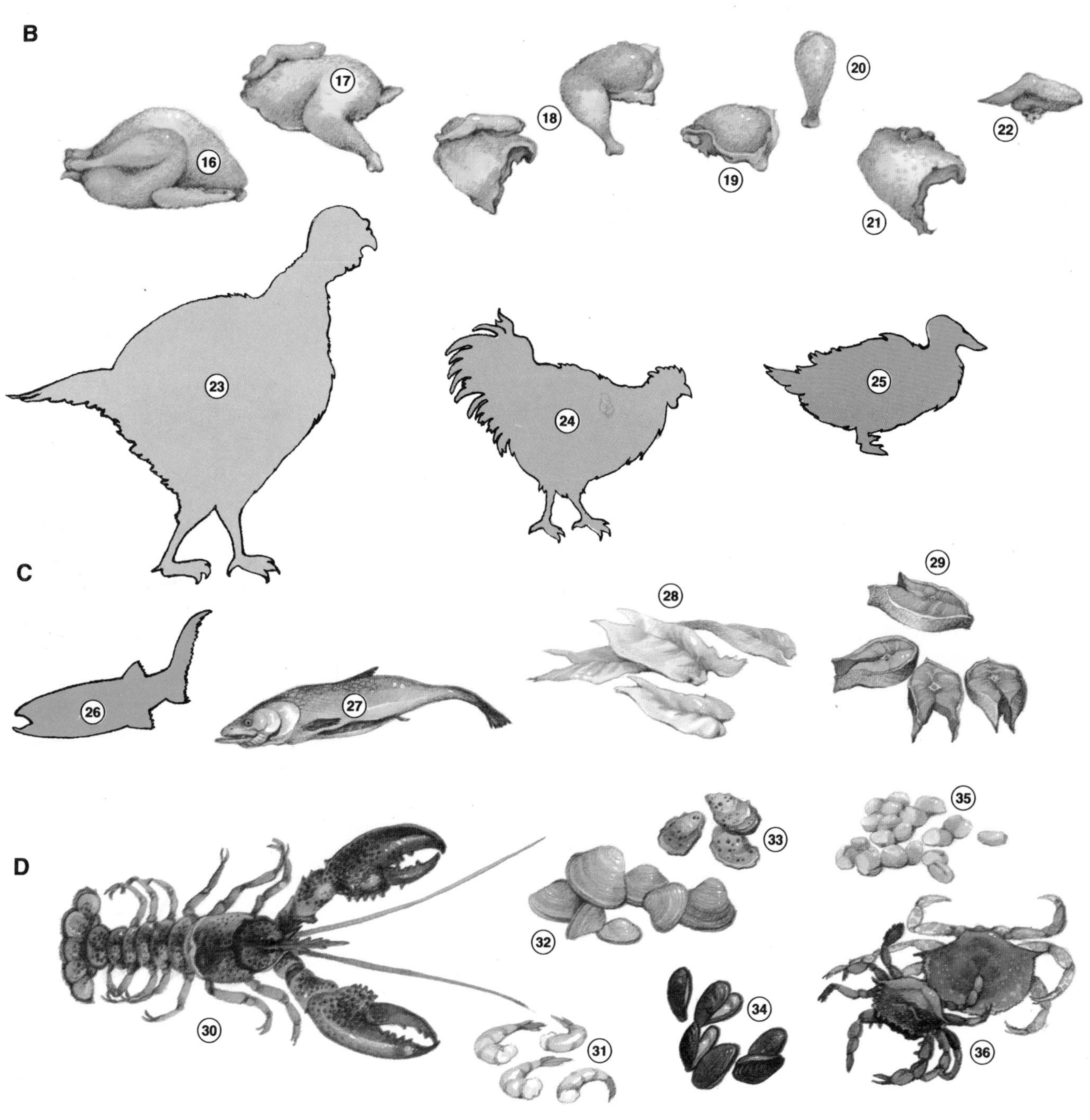

Домашняя птица	**B. Poultry**
целая (курица)	**16.** whole (chicken)
половина (курицы)	**17.** split
четверть (курицы)	**18.** quarter
бедро (курицы)	**19.** thigh
нога (курицы)	**20.** leg
грудь (курицы)	**21.** breast
крыло (курицы)	**22.** wing
индюк	**23.** turkey
курица	**24.** chicken
утка	**25.** duck
Морские продукты	**C. Seafood**
рыба	**26.** fish
целая рыба	**27.** whole
филе	**28.** filet
кусок рыбы для жаренья	**29.** steak
Моллюски	**D. Shellfish**
омар	**30.** lobster
креветка	**31.** shrimp
съедобный морской моллюск	**32.** clam(s)
устрица (-ы)	**33.** oyster(s)
моллюск (-и)	**34.** mussel(s)
гребешок (-шки)	**35.** scallop(s)
краб (-ы)	**36.** crab(s)

Упаковки, количества и деньги

картонная коробка	**1.** carton	батон, буханка, пакет (хлеба)	**7.** loaf
баночка	**2.** container	пакет	**8.** bag
бутылка	**3.** bottle	банка (обычно стеклянная)	**9.** jar
пачка	**4.** package	банка (металлическая)	**10.** can
пачка (масла)	**5.** stick	рулон	**11.** roll
банка	**6.** tub		

коробка (картонная) **12.** box
пакет (шести банок) **13.** six-pack
обик с насосом (зубной пасты, жидкого мыла) **14.** pump
тюбик (зубной пасты) **15.** tube
пачка, пакет **16.** pack
книжечка **17.** book
плитка, кусок **18.** bar
чашка **19.** cup
стакан **20.** glass
кусок **21.** slice
кусок **22.** piece

глубокая тарелка **23.** bowl
пульверизаторная банка **24.** spray can

Деньги **Money**
долларовые купюры **25.** dollar bills
монеты **26.** coins
цент **27.** penny
пять центов **28.** nickel
десять центов **29.** dime
двадцать пять центов **30.** quarter

14 The Supermarket

Гастроном

кулинарно-гастрономический отдел **1.** deli counter
свежезамороженные продукты **2.** frozen foods
морозильник **3.** freezer
молочные продукты **4.** dairy products
молоко **5.** milk
полка **6.** shelf
весы **7.** scale

корзина **8.** shopping basket
овощи и фрукты **9.** produce
проход **10.** aisle
печеные продукты **11.** baked goods
хлеб **12.** bread
консервы **13.** canned goods
напитки **14.** beverages

предметы домашнего обихода	**15.** household items
ларь	**16.** bin
покупатель(-ница)	**17.** customer
легкие закуски	**18.** snacks
тележка	**19.** shopping cart
счет	**20.** receipt
касса	**21.** cash register
кассирша	**22.** cashier
конвейерная лента	**23.** conveyor belt
бакалея	**24.** groceries
кулек (бумажный)	**25.** bag
касса	**26.** checkout counter
чек	**27.** check

Ресторан и бар

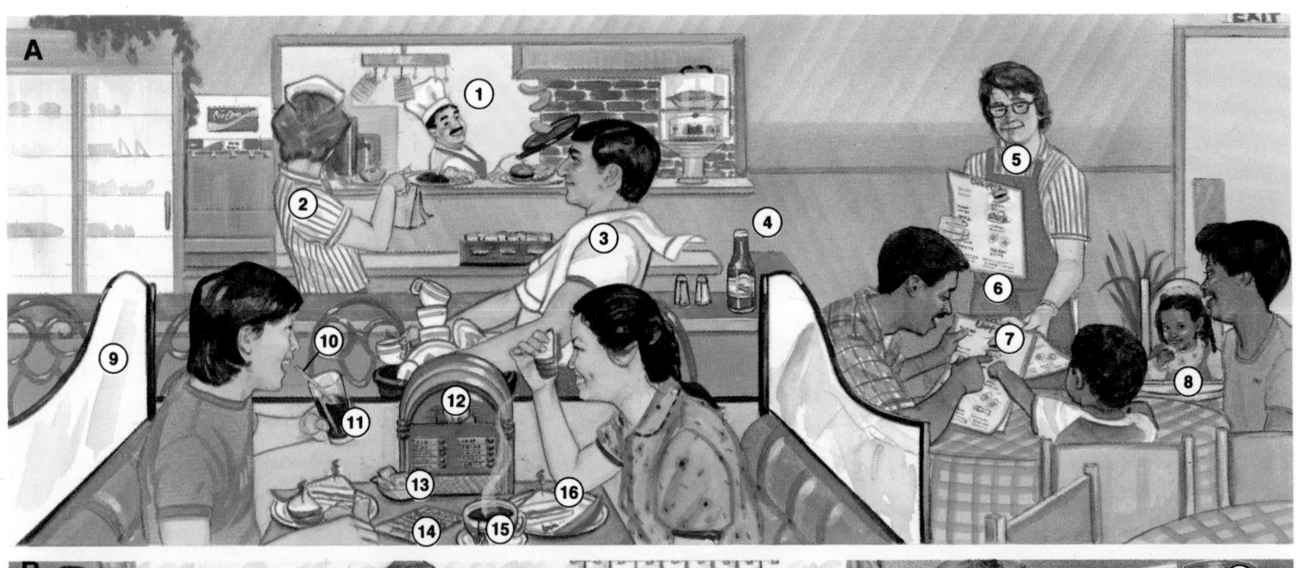

Ресторан	**A.**	**Family Restaurant**
повар	**1.**	cook
официантка	**2.**	waitress
младший официант	**3.**	busboy
кетчуп	**4.**	ketchup
официант	**5.**	waiter
фартук	**6.**	apron
меню	**7.**	menu
детский стул	**8.**	high chair
стол за перегородкой	**9.**	booth
соломинка	**10.**	straw
безалкогольный напиток	**11.**	soft drink
музыкальный автомат	**12.**	jukebox
сахар (в бумажном пакете)	**13.**	sugar (packet)
счет	**14.**	check
чай	**15.**	tea
бутерброд	**16.**	sandwich

Бар	**B.**	**Cocktail Lounge**
штопор	**17.**	corkscrew
пробка	**18.**	cork
вино	**19.**	wine
кран	**20.**	tap
бармен	**21.**	bartender
спиртной напиток (в бутылке)	**22.**	liquor (bottle)
пиво	**23.**	beer
прилавок, стойка	**24.**	bar
табурет у прилавка	**25.**	bar stool
трубка	**26.**	pipe
подставка	**27.**	coaster
(книжечка) спичек	**28.**	(book of) matches
пепельница	**29.**	ashtray
зажигалка	**30.**	lighter
сигарета	**31.**	cigarette
официантка	**32.**	cocktail waitress
поднос	**33.**	tray

Глаголы, употребляемые в ресторане

есть	**1.** eat
пить	**2.** drink
подавать	**3.** serve
готовить, варить	**4.** cook
заказывать	**5.** order
убирать (посуду со стола)	**6.** clear
платить	**7.** pay
накрывать (на стол)	**8.** set (the table)
давать	**9.** give
принимать, брать	**10.** take
намазывать	**11.** spread
держать	**12.** hold
зажигать	**13.** light
обжигаться	**14.** burn

Common Prepared Foods

Основные готовые продукты

горчица	**1. mustard**	печеная картошка	**20. baked potato**
«хот дог» (булочка с сосиской)	**2. hot dog**	бифштекс	**21. steak**
бобы в томатном соусе	**3. baked beans**	печенье	**22. cookie**
«чипсы» (жареная хрустящая картошка)	**4. potato chips**	мороженое с фруктами, сиропом и орехами	**23. sundae**
блины	**5. pancakes**	«тако» (жареная кукурузная лепешка с рубленым мясом и овощами)	**24. taco**
сироп	**6. syrup**	«эгг рол» (китайский блин, фаршированный мясом и овощами)	**25. egg roll**
булочка	**7. bun**	слоеный торт с клубникой	**26. strawberry shortcake**
соленый огурец	**8. pickle**	сухое печенье	**27. biscuit**
«гамбургер» (булочка с бифштексом)	**9. hamburger**	картофель жареный (соломка)	**28. french fries**
макароны	**10. spaghetti**	жареная курица	**29. fried chicken**
фрикадельки	**11. meatballs**	пицца	**30. pizza**
заправка к салату	**12. salad dressing**	желе	**31. jelly**
овощной салат	**13. tossed salad**	яичница (глазунья)	**32. (sunnyside-up) egg**
жаркое (из говядины)	**14. beef stew**	бекон	**33. bacon**
свиные отбивные	**15. pork chops**	гренки, тост	**34. toast**
овощной гарнир	**16. mixed vegetables**	кофе	**35. coffee**
картофельное пюре	**17. mashed potatoes**	мороженое в вафельном стаканчике	**36. ice cream cone**
масло	**18. butter**		
булочка	**19. roll**		

Outdoor Clothe

Зимняя одежд

перчатки	1. gloves
кепка	2. cap
фланелевая рубашка	3. flannel shirt
рюкзак	4. backpack
непромокаемая куртка	5. windbreaker
джинсы	6. (blue) jeans
свитер	7. (crewneck) sweater
куртка с капюшоном	8. parka
ботинки	9. hiking boots
наушники	10. earmuffs
рукавицы, варежки	11. mittens
стеганый жилет	12. down vest
свитер с высоким воротом	13. (turtleneck) sweater
колготки	14. tights
коньки	15. ice skates
вязаная шапка	16. ski cap
куртка	17. jacket
шляпа	18. hat
шарф	19. scarf
пальто	20. overcoat
сапоги	21. boots
берет	22. beret
свитер	23. (V-neck) sweater
зимний жакет	24. coat
резиновые сапоги	25. rain boots

Одежда

отворот	1. lapel
пиджак	2. blazer
пуговица	3. button
брюки	4. slacks
каблук	5. heel
подметка	6. sole
шнурок	7. shoelace
спортивный свитер	8. sweatshirt
бумажник	9. wallet
спортивные брюки	10. sweatpants
кроссовки	11. sneakers
повязка для головы	12. sweatband
майка	13. tank top
шорты	14. shorts
длинный рукав	15. long sleeve
пояс	16. belt
пряжка	17. buckle
сумка для покупок	18. shopping bag
босоножки	19. sandal
воротник	20. collar
короткий рукав	21. short sleeve
платье	22. dress
кошелек	23. purse
зонт	24. umbrella
туфли на высоких каблуках	25. (high) heels

шерстяная кофта	**26.** cardigan
вельветовые брюки	**27.** (corduroy) pants
шлем	**28.** hard hat
футболка, майка	**29.** T-shirt
комбинезон (рабочий)	**30.** overalls
сумка для завтрака, обеда	**31.** lunch box
рабочие ботинки	**32.** (construction) boots
жакет	**33.** jacket
блузка	**34.** blouse
сумка	**35.** (shoulder) bag
юбка	**36.** skirt
портфель	**37.** briefcase
плащ, дождевик	**38.** raincoat
жилет	**39.** vest
мужской костюм с жилетом	**40.** three-piece suit
карман	**41.** pocket
кожаный ботинок типа мокасина	**42.** loafer
фуражка	**43.** cap
очки	**44.** glasses
форма	**45.** uniform
рубашка	**46.** shirt
галстук	**47.** tie
газета	**48.** newspaper
туфля	**49.** shoe

22 Underwear and Sleepwear

Ннжнее белье

майка	**1.** undershirt
мужские трусы	**2.** boxer shorts
трусы	**3.** underpants
суспензорий	**4.** athletic supporter
колготки	**5.** pantyhose
чулки	**6.** stockings
кальсоны	**7.** long johns
нижняя юбка	**8.** half slip
нижняя рубашка	**9.** camisole
комбинация	**10.** full slip
трусики-бикини	**11.** (bikini) panties
трусики	**12.** briefs
бюстгальтер, лифчик	**13.** bra(ssiere)
пояс для чулок	**14.** garter belt
резиновый пояс	**15.** girdle
гольфы	**16.** knee socks
носки	**17.** socks
тапочки	**18.** slippers
пижама	**19.** pajamas
купальный халат	**20.** bathrobe
ночная сорочка	**21.** nightgown

Ювелирные изделия	**A. Jewelry**
серьги	**1.** earrings
кольцо(-а)	**2.** ring(s)
кольцо невесты	**3.** engagement ring
обручальное кольцо	**4.** wedding ring
цепочка	**5.** chain
ожерелье	**6.** necklace
бусы	**7.** (strand of) beads
брошь	**8.** pin
браслет	**9.** bracelet
часы	**10.** watch
ремешок для часов	**11.** watchband
запонки	**12.** cuff links
булавка для галстука	**13.** tie pin
зажим для галстука	**14.** tie clip
клипсы	**15.** clip-on earring
серьга	**16.** pierced earring
застежка	**17.** clasp
серьги на стержне, стержень	**18.** post
зажим	**19.** back

Принадлежности туалета и косметика	**B. Toiletries and Makeup**
бритва	**20.** razor
лосьон после бритья	**21.** after-shave lotion
крем для бритья	**22.** shaving cream
лезвия для бритья	**23.** razor blades
пилочка (для ногтей)	**24.** emery board
лак для ногтей	**25.** nail polish
карандаш для бровей	**26.** eyebrow pencil
духи	**27.** perfume
тушь для ресниц	**28.** mascara
губная помада	**29.** lipstick
тени для век	**30.** eye shadow
ножницы для ногтей	**31.** nail clippers
румяна	**32.** blush
тени, карандаш	**33.** eyeliner

Describing Clothes
Описание одежды

короткий	1.	short
длинный	2.	long
тесный	3.	tight
широкий	4.	loose
грязный	5.	dirty
чистый	6.	clean
маленький	7.	small
большой	8.	big
светлый	9.	light
темный	10.	dark
высокий	11.	high
низкий	12.	low
новый	13.	new
старый	14.	old
открытый	15.	open
закрытый	16.	closed
полосатый	17.	striped
клетчатый	18.	checked
в горошек	19.	polka dot
однотонная (ткань)	20.	solid
узор	21.	print
клетка	22.	plaid

Прилагательные, описывающие погоду

дождливый	**1.** rainy
облачный	**2.** cloudy
снежный	**3.** snowy
солнечный	**4.** sunny
термометр	**5.** thermometer
температура	**6.** temperature
жаркий	**7.** hot
теплый	**8.** warm
прохладный	**9.** cool
холодный	**10.** cold
морозный	**11.** freezing
туманный	**12.** foggy
ветреный	**13.** windy
сухой	**14.** dry
мокрый, мокрая (дорога)	**15.** wet
ледяной, ледяная (дорога)	**16.** icy

Seasonal Verbs

Глаголы, употребляемые в соответствии с временем года

Весна	Spring	Лето	Summer	Осень	Fall	Зима	Winter
красить	1. paint	поливать	5. water	наполнять	9. fill	сгребать (снег)	13. shovel
мыть	2. clean	косить	6. mow	сгребать, загребать	10. rake	посыпать песком	14. sand
копать	3. dig	рвать (цветы)	7. pick	рубить	11. chop	скоблить, скрести	15. scrape
сажать	4. plant	подрезать	8. trim	двигать	12. push	носить	16. carry

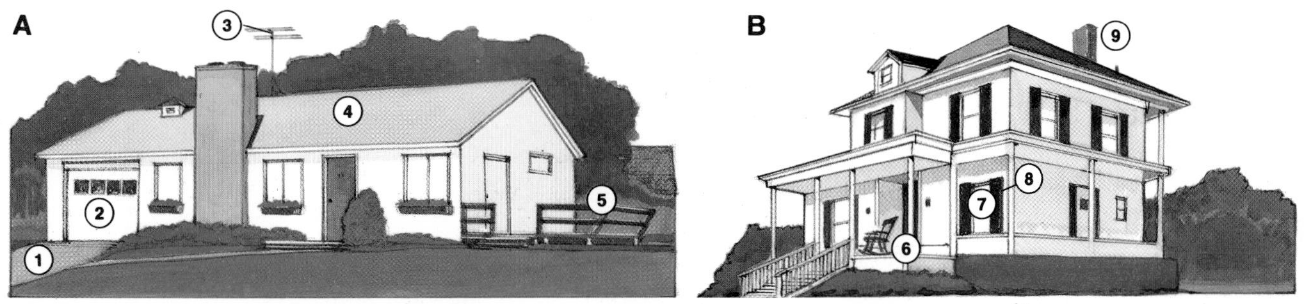

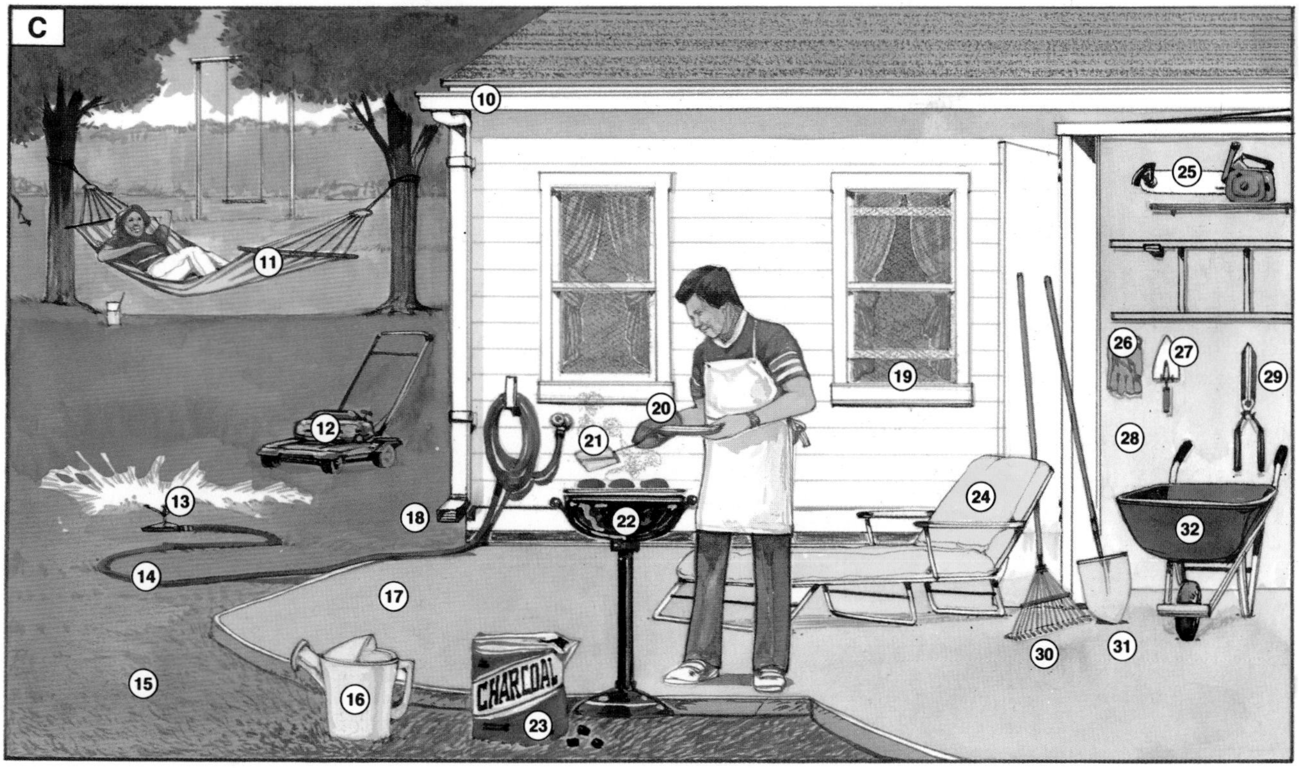

Одноэтажный дом	**A. Ranch House**
подъездная аллея	1. driveway
гараж	2. garage
телевизионная антенна	3. TV antenna
крыша	4. roof
веранда	5. deck
Двухэтажный дом «колониального» стиля	**B. Colonial-style House**
крыльцо	6. porch
окно	7. window
ставень	8. shutter
труба (дымовая)	9. chimney
Двор	**C. The Backyard**
водосточный желоб	10. gutter
гамак	11. hammock
косилка (для травы)	12. lawn mower
ороситель (для поливки газона)	13. sprinkler
шланг	14. garden hose

трава	15. grass
лейка	16. watering can
веранда	17. patio
дренажная труба, водосток	18. drainpipe
сетка	19. screen
рукавица	20. mitt
лопатка	21. spatula
гриль	22. grill
брикеты угля	23. charcoal briquettes
шезлонг	24. lounge chair
электрическая пила	25. power saw
рабочие перчатки	26. work gloves
садовый совок	27. trowel
сарай для инструментов	28. toolshed
садовые ножницы	29. hedge clippers
грабли	30. rake
лопата	31. shovel
тачка	32. wheelbarrow

Гостиная

вентилятор **1.** ceiling fan
потолок **2.** ceiling
стена **3.** wall
рама (для картины) **4.** frame
картина **5.** painting
ваза **6.** vase
каминная полка **7.** mantel
камин **8.** fireplace
огонь **9.** fire
бревно **10.** log
перила **11.** banister
лестница **12.** staircase
ступень **13.** step
письменный стол **14.** desk
ковер **15.** wall-to-wall carpeting

кресло с откидно
дистанционное уп
стереофоническа
громког
книж
диванн
коф
угл

Столовая

- посуда **1.** china
- посудный шкаф **2.** china closet
- люстра **3.** chandelier
- кувшин **4.** pitcher
- рюмка, бокал, фужер для вина **5.** wine glass
- стакан (для воды) **6.** water glass
- стол **7.** table
- ложка **8.** spoon
- перечница **9.** pepper shaker
- солонка **10.** salt shaker
- тарелка для хлеба **11.** bread and butter plate
- вилка **12.** fork
- тарелка **13.** plate
- салфетка **14.** napkin
- нож **15.** knife
- скатерть **16.** tablecloth
- стул **17.** chair
- кофейник **18.** coffeepot
- чайник **19.** teapot
- чашка **20.** cup
- блюдце **21.** saucer
- столовое серебро **22.** silverware
- сахарница **23.** sugar bowl
- кувшинчик для сливок **24.** creamer
- салатница **25.** salad bowl
- пламя **26.** flame
- свеча **27.** candle
- подсвечник **28.** candlestick
- буфет **29.** buffet

The Kitchen

Кухня

посудомоечная машина	**1.** dishwasher
сушилка	**2.** dish drainer
пароварка	**3.** steamer
консервный нож	**4.** can opener
сковорода	**5.** frying pan
нож для открывания бутылок	**6.** bottle opener
дуршлаг	**7.** colander
кастрюля (с ручкой)	**8.** saucepan
крышка	**9.** lid
жидкое мыло (для посуды)	**10.** dishwashing liquid
мочалка	**11.** scouring pad
миксер, смеситель	**12.** blender
кастрюля	**13.** pot
сотейник	**14.** casserole dish
банка	**15.** canister
тостер	**16.** toaster
форма (для запекания мяса)	**17.** roasting pan
посудное полотенце	**18.** dish towel
холодильник	**19.** refrigerator
морозильник	**20.** freezer
форма для льда	**21.** ice tray
шкафчик	**22.** cabinet
микроволновая духовка	**23.** microwave oven
миска	**24.** mixing bowl
скалка	**25.** rolling pin
доска	**26.** cutting board
кухонный стол	**27.** counter
чайник	**28.** teakettle
конфорка	**29.** burner
газовая (электрическая) плита	**30.** stove
кофейник	**31.** coffeemaker
духовка	**32.** oven
бройлер (нижняя часть плиты)	**33.** broiler
рукавица, прихватка	**34.** pot holder

Глаголы, употребляемые в кухне

мешать **1.** stir
тереть **2.** grate
открывать **3.** open
наливать **4.** pour
снимать (кожицу) **5.** peel
нарезать **6.** carve
разбивать **7.** break
взбивать **8.** beat

разрезать, резать **9.** cut
шинковать **10.** slice
крошить, рубить **11.** chop
варить на пару **12.** steam
жарить на открытом огне **13.** broil
печь **14.** bake
жарить **15.** fry
кипятить (воду), варить **16.** boil

Спальня

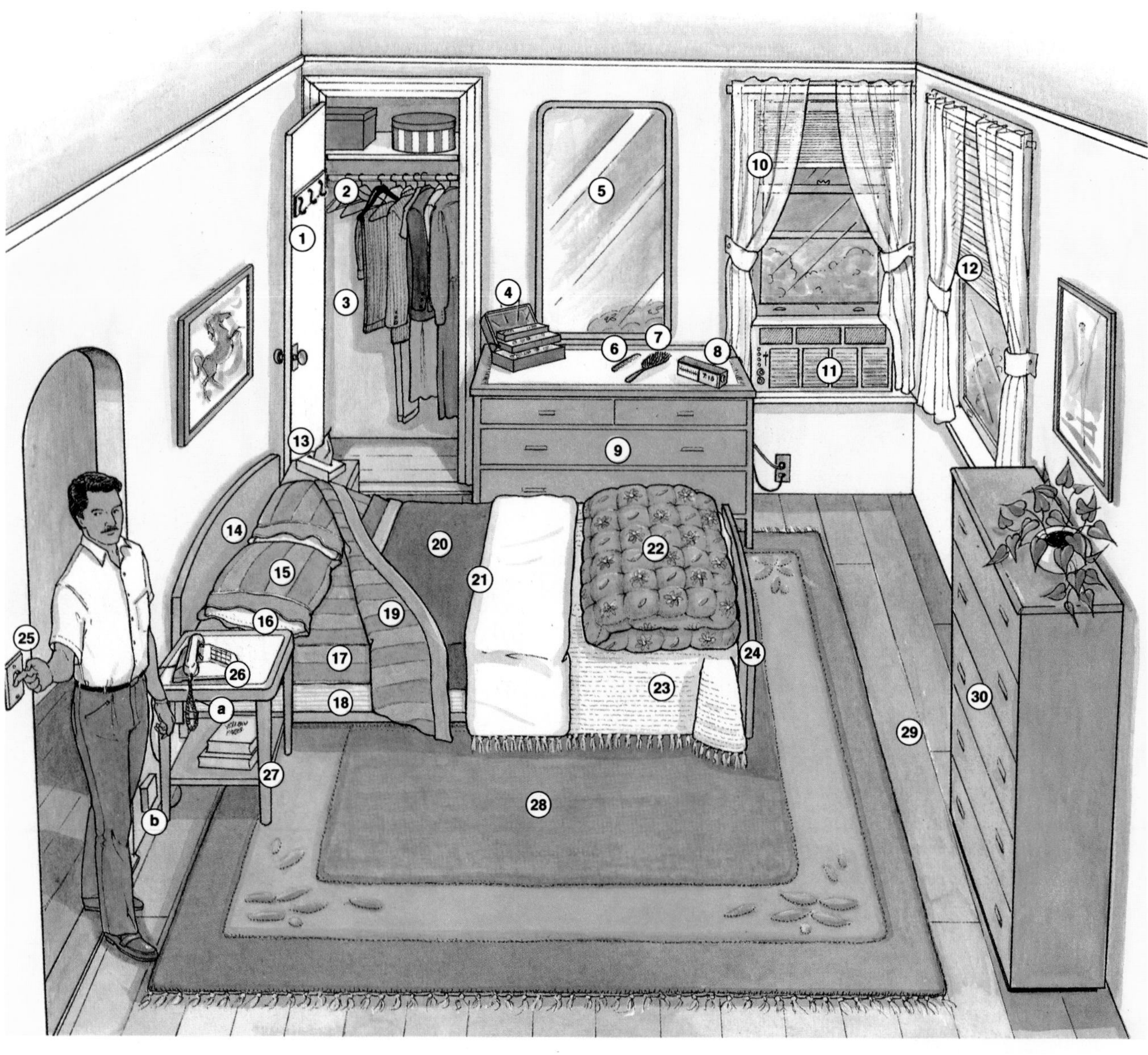

крючок	**1.** hook
вешалка	**2.** hanger
шкаф (стенной)	**3.** closet
шкатулка для драгоценностей	**4.** jewelry box
зеркало	**5.** mirror
расческа, гребенка	**6.** comb
щетка для волос	**7.** hairbrush
будильник	**8.** alarm clock
комод, туалет	**9.** bureau
занавес	**10.** curtain
кондиционер	**11.** air conditioner
шторы	**12.** blinds
косметические салфетки	**13.** tissues
передняя спинка	**14.** headboard
наволочка	**15.** pillowcase
подушка	**16.** pillow
матрац	**17.** mattress
пружинный матрац	**18.** box spring
простыня	**19.** (flat) sheet
одеяло	**20.** blanket
постель, кровать	**21.** bed
стеганое одеяло	**22.** comforter
постельное покрывало	**23.** bedspread
задняя спинка	**24.** footboard
включатель	**25.** light switch
телефон	**26.** phone
шнур	**a.** cord
розетка	**b.** jack
тумбочка	**27.** night table
ковер	**28.** rug
пол	**29.** floor
комод	**30.** chest of drawers

штора	**1.**	shade
подвесная карусель с игрушками	**2.**	mobile
мишка	**3.**	teddy bear
детская кроватка	**4.**	crib
предохранительная загородка	**5.**	bumper
детский лосьон	**6.**	baby lotion
тальк	**7.**	baby powder
детские салфетки	**8.**	baby wipes
стол для пеленания	**9.**	changing table
палочки с ватой	**10.**	cotton swab
булавка	**11.**	safety pin
пеленка одноразового пользования	**12.**	disposable diaper
пеленка	**13.**	cloth diaper
складная коляска	**14.**	stroller
устройство для сигнала при пожаре	**15.**	smoke detector
кресло-качалка	**16.**	rocking chair
бутылка (для кормления ребенка)	**17.**	bottle
соска для бутылки	**18.**	nipple
детский комбинезон	**19.**	stretchie
нагрудник	**20.**	bib
погремушка	**21.**	rattle
пустышка	**22.**	pacifier
ходунок	**23.**	walker
детские качели	**24.**	swing
кукольный домик	**25.**	doll house
колыбель	**26.**	cradle
мягкая игрушка	**27.**	stuffed animal
кукла	**28.**	doll
сундук для игрушек	**29.**	toy chest
детский манеж	**30.**	playpen
головоломка (игра)	**31.**	puzzle
кубик	**32.**	block
детский горшок	**33.**	potty

Ванная

карниз	1.	curtain rod
крючки для занавески	2.	curtain rings
шапочка для душа	3.	shower cap
душ	4.	shower head
занавеска	5.	shower curtain
мыльница	6.	soap dish
мочалка, губка	7.	sponge
шампунь	8.	shampoo
сток	9.	drain
пробка	10.	stopper
ванна	11.	bathtub
коврик	12.	bath mat
корзина для мусора	13.	wastepaper basket
аптечка	14.	medicine chest
мыло	15.	soap
зубная паста	16.	toothpaste
кран горячей воды	17.	hot water faucet
кран холодной воды	18.	cold water faucet
умывальная раковина	19.	sink
щеточка для ногтей	20.	nailbrush
зубная щетка	21.	toothbrush
тряпочка для мытья тела	22.	washcloth
ручное полотенце	23.	hand towel
ванное (-ая) полотенце (простыня)	24.	bath towel
вешалка для полотенец	25.	towel rack
ручной фен	26.	hair dryer
кафельная плитка	27.	tile
корзина для грязного белья	28.	hamper
унитаз	29.	toilet
туалетная бумага	30.	toilet paper
туалетная щетка	31.	toilet brush
весы	32.	scale

Подсобное помещение

стремянка, лестница	**1.** stepladder
метелка из перьев	**2.** feather duster
фонарь	**3.** flashlight
тряпки	**4.** rags
автоматический прерыватель	**5.** circuit breaker
швабра с губкой	**6.** (sponge) mop
метла	**7.** broom
совок для мусора	**8.** dustpan
чистящее средство	**9.** cleanser
раствор для мытья окон	**10.** window cleaner
запасная губка к швабре	**11.** (mop) refill
утюг	**12.** iron
гладильная доска	**13.** ironing board
плунжер, вантуз	**14.** plunger
ведро	**15.** bucket
пылесос	**16.** vacuum cleaner
приспособления к пылесосу	**17.** attachments

водопровод	**18.** pipe
бельевая веревка	**19.** clothesline
прищепки	**20.** clothespins
крахмал	**21.** spray starch
лампочка	**22.** lightbulb
бумажные полотенца	**23.** paper towels
машина для сушки белья	**24.** dryer
стиральный порошок	**25.** laundry detergent
отбеливатель	**26.** bleach
смягчитель для белья	**27.** fabric softener
грязное белье	**28.** laundry
корзина для белья	**29.** laundry basket
стиральная машина	**30.** washing machine
мусорная корзина	**31.** garbage can
мышеловка	**32.** mousetrap

Мастерская

складная линейка	**1.**	carpenter's rule
зажим	**2.**	C-clamp
механический лобзик	**3.**	jigsaw
древесина	**4.**	wood
удлинительный шнур	**5.**	extension cord
розетка	**6.**	outlet
заземлительный штепсель	**7.**	grounding plug
ручная пила	**8.**	saw
тиски	**9.**	brace
гаечный ключ	**10.**	wrench
резиновый молоток	**11.**	mallet
разводной ключ	**12.**	monkey wrench
молоток	**13.**	hammer
скрепер	**14.**	scraper
подвесная доска с крючками	**15.**	pegboard
крючок	**16.**	hook
топор	**17.**	hatchet
ножовка (для металла)	**18.**	hacksaw
плоскогубцы	**19.**	pliers
дисковая пила	**20.**	circular saw
рулетка	**21.**	tape measure
верстак	**22.**	workbench
ящик для инструментов	**23.**	toolbox

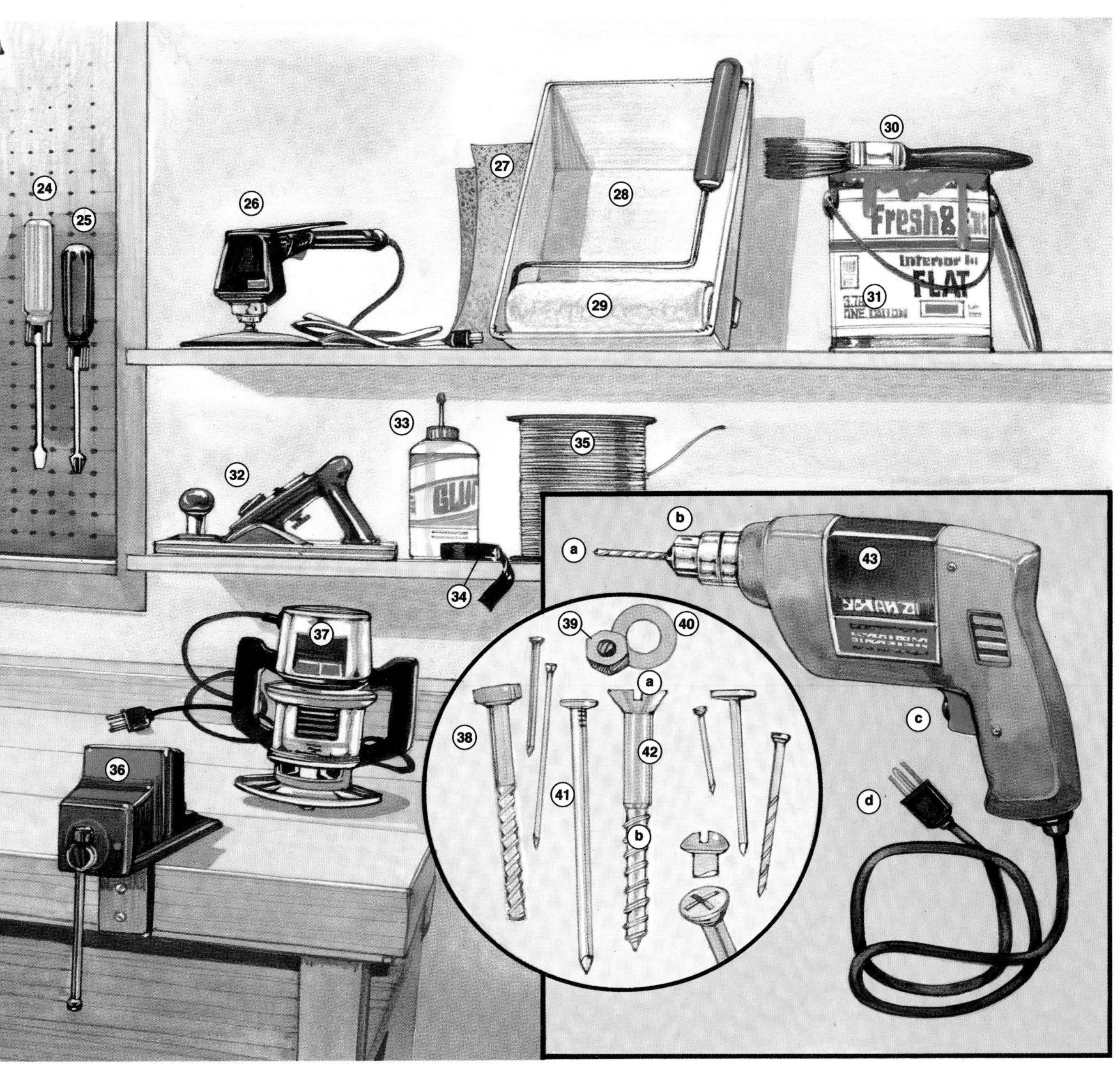

отвертка	**24.** screwdriver
отвертка для винта с крестовым шлипцом	**25.** Phillips screwdriver
шлифовальный станок	**26.** power sander
наждачная бумага	**27.** sandpaper
корыто для краски	**28.** pan
малярный ролик	**29.** roller
кисть	**30.** paintbrush
краска	**31.** paint
рубанок	**32.** wood plane
клей	**33.** glue
изоляционная лента	**34.** electrical tape
проволока	**35.** wire
слесарные тиски	**36.** vise
фрезерный станок	**37.** router
болт	**38.** bolt
гайка	**39.** nut
шайба	**40.** washer
гвоздь	**41.** nail
винт	**42.** screw
головка	**a.** head
резьба	**b.** thread
электрическая дрель	**43.** electric drill
сверло	**a.** bit
ствол	**b.** shank
включатель	**c.** switch
штепсельная вилка	**d.** plug

Housework and Repair Verbs

Глаголы, относящиеся к домашней работе и к ремонту

складывать	**1.** fold		вытирать	**9.** dry
чистить	**2.** scrub		ремонтировать	**10.** repair
полировать, шлифовать	**3.** polish		гладить	**11.** iron
затягивать	**4.** tighten		смазывать	**12.** oil
вытирать	**5.** wipe		менять постель	**13.** change (the sheets)
вешать	**6.** hang		пылесосить	**14.** vacuum
мести	**7.** sweep		вытирать (пыль)	**15.** dust
стелить (постель)	**8.** make (the bed)		стирать	**16.** wash

Медицинское и зубоврачебное обслуживание

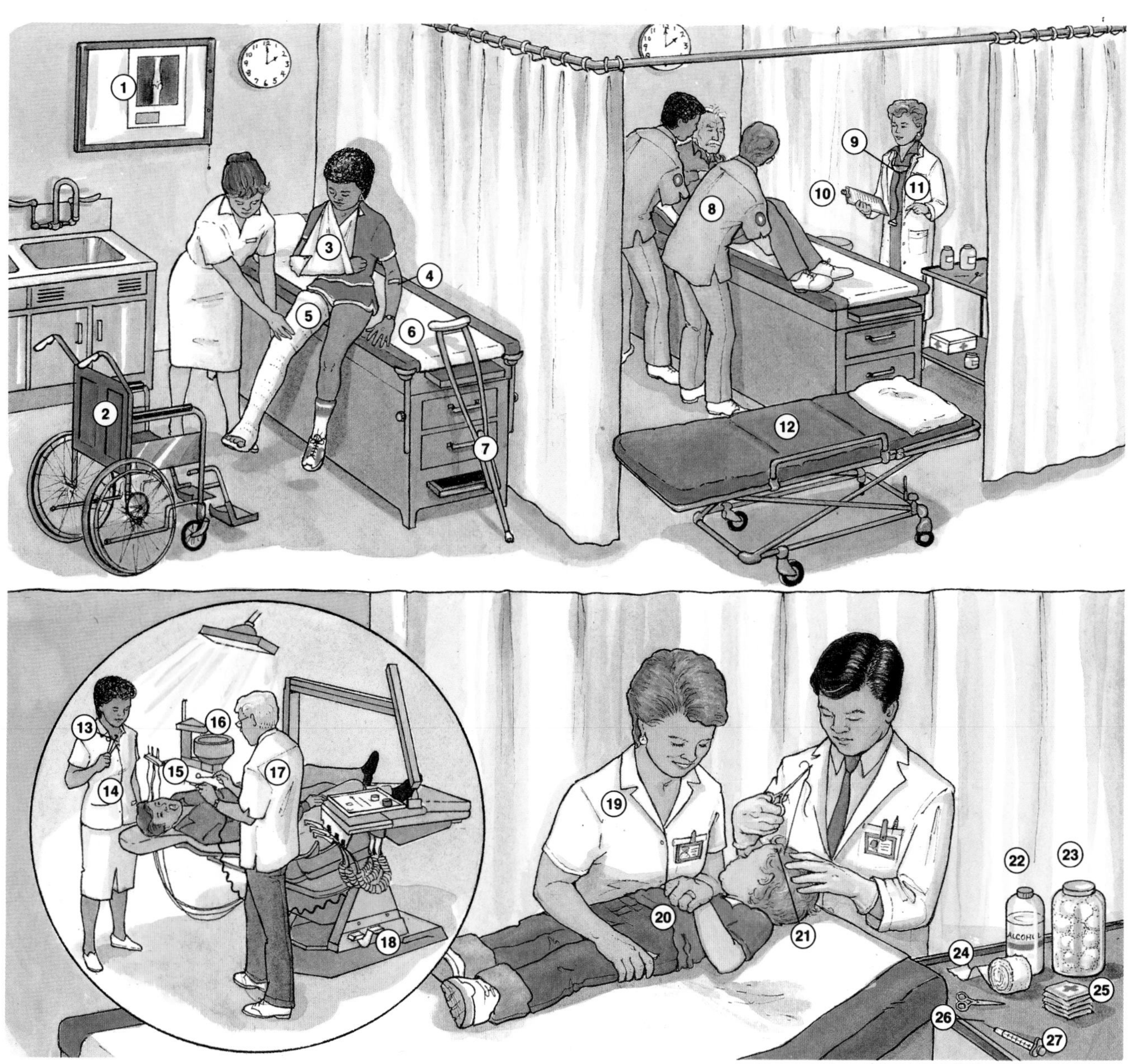

рентгеновский снимок	1.	X-ray
кресло на колесах, инвалидная коляска	2.	wheelchair
повязка	3.	sling
лейкопластырь	4.	Band-Aid
гипсовая повязка (гипс)	5.	cast
кушетка (для медицинского осмотра)	6.	examining table
костыль	7.	crutch
санитарка	8.	attendant
стетоскоп	9.	stethoscope
история болезни	10.	chart
врач	11.	doctor
носилки	12.	stretcher
зубоврачебные инструменты	13.	instruments
зубной врач-гигиенист	14.	oral hygienist
бор-машина	15.	drill
плевательница	16.	basin
зубной врач	17.	dentist
педаль	18.	pedal
медсестра	19.	nurse
больной, пациент	20.	patient
швы	21.	stitches
медицинский спирт	22.	alcohol
ватные тампоны	23.	cotton balls
бинт	24.	(gauze) bandage
марлевые прокладки	25.	gauze pads
игла	26.	needle
шприц	27.	syringe

40 Ailments and Injuries

Болезни и (телесные) повреждения

сыпь	**1.** rash
температура, жар	**2.** fever
укус насекомого	**3.** insect bite
озноб	**4.** chills
синяк под глазом	**5.** black eye
головная боль	**6.** headache
боль в желудке, животе	**7.** stomachache
боль в спине	**8.** backache
зубная боль	**9.** toothache
гипертония, повышенное кровяное давление	**10.** high blood pressure
насморк	**11.** cold
боль в горле	**12.** sore throat
медицинская лопатка	**a.** tongue depressor
растяжение связок	**13.** sprain
резиновый бинт	**a.** stretch bandage
инфекция, заражение	**14.** infection
перелом кости	**15.** broken bone
порез	**16.** cut
ушиб, синяк	**17.** bruise
ожог	**18.** burn

Treatments and Remedies

Лечения и лекарства

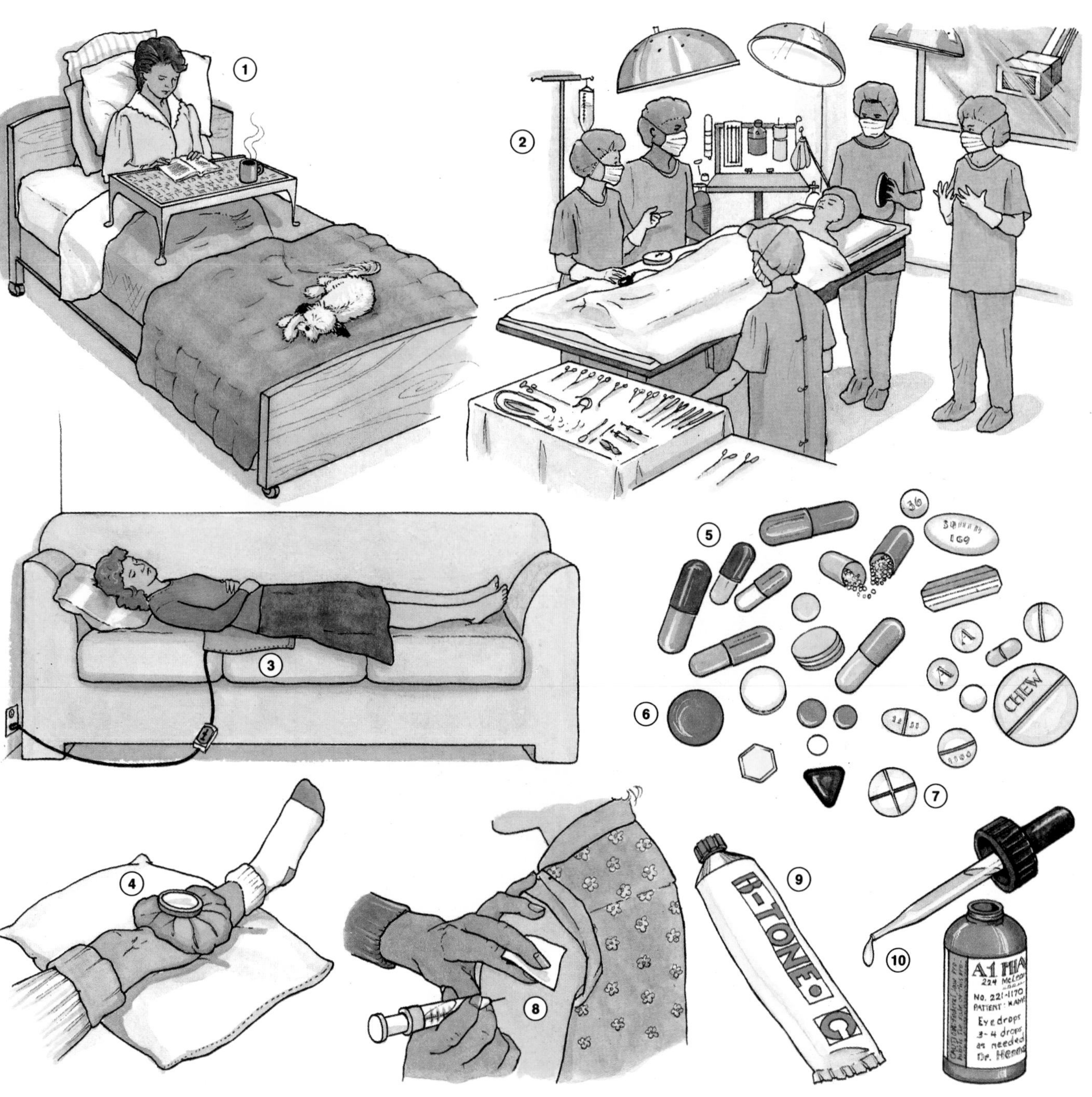

постельный режим	**1.** bed rest
операция	**2.** surgery
грелка	**3.** heating pad
ледяной компресс	**4.** ice pack

Лекарство	**Medicine**
капсула	**5.** capsule
таблетка	**6.** tablet
пилюля	**7.** pill
укол, инъекция	**8.** injection
мазь, притирание	**9.** ointment
глазные капли	**10.** eye drops

Firefighting and Rescue

Пожар и спасение при пожаре

лестница	**1.** ladder
пожарный насос	**2.** fire engine
пожарная машина	**3.** fire truck
пожарная лестница	**4.** fire escape
огонь, пожар	**5.** fire
скорая помощь	**6.** ambulance
медработник	**7.** paramedic
пожарный рукав, шланг	**8.** hose
гидрант	**9.** fire hydrant
пожарник	**10.** fire fighter
огнетушитель	**11.** fire extinguisher
каска	**12.** helmet
огнеупорное пальто пожарника	**13.** coat
топор	**14.** ax
дым	**15.** smoke
вода	**16.** water
брандспойт	**17.** nozzle

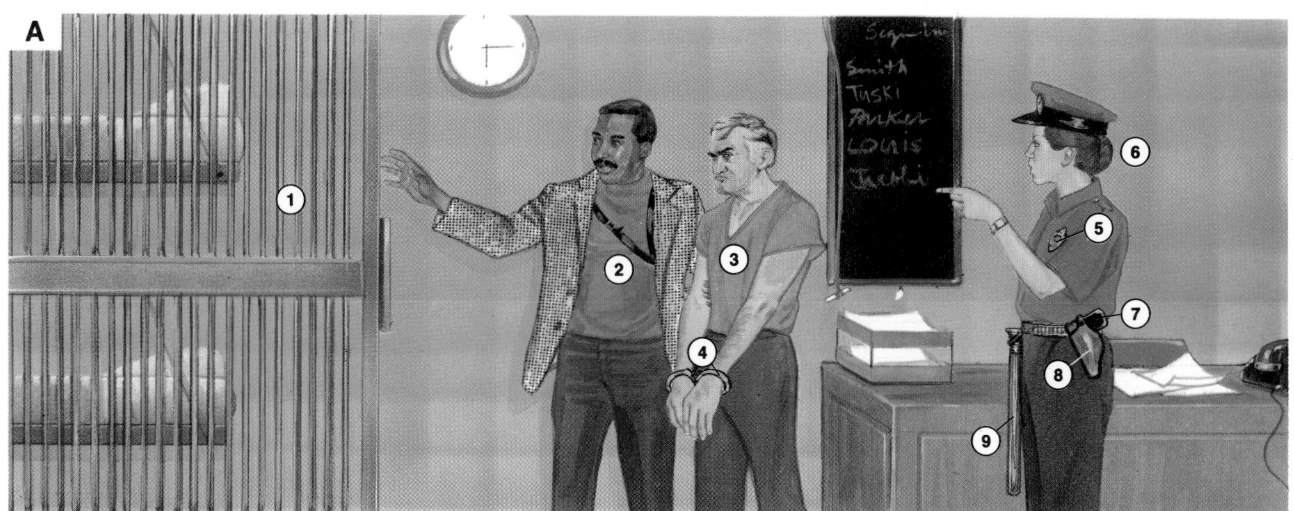

Полицейский участок	**A. Police Station**
тюрьма	**1.** jail
следователь, детектив	**2.** detective
подозреваемый	**3.** suspect
наручники	**4.** handcuffs
значок, жетон	**5.** badge
полицейский	**6.** police officer
пистолет	**7.** gun
кобура	**8.** holster
дубинка	**9.** nightstick
Суд	**B. Court**
судья	**10.** judge
судейская мантия	**11.** robes
молоток	**12.** gavel
свидетель	**13.** witness
секретарь судебного заседания	**14.** court reporter
протокол	**15.** transcript
судейский стол	**16.** bench
прокурор	**17.** prosecuting attorney
место для свидетелей	**18.** witness stand
судебный пристав	**19.** court officer
скамья присяжных	**20.** jury box
присяжные	**21.** jury
адвокат	**22.** defense attorney
обвиняемый	**23.** defendant
отпечатки пальцев	**24.** fingerprints

Город

административное здание	**1.** office building	почта	**9.** post office
вестибюль	**2.** lobby	регулировщик	**10.** traffic cop
угол (улицы)	**3.** corner	перекресток	**11.** intersection
переход	**4.** crosswalk	пешеход	**12.** pedestrian
универмаг	**5.** department store	автобусная остановка	**13.** bus stop
булочная	**6.** bakery	скамья	**14.** bench
телефон-автомат	**7.** public telephone	урна	**15.** trash basket
уличный указатель	**8.** street sign	станция метро	**16.** subway station

лифт	**17.** elevator	тротуар	**25.** sidewalk
книжный магазин	**18.** bookstore	обочина	**26.** curb
стоянка	**19.** parking garage	прогулочная коляска	**27.** baby carriage
стояночный счетчик	**20.** parking meter	овощной магазин	**28.** fruit and vegetable market
светофор	**21.** traffic light	уличный фонарь	**29.** streetlight
аптека	**22.** drugstore	газетный киоск	**30.** newsstand
жилое здание	**23.** apartment house	улица	**31.** street
номер дома	**24.** building number	канализационный колодец	**32.** manhole

The U.S. Postal System

Почта Соединенных Штатов

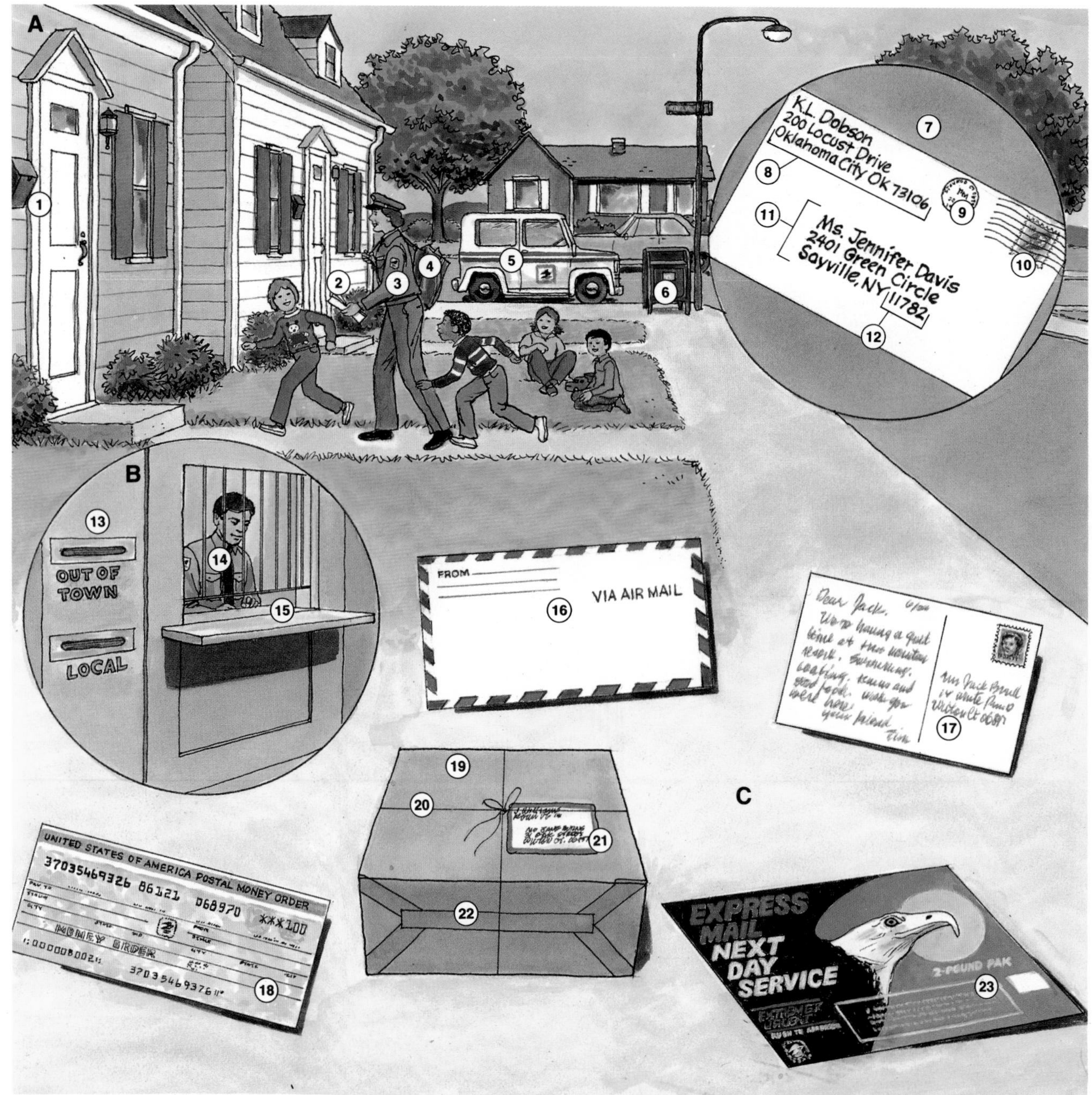

Доставка почты	**A. Delivering Mail**
почтовый ящик	1. mailbox
почта	2. mail
почтальон	3. letter carrier
почтовая сумка	4. mailbag
почтовый грузовик	5. mail truck
почтовый ящик	6. U.S. mailbox
письмо	7. letter
обратный адрес	8. return address
почтовый штемпель	9. postmark
марка	10. stamp
адрес	11. address
почтовый индекс	12. zip code
Почта	**B. The Post Office**
отверстие для почты	13. mail slot
почтовый работник	14. postal worker
окно	15. window
Виды почты	**C. Types of Mail**
конверт (для авиапочты)	16. (airmail) envelope
почтовая открытка	17. postcard
денежный перевод	18. money order
посылка	19. package
веревка	20. string
этикетка, наклейка	21. label
упаковочная лента	22. tape
посылка срочной почты	23. Express Mail (package)

Библиотека

библиотекарь **1.** library clerk
контрольный стол **2.** checkout desk
библиотечный билет **3.** library card
картотека **4.** card catalog
выдвижной ящик **5.** drawer
картотечная карточка **6.** call card
шифр **7.** call number
автор **8.** author
название **9.** title
предмет **10.** subject
полка **11.** row
бланк заказа **12.** call slip
микрофильм **13.** microfilm
аппарат для чтения микрофильмов **14.** microfilm reader

секция периодики **15.** periodicals section
журнал **16.** magazine
полка **17.** rack
копировальная машина **18.** photocopy machine
глобус **19.** globe
атлас **20.** atlas
справочный отдел **21.** reference section
справочный стол **22.** information desk
библиотекарша **23.** (reference) librarian
словарь **24.** dictionary
энциклопедия **25.** encyclopedia
полка **26.** shelf

The Armed Forces

Вооруженные силы

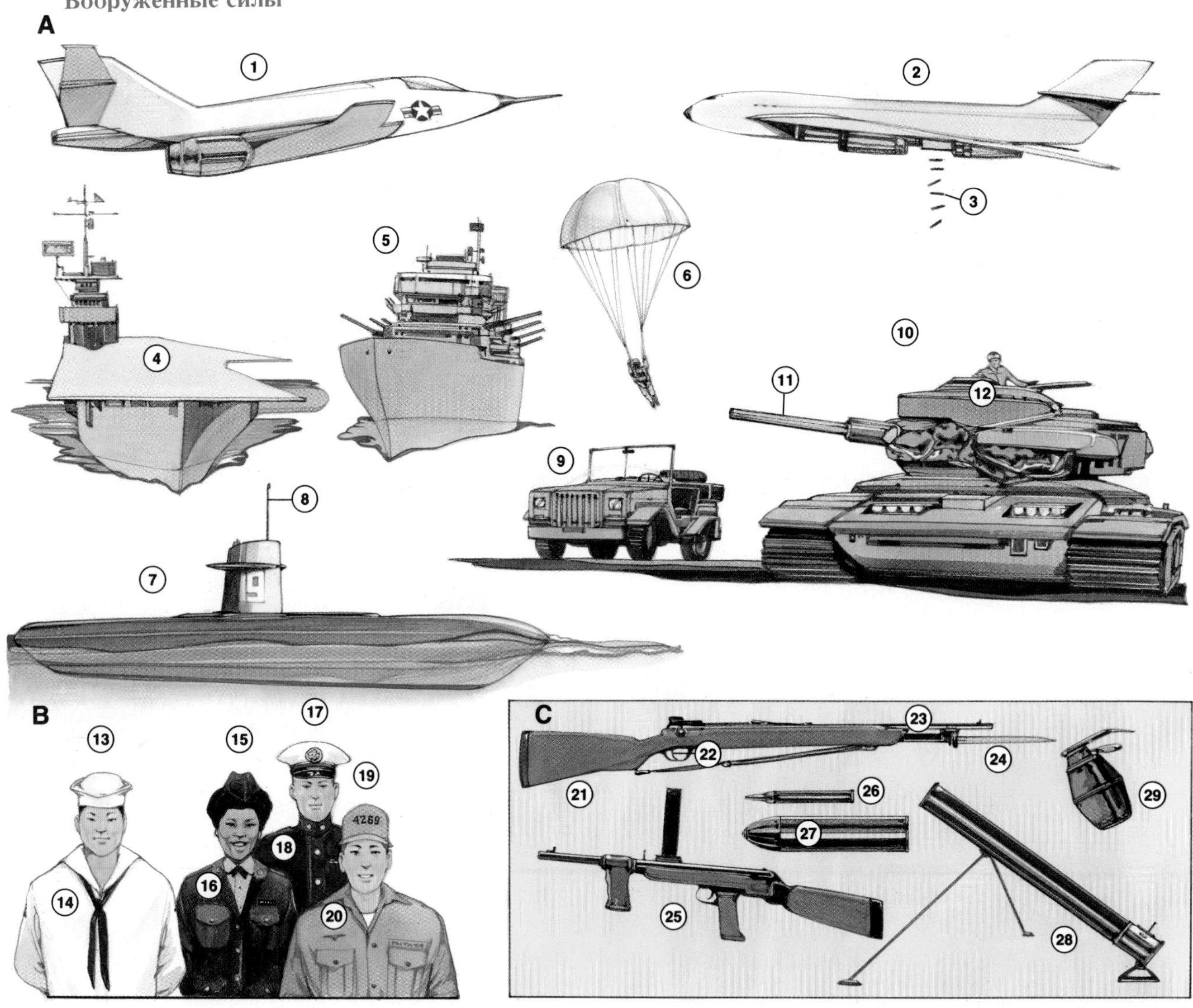

Машины и боевая техника	**A. Vehicles and Equipment**
истребитель	**1.** fighter plane
бомбардировщик	**2.** bomber
бомба	**3.** bomb
авианосец	**4.** aircraft carrier
линейный корабль	**5.** battleship
парашют	**6.** parachute
подводная лодка	**7.** submarine
перископ	**8.** periscope
джип	**9.** jeep
танк	**10.** tank
пушка	**11.** cannon
орудийная башня	**12.** gun turret
Личный состав	**B. Personnel**
военно-морской флот	**13.** Navy
матрос	**14.** sailor
армия	**15.** Army
солдат	**16.** soldier
морская пехота	**17.** Marines
морской пехотинец	**18.** marine
военно-воздушные силы	**19.** Air Force
рядовой военно-воздушных сил	**20.** airman
Оружие и боеприпасы	**C. Weapons and Ammunition**
винтовка	**21.** rifle
спусковой крючок	**22.** trigger
ствол	**23.** barrel
штык	**24.** bayonet
пулемет	**25.** machine gun
пуля	**26.** bullet
снаряд	**27.** shell
бомбомет	**28.** mortar
ручная граната	**29.** hand grenade

Грузовики

автоуборщик **1.** street cleaner
буксировщик **2.** tow truck
бензовоз, автоцистерна **3.** fuel truck
пикап **4.** pickup truck
снегоочиститель **5.** snow plow
мусоровоз **6.** garbage truck
мусорщик **7.** sanitation worker
передвижной буфет **8.** lunch truck
грузовик-фургон **9.** panel truck

доставщик **10.** delivery person
грузовик **11.** moving van
грузчик **12.** mover
бетоновоз **13.** cement truck
самосвал **14.** dump truck
тягач **15.** tractor trailer
шофер **16.** truck driver
транспортировщик автомобилей **17.** transporter
грузовая платформа **18.** flatbed

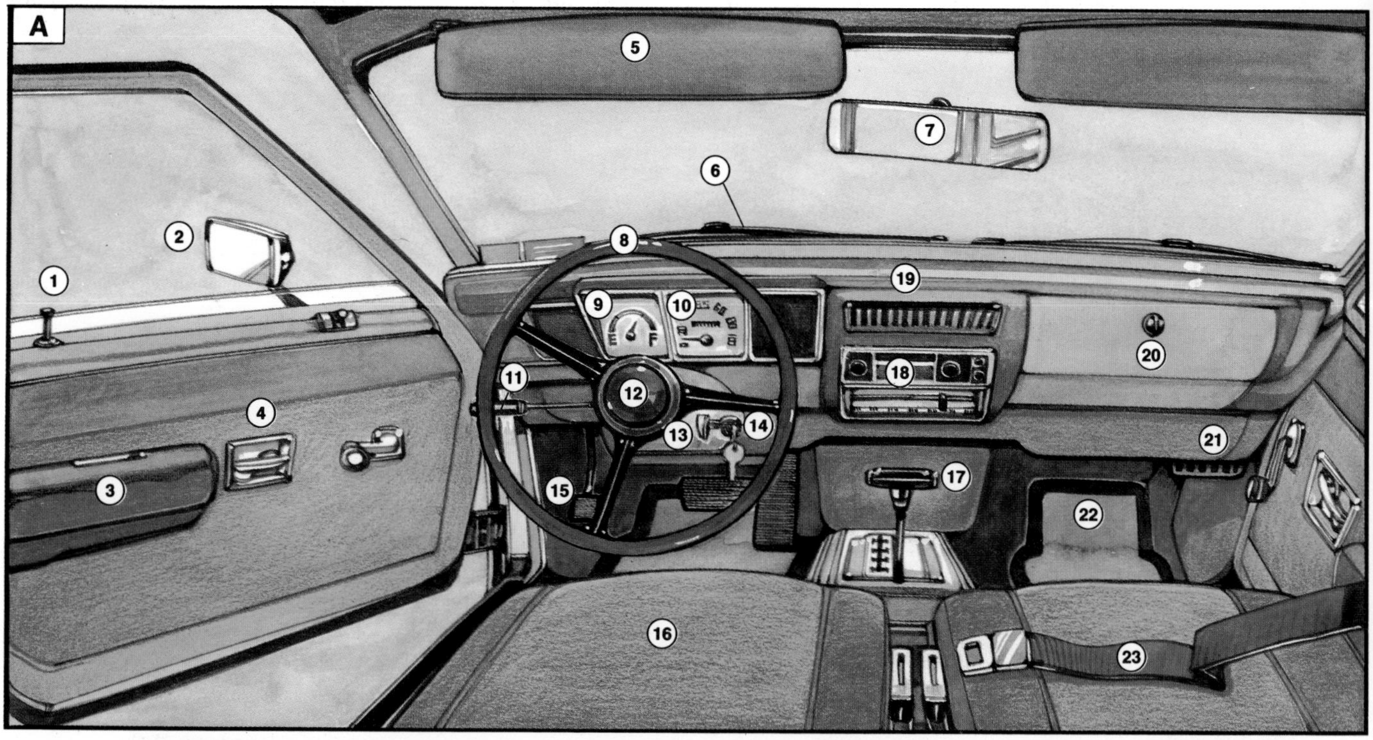

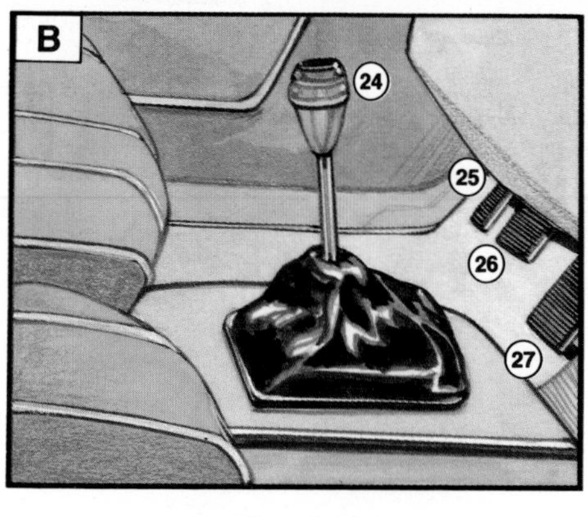

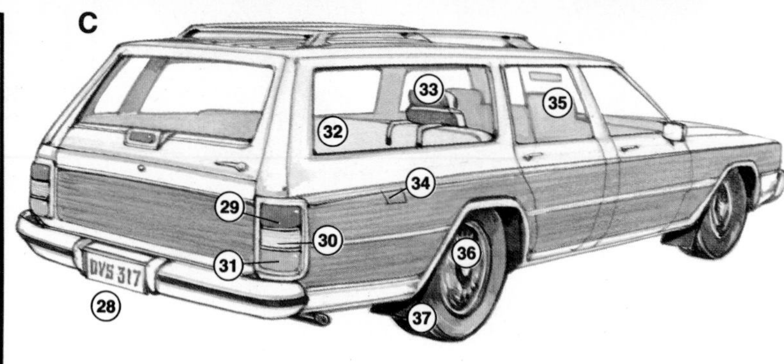

Автомобили с автоматической коробкой передач	A. Automatic Transmission
замок	1. door lock
боковое зеркало	2. side mirror
подлокотник	3. armrest
дверная ручка	4. door handle
противосолнечный щиток	5. visor
стеклоочиститель, «дворник»	6. windshield wiper
зеркало заднего обзора	7. rearview mirror
руль	8. steering wheel
указатель уровня бензина	9. gas gauge
спидометр	10. speedometer
переключатель сигнала поворота	11. turn signal lever
звуковой сигнал	12. horn
рулевая колонка	13. column
зажигание	14. ignition
стояночный тормоз	15. emergency brake
сиденье	16. bucket seat
переключатель скоростей	17. gearshift
радио	18. radio
приборная панель	19. dashboard
перчаточный ящик	20. glove compartment
вентилятор	21. vent
коврик	22. mat
ремень безопасности	23. seat belt

Автомобили с ручной коробкой передач	B. Manual Transmission
ручка управления	24. stick shift
педаль сцепления	25. clutch
педаль тормоза	26. brake
педаль газа	27. accelerator

Фургон	C. Station Wagon
номерной знак	28. license plate
стоп-сигнал	29. brake light
сигнал заднего хода	30. backup light
задние габаритные огни	31. taillight
заднее сиденье	32. backseat
детское кресло	33. child's seat
бензобак	34. gas tank
подголовник	35. headrest
колпак	36. hubcap
шина	37. tire

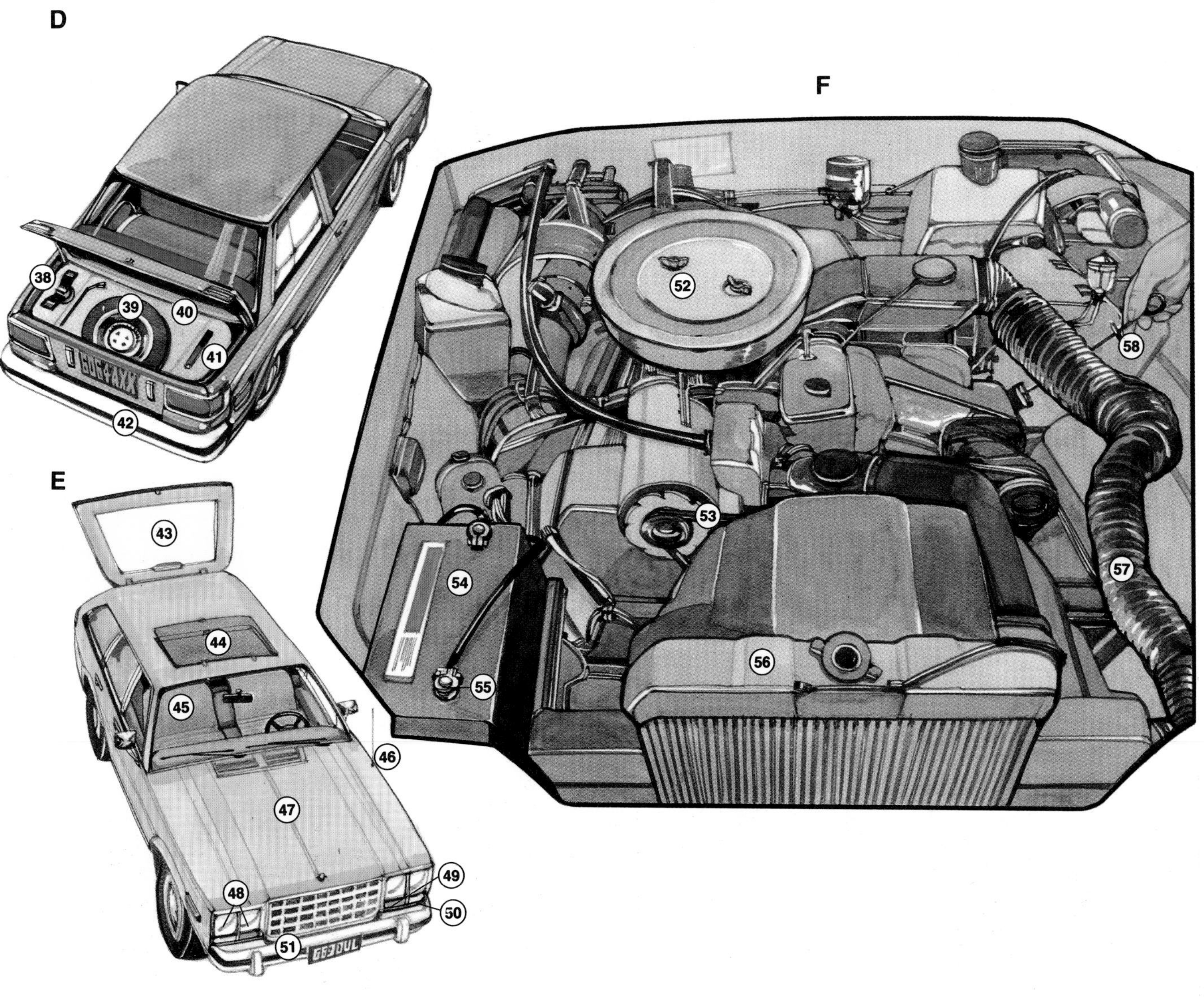

Двухдверный седан	**D. (Two-door) Sedan**
домкрат	**38.** jack
запасное колесо	**39.** spare tire
багажник	**40.** trunk
аварийный знак	**41.** flare
задний бампер	**42.** rear bumper
ятидверный автомобиль·комби	**E. Four-door Hatchback**
дверь багажника	**43.** hatchback
окно на крыше	**44.** sunroof
ветровое стекло	**45.** windshield
антенна	**46.** antenna
капот	**47.** hood
передние фары	**48.** headlights
стояночные огни	**49.** parking lights
сигналы поворота	**50.** turn signal (lights)
передний бампер	**51.** front bumper
Двигатель	**F. Engine**
воздушный фильтр	**52.** air filter
вентиляторный ремень	**53.** fan belt
аккумулятор	**54.** battery
полюс аккумулятора	**55.** terminal
радиатор	**56.** radiator
шланг	**57.** hose
указатель уровня масла	**58.** dipstick

Bikes

Велосипеды

тренировочные колеса	1.	training wheels
руль (гоночный)	2.	(racing) handlebars
женская рама	3.	girl's frame
колесо	4.	wheel
звонок, клаксон	5.	horn
трехколесный велосипед	6.	tricycle
шлем	7.	helmet
велосипед-вездеход	8.	dirt bike
опора	9.	kickstand
крыло	10.	fender
мужская рама	11.	boy's frame
руль (туристический)	12.	touring handlebars
замок	13.	lock
стенд для велосипеда	14.	bike stand
велосипед	15.	bicycle
сиденье	16.	seat
тормоз	17.	brake
цепь	18.	chain
педаль	19.	pedal
звездочка	20.	sprocket
насос	21.	pump
переключатель скоростей	22.	gear changer
трос	23.	cable
ручной тормоз	24.	hand brake
рефлектор	25.	reflector
спица	26.	spoke
нипель	27.	valve
шина	28.	tire
мотороллер	29.	motor scooter
мотоцикл	30.	motorcycle
амортизаторы	31.	shock absorbers
мотор	32.	engine
выхлопная труба	33.	exhaust pipe

междугородная автострада, (-ое) шоссе	**1.** interstate highway	пассажирская машина	**15.** passenger car
выход с шоссе	**2.** exit ramp	жилой автофургон	**16.** camper
путепровод	**3.** overpass	спортивная машина	**17.** sports car
пересечение по типу «кленового листа»	**4.** cloverleaf	средняя разделительная баррикада	**18.** center divider
левый ряд	**5.** left lane	мотоцикл	**19.** motorcycle
средний ряд	**6.** center lane	автобус	**20.** bus
правый ряд	**7.** right lane	въезд на шоссе	**21.** entrance ramp
знак ограничения скорости	**8.** speed limit sign	обочина	**22.** shoulder
путешествующий на попутных машинах, автостопом	**9.** hitchhiker	дорожный знак	**23.** road sign
прицеп (жилой)	**10.** trailer	знак съезда с шоссе	**24.** exit sign
станция технического обслуживания	**11.** service area	грузовик	**25.** truck
обслуживающий персонал	**12.** attendant	фургон	**26.** van
воздушный насос	**13.** air pump	киоск (будка) по сбору платы за пользование дорогой	**27.** tollbooth
колонка	**14.** gas pump		

Public Transportation

Городской транспорт

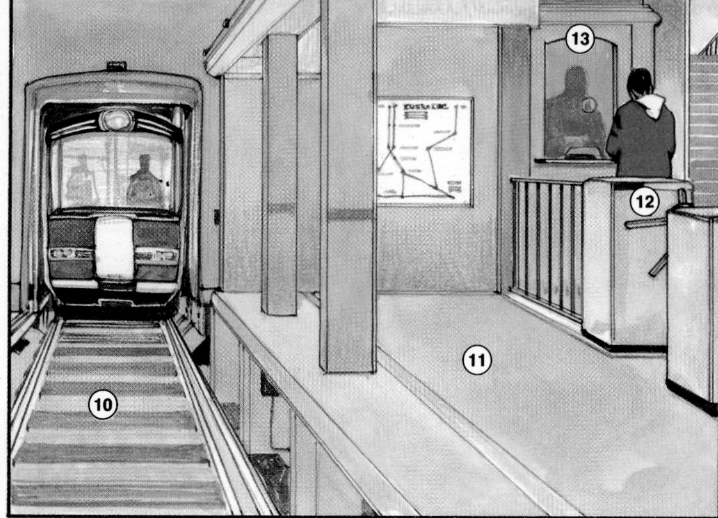

Автобус	**A. Bus**
шнур для сигнала остановки	**1.** cord
сиденье	**2.** seat
водитель	**3.** bus driver
пересадочный билет	**4.** transfer
касса платы	**5.** fare box
пассажир	**6.** rider

Метро	**B. Subway**
кондуктор	**7.** conductor
ремень	**8.** strap
вагон	**9.** car
рельсы	**10.** track
платформа	**11.** platform
турникет	**12.** turnstile
касса для продажи жетонов	**13.** token booth

Поезд	**C. Train**
пригородный поезд	**14.** commuter train
машинист	**15.** engineer
билет	**16.** ticket
ежедневный пассажир	**17.** commuter
вокзал	**18.** station
билетная касса	**19.** ticket window
расписание	**20.** timetable
Такси	**D. Taxi**
стоимость проезда	**21.** fare
чаевые	**22.** tip
счетчик	**23.** meter
счет	**24.** receipt
пассажир	**25.** passenger
таксист, водитель такси	**26.** cab driver
такси	**27.** taxicab
стоянка такси	**28.** taxi stand
Другие виды транспорта	**E. Other Forms of Transportation**
монорейльс	**29.** monorail
трамвай	**30.** streetcar
канатная дорога	**31.** aerial tramway
фуникулер	**32.** cable car
лошадиная упряжка	**33.** horse-drawn carriage

Air Travel

Воздушный транспорт

Стойка регистрации	Airport Check-In
складной саквояж	**1.** garment bag
ручной багаж, сумка	**2.** carry-on bag
пассажир	**3.** traveler
билет	**4.** ticket
носильщик	**5.** porter
тележка	**6.** dolly
чемодан	**7.** suitcase
багаж	**8.** baggage

Охрана	Security
охранник	**9.** security guard
детектор металла	**10.** metal detector
рентгеновский детектор	**11.** X-ray screener
транспортер	**12.** conveyor belt

На борту	Boarding
кабина пилота	**13.** cockpit
приборы	**14.** instruments
пилот, летчик	**15.** pilot
второй летчик	**16.** copilot
инженер	**17.** flight engineer
посадочный талон	**18.** boarding pass
кабина	**19.** cabin
бортпроводник	**20.** flight attendant
багажное отделение	**21.** luggage compartment
откидной столик	**22.** tray table
проход	**23.** aisle

Виды самолетов — **A. Aircraft Types**
- воздушный шар — **1.** hot air balloon
- вертолет — **2.** helicopter
- несущий винт — **a.** rotor
- частный самолет — **3.** private jet
- планер — **4.** glider
- дирижабль — **5.** blimp
- дельтаплан — **6.** hang glider
- самолет с винтовым двигателем — **7.** propeller plane
- носовая часть — **8.** nose
- крыло — **9.** wing
- хвостовая часть — **10.** tail

Взлет — **B. Takeoff**
- реактивный двигатель — **11.** jet engine
- грузовой отсек — **12.** cargo area
- дверь грузового отделения — **13.** cargo door
- фюзеляж — **14.** fuselage
- шасси — **15.** landing gear
- аэропорт — **16.** terminal building
- ангар — **17.** hangar
- реактивный самолет — **18.** (jet) plane
- взлетно-посадочная полоса — **19.** runway
- контрольная башня — **20.** control tower

В порту

рыболовное судно	1.	fishing boat	буй	16.	buoy
рыбак	2.	fisherman	паром	17.	ferry
пирс, причал	3.	pier	дымовая труба	18.	smokestack
автопогрузчик	4.	forklift	спасательная шлюпка	19.	lifeboat
нос	5.	bow	сходня, трап	20.	gangway
кран	6.	crane	иллюминатор	21.	porthole
контейнер	7.	container	палуба	22.	deck
грузовой отсек, трюм	8.	hold	лебедка	23.	windlass
контейнеровоз	9.	(container)ship	якорь	24.	anchor
груз	10.	cargo	трос, канат	25.	line
корма	11.	stern	швартовная тумба, кнехт	26.	bollard
баржа	12.	barge	океанский лайнер	27.	ocean liner
буксир	13.	tugboat	док, верфь	28.	dock
маяк	14.	lighthouse	морской вокзал	29.	terminal
танкер	15.	tanker			

Лодочный спорт

спасательный жилет	1. life jacket
каноэ	2. canoe
байдарочное весло	3. paddle
парусная лодка	4. sailboat
руль	5. rudder
опускной киль, шверт	6. centerboard
бум	7. boom
мачта	8. mast
парус	9. sail
воднолыжник	10. water-skier
буксирный трос	11. towrope
подвесной мотор	12. outboard motor
моторная лодка	13. motorboat
спортсмен, занимающийся серфингом с парусом	14. windsurfer
доска с парусом	15. sailboard
катер	16. cabin cruiser
каяк, байдарка	17. kayak
лодка, ялик	18. dinghy
швартовная бочка	19. mooring
надувной плот	20. inflatable raft
уключина	21. oarlock
весло	22. oar
гребная шлюпка	23. rowboat

Растения и деревья

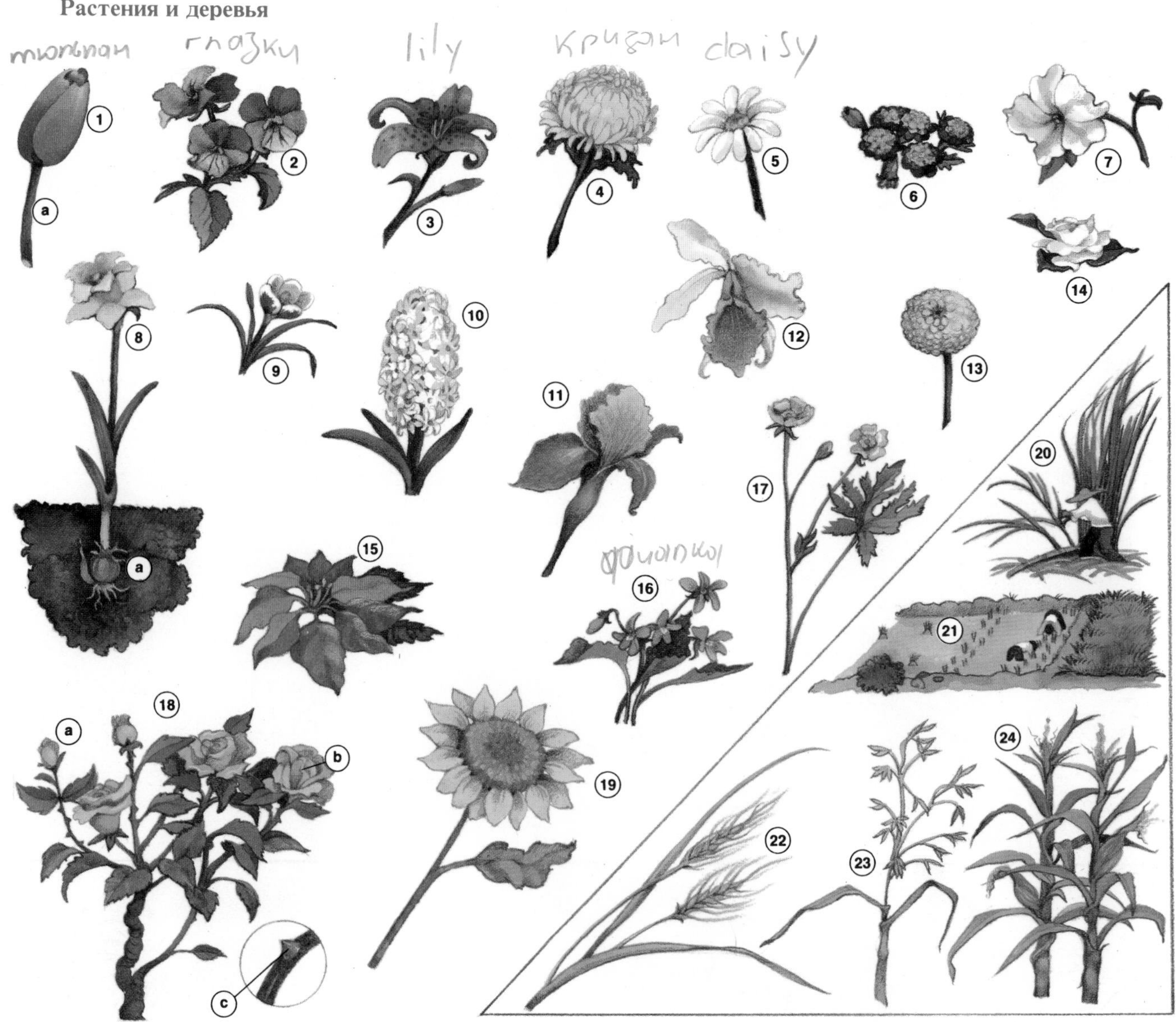

Цветы	Flowers
тюльпан	1. tulip
стебель	a. stem
анютины глазки	2. pansy
лилия	3. lily
кризантема	4. (chrysanthe)mum
ромашка	5. daisy
ноготок	6. marigold
петуния	7. petunia
желтый нарцисс	8. daffodil
луковица	a. bulb
крокус	9. crocus
гиацинт	10. hyacinth
ирис	11. iris
орхидея	12. orchid
цинния	13. zinnia
гардения	14. gardenia
рождественские цветы	15. poinsettia
фиалка	16. violet
лютик	17. buttercup
роза	18. rose
бутон розы	a. bud
лепесток	b. petal
колючка, шип	c. thorn
подсолнечник	19. sunflower

Травы и зерна	Grasses and Grains
сахарный тростник	20. sugarcane
рис	21. rice
пшеница	22. wheat
овес	23. oats
кукуруза, маис	24. corn

Деревья		Trees
красное дерево	25.	redwood
пальма	26.	palm
эвкалипт	27.	eucalyptus
кизил	28.	dogwood
магнолия	29.	magnolia
тополь	30.	poplar
ива	31.	willow
береза	32.	birch
дуб	33.	oak
ветвь, веточка	a.	twig
желудь	b.	acorn
сосна	34.	pine
хвоя	a.	needle
сосновая шишка	b.	cone
дерево	35.	tree
ветвь, сук	a.	branch
ствол	b.	trunk
кора	c.	bark
корень	d.	root
ильм, вяз	36.	elm
лист	a.	leaf
падуб, остролист	37.	holly
клен	38.	maple

Другие растения		Other Plants
комнатные растения	39.	house plants
кактус	40.	cactus
кусты	41.	bushes
вьющееся, ползучее растение	42.	vine

Ядовитые растения		Poisonous Plants
дуб ядоносный	43.	poison oak
сумах ядоносный	44.	poison sumac
плющ ядоносный	45.	poison ivy

Простые животные

улитка	**1.** snail
ракушка	**a.** shell
антенна, рога, рожки	**b.** antenna
устрица	**2.** oyster
моллюск	**3.** mussel
слизняк	**4.** slug
кальмар	**5.** squid
осьминог	**6.** octopus
морская звезда	**7.** starfish
креветка	**8.** shrimp
краб	**9.** crab
гребешок	**10.** scallop
червь, червяк	**11.** worm
медуза	**12.** jellyfish
щупальце	**a.** tentacle
омар	**13.** lobster
клешня	**a.** claw

Насекомые

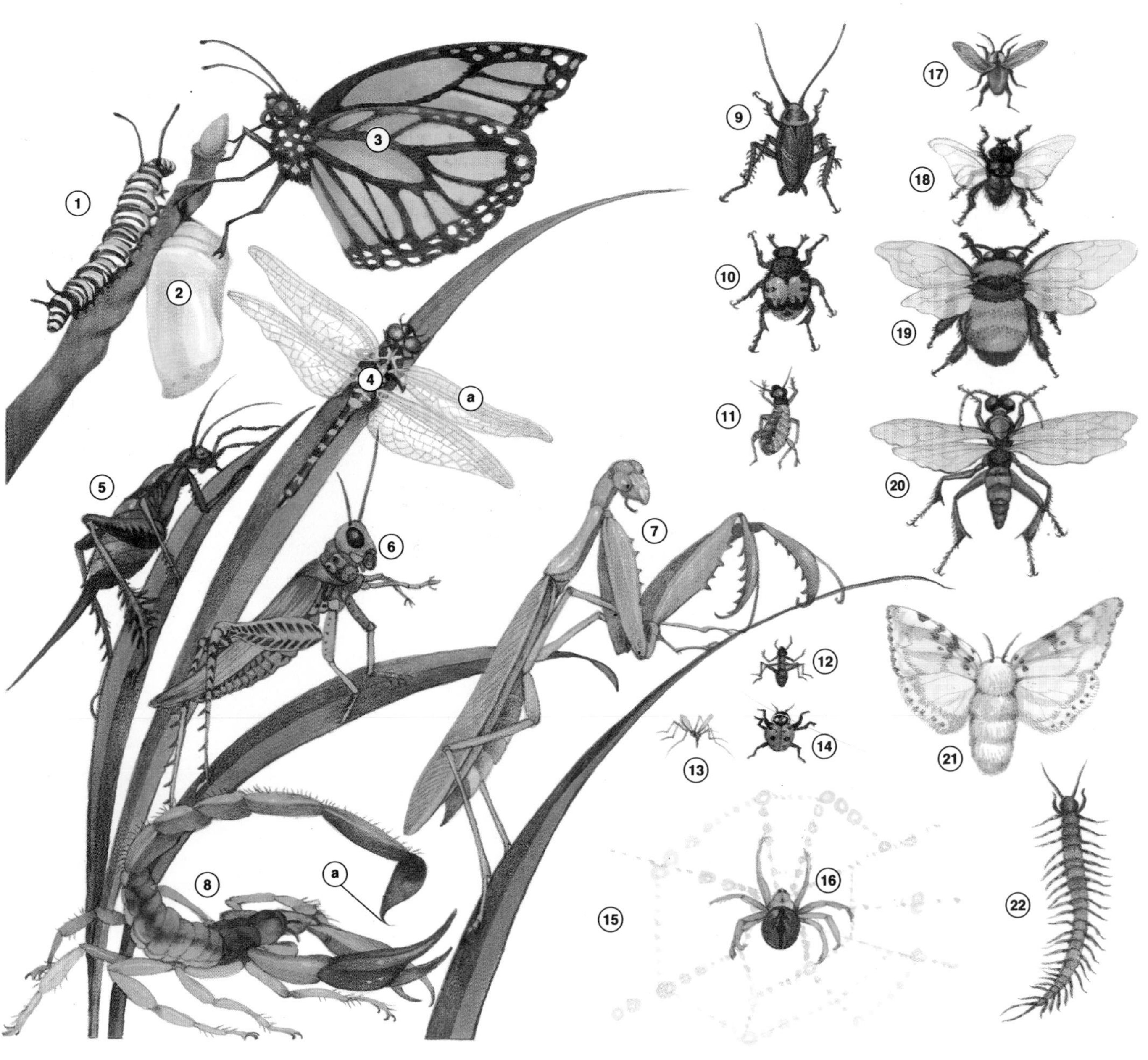

гусеница	**1.** caterpillar
кокон	**2.** cocoon
бабочка	**3.** butterfly
стрекоза	**4.** dragonfly
крыло	**a.** wing
сверчок	**5.** cricket
кузнечик	**6.** grasshopper
богомол	**7.** mantis
скорпион	**8.** scorpion
жало	**a.** sting
таракан	**9.** cockroach
жук	**10.** beetle
термит	**11.** termite
муравей	**12.** ant
комар	**13.** mosquito
божья коровка	**14.** ladybug
паутина	**15.** web
паук	**16.** spider
светлячок	**17.** firefly
муха	**18.** fly
пчела	**19.** bee
оса	**20.** wasp
моль	**21.** moth
многоножка	**22.** centipede

Птицы

голубь	**1.** pigeon
крыло	**a.** wing
колибри	**2.** hummingbird
ворона	**3.** crow
клюв	**a.** beak
чайка	**4.** sea gull
орел	**5.** eagle
сова	**6.** owl
ястреб	**7.** hawk
перо	**a.** feather
ронжа, сойка	**8.** blue jay
малиновка	**9.** robin
воробей	**10.** sparrow
кардинал	**11.** cardinal
страус	**12.** ostrich
яйцо	**13.** egg
канарейка	**14.** canary
длиннохвостый попугай	**15.** parakeet
попугай	**16.** parrot
дятел	**17.** woodpecker
павлин	**18.** peacock
фазан	**19.** pheasant
индюк	**20.** turkey
петух	**21.** rooster
птенец, цыпленок	**22.** chick
курица	**23.** chicken
пеликан	**24.** pelican
клюв	**a.** bill
утка	**25.** duck
гусь	**26.** goose
пингвин	**27.** penguin
лебедь	**28.** swan
фламинго	**29.** flamingo
аист	**30.** stork
гнездо	**31.** nest
дрофа	**32.** roadrunner

Рыбы	A. Fish
морской конек	1. sea horse
форель	2. trout
меч-рыба	3. swordfish
хвост	a. tail
плавник	b. fin
жабры	c. gill
угорь	4. eel
акула	5. shark
скат	6. stingray
камбала	7. flounder

Амфибии и пресмыкающиеся	B. Amphibians and Reptiles
аллигатор	8. alligator
змея	9. (garter) snake
гремучая змея	10. rattlesnake
кобра, очковая змея	11. cobra
черепаха	12. turtle
игуана	13. iguana
саламандра	14. salamander
ящерица	15. lizard
головастик	16. tadpole
лягушка	17. frog
черепаха	18. tortoise
панцирь	a. shell

Млекопитающие 1

Сумчатые, беззубые или летающие млекопитающие	**Pouched, Toothless, or Flying Mammals**
коала	**1.** koala
броненосец	**2.** armadillo
кенгуру	**3.** kangaroo
хвост	**a.** tail
задние ноги	**b.** hind legs
сумка	**c.** pouch
передние ноги	**d.** forelegs
летучая мышь	**4.** bat
муравьед	**5.** anteater
Грызуны	**Rodents**
бурундук	**6.** chipmunk
крыса	**7.** rat
мешетчатая крыса, «гофер»	**8.** gopher
мышь	**9.** mouse
белка	**10.** squirrel
дикобраз	**11.** porcupine
игла	**a.** quill
бобр	**12.** beaver
кролик	**13.** rabbit
Копытные млекопитающие	**Hoofed Mammals**
гиппопотам, бегемот	**14.** hippopotamus
лама	**15.** llama
носорог	**16.** rhinoceros
рог	**a.** horn
слон	**17.** elephant
хобот	**a.** trunk
клык, бивень	**b.** tusk
зебра	**18.** zebra

бизон	**19.** bison
пони	**20.** pony
лошадь	**21.** horse
грива	**a.** mane
жеребенок	**22.** foal
осел	**23.** donkey
ягненок	**24.** lamb
овца	**25.** sheep
олень	**26.** deer
молодой олень	**27.** fawn
коза, козел	**28.** goat
жираф	**29.** giraffe
свинья, боров	**30.** hog
теленок	**31.** calf
корова	**32.** cow
верблюд	**33.** camel
горб	**a.** hump
бык	**34.** bull
американский лось	**35.** moose
рог	**a.** antler
копыто	**b.** hoof

68 Mammals II

Млекопитающие 2

леопард	**1.** leopard
тигр	**2.** tiger
коготь	**a.** claw
лев	**3.** lion
кот	**4.** cat
котенок	**5.** kitten
лиса	**6.** fox
енот	**7.** raccoon
скунс	**8.** skunk

Морские млекопитающие	**Aquatic Mammals**
кит	**9.** whale
выдра	**10.** otter
морж	**11.** walrus
тюлень	**12.** seal
плавник, ласт	**a.** flipper
дельфин	**13.** dolphin

Приматы		**Primates**
обезьяна	**14.**	monkey
гиббон	**15.**	gibbon
шимпанзе	**16.**	chimpanzee
горилла	**17.**	gorilla
орангутан	**18.**	orangutan
бабуин	**19.**	baboon

Медведи		**Bears**
панда	**20.**	panda
черный медведь	**21.**	black bear
белый, полярный медведь	**22.**	polar bear
медведь-гризли	**23.**	grizzly bear

Собаки		**Dogs**
спаниель	**24.**	spaniel
терьер	**25.**	terrier
охотничья поисковая собака	**26.**	retriever
щенок	**27.**	puppy
овчарка	**28.**	shepherd

волк	**29.**	wolf
лапа	**a.**	paw
гиена	**30.**	hyena

Карта мира

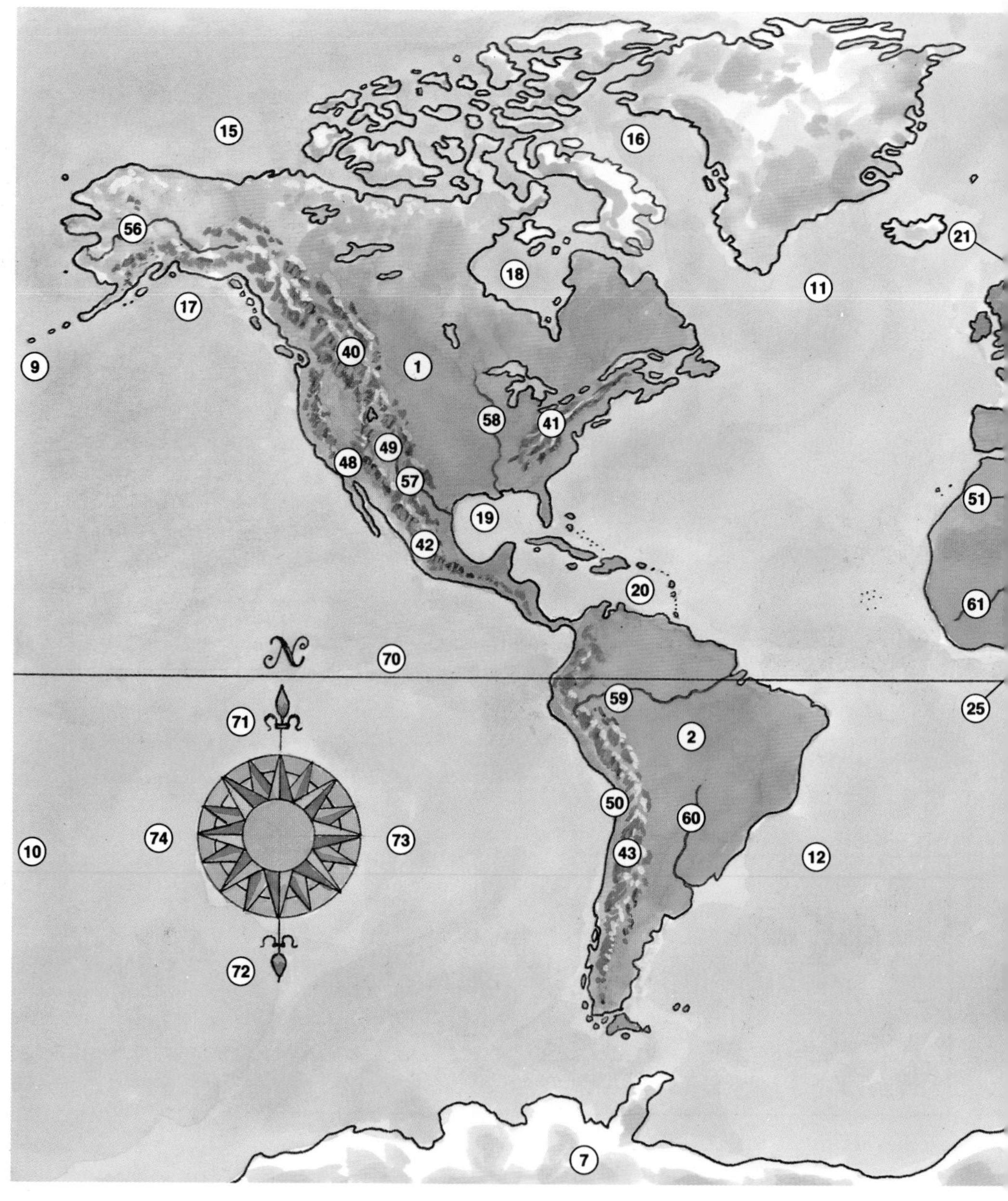

Материки		Continents
Северная Америка	1.	North America
Южная Америка	2.	South America
Европа	3.	Europe
Африка	4.	Africa
Азия	5.	Asia
Австралия	6.	Australia
Антарктика	7.	Antarctica

Океаны		Oceans
Северный Ледовитый океан	8.	Arctic
Северный Тихий океан	9.	North Pacific
Южный Тихий океан	10.	South Pacific
Северный Атлантический океан	11.	North Atlantic
Южный Атлантический океан	12.	South Atlantic
Индийский океан	13.	Indian
Антарктический океан	14.	Antarctic

Моря, бухты, заливы		Seas, Gulfs, and Bays
море Бофорта	15.	Beaufort Sea
залив Баффина	16.	Baffin Bay
залив Аляска	17.	Gulf of Alaska
Гудзонов залив	18.	Hudson Bay
Мексиканский залив	19.	Gulf of Mexico
Карибское море	20.	Caribbean Sea
Северное море	21.	North Sea
Балтийское море	22.	Baltic Sea
Баренцево море	23.	Barents Sea
Средиземное море	24.	Mediterranean Sea
Гвинейский залив	25.	Gulf of Guinea

Черное море	26.	Black Sea
Каспийское море	27.	Caspian Sea
Персидский залив	28.	Persian Gulf
Красное море	29.	Red Sea
Арабское море	30.	Arabian Sea
Карское море	31.	Kara Sea
Бенгальский залив	32.	Bay of Benga
море Лаптевых	33.	Laptev Sea
Берингово море	34.	Bering Sea
Охотское море	35.	Sea of Okhots
Японское море	36.	Sea of Japan
желтое море	37.	Yellow Sea
Восточно-Китайское море	38.	East China Se
Южно-Китайское море	39.	South China S

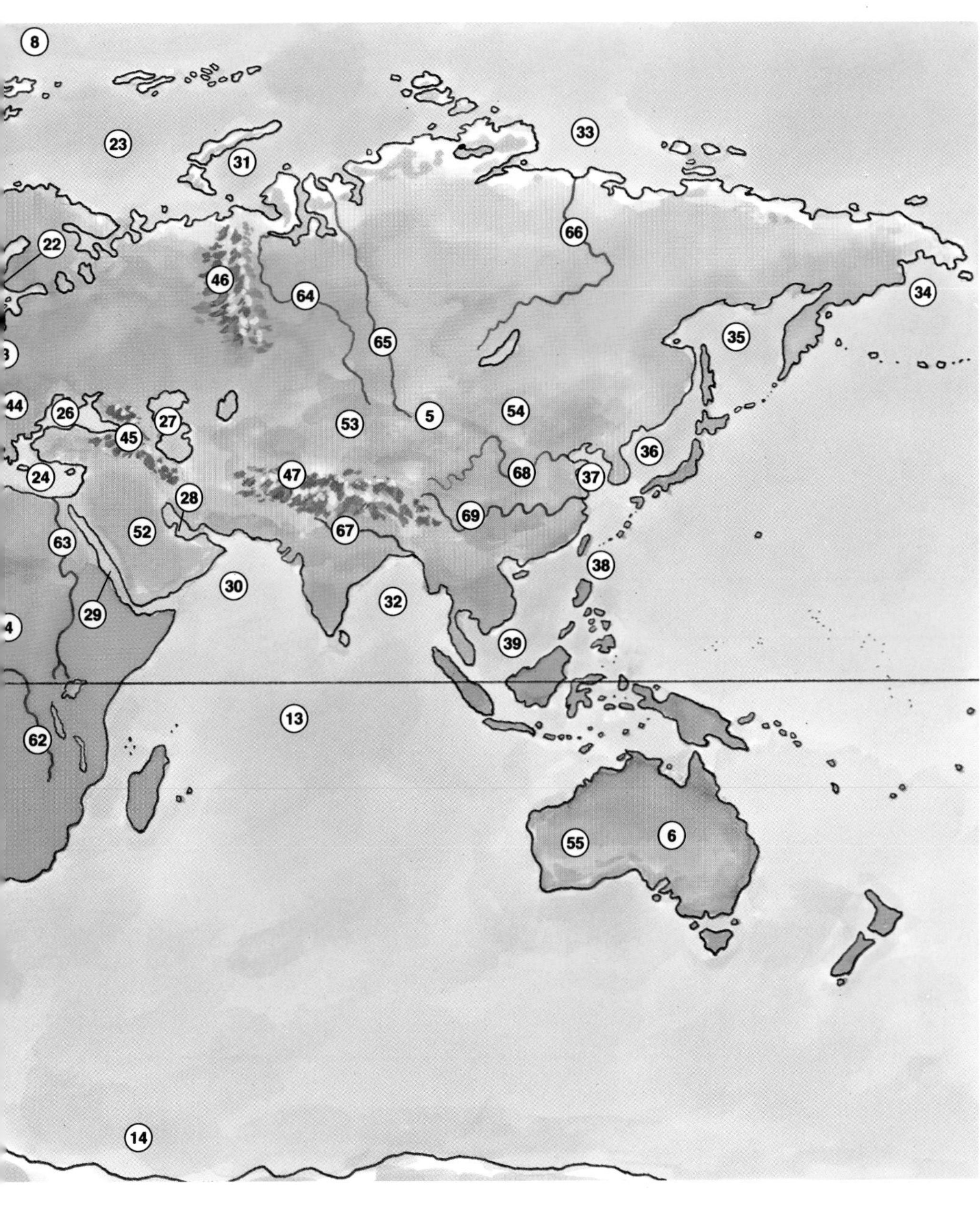

Горные хребты	Mountain Ranges
Скалистые горы	**40.** Rocky Mountains
Аппалачи	**41.** Appalachian Mountains
Сьерра-Мадре	**42.** Sierra Madre
Анды	**43.** Andes
Альпы	**44.** Alps
Кавказ	**45.** Caucasus
Урал	**46.** Urals
Гималаи	**47.** Himalayas

Пустыни	Deserts
пустыня Мохаве	**48.** Mojave
Окрашенная пустыня	**49.** Painted
пустыня Атакама	**50.** Atacama
пустыня Сахара	**51.** Sahara
пустыня Руб-эль-Хали	**52.** Rub' al Khali
пустыня Такла Макан	**53.** Takla Makan
пустыня Гоби	**54.** Gobi
Большая Песчаная пустыня	**55.** Great Sandy

Реки	Rivers
Юкон	**56.** Yukon
Рио-Гранде	**57.** Rio Grande
Миссисипи	**58.** Mississippi
Амазонка	**59.** Amazon
Парана	**60.** Paraná
Нигер	**61.** Niger
Конго	**62.** Congo
Нил	**63.** Nile
Обь	**64.** Ob
Енисей	**65.** Yenisey
Лена	**66.** Lena
Ганг	**67.** Ganges
Хуанхэ	**68.** Huang
Янцзы	**69.** Yangtze

экватор	**70.** equator
север	**71.** north
юг	**72.** south
восток	**73.** east
запад	**74.** west

Соединенные Штаты Америки

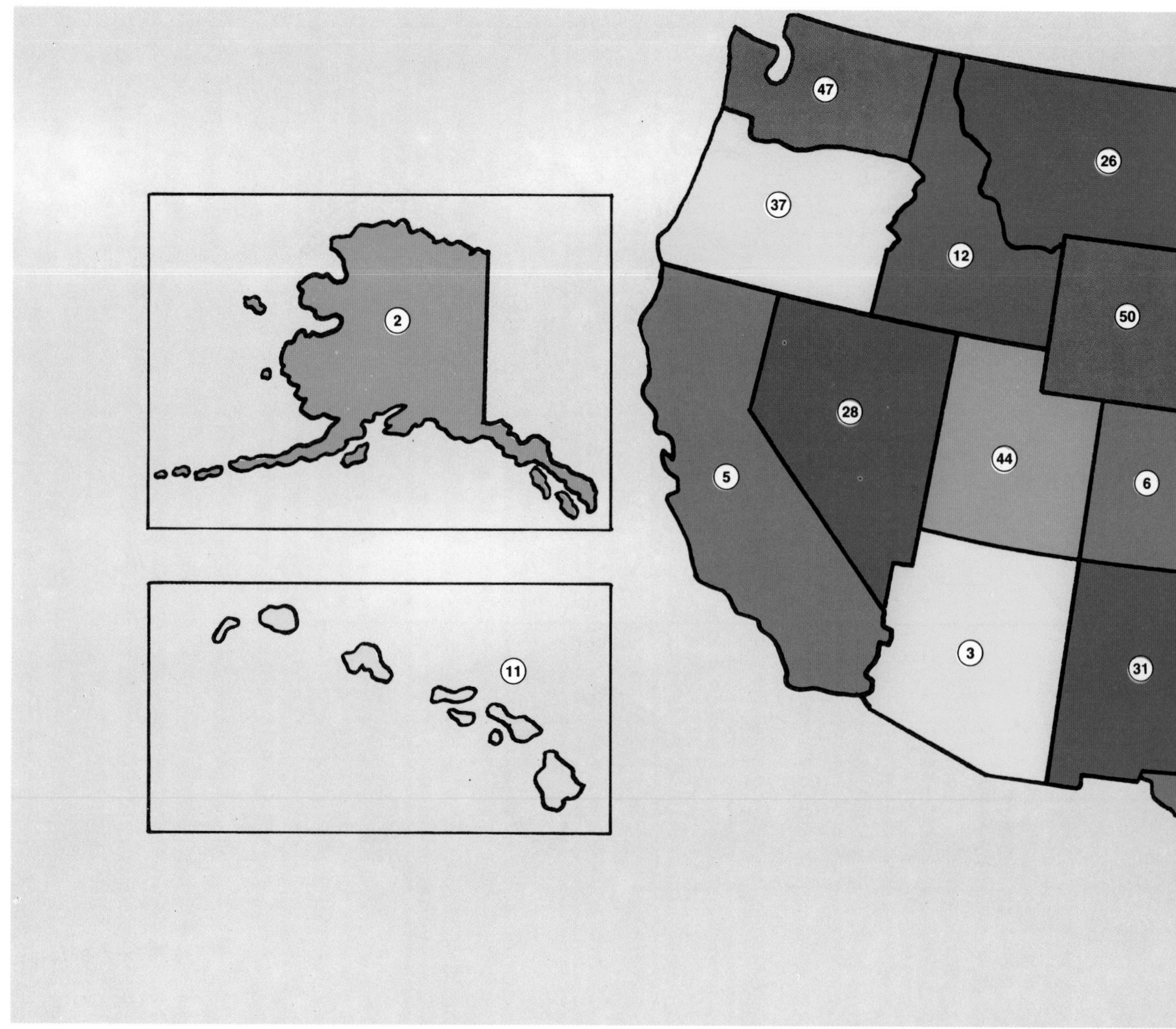

Алабама	**1.**	Alabama
Аляска	**2.**	Alaska
Аризона	**3.**	Arizona
Арканзас	**4.**	Arkansas
Калифорния	**5.**	California
Колорадо	**6.**	Colorado
Коннектикут	**7.**	Connecticut
Делавер	**8.**	Delaware
Флорида	**9.**	Florida
Джорджия	**10.**	Georgia
Гавайи	**11.**	Hawaii
Айдахо	**12.**	Idaho
Иллинойс	**13.**	Illinois
Индиана	**14.**	Indiana
Айова	**15.**	Iowa
Канзас	**16.**	Kansas
Кентукки	**17.**	Kentucky
Луизиана	**18.**	Louisiana
Мэн	**19.**	Maine
Мариленд	**20.**	Maryland
Массачусетс	**21.**	Massachusetts
Мичиган	**22.**	Michigan
Миннесота	**23.**	Minnesota
Миссисипи	**24.**	Mississippi

Соединенные Штаты Америки

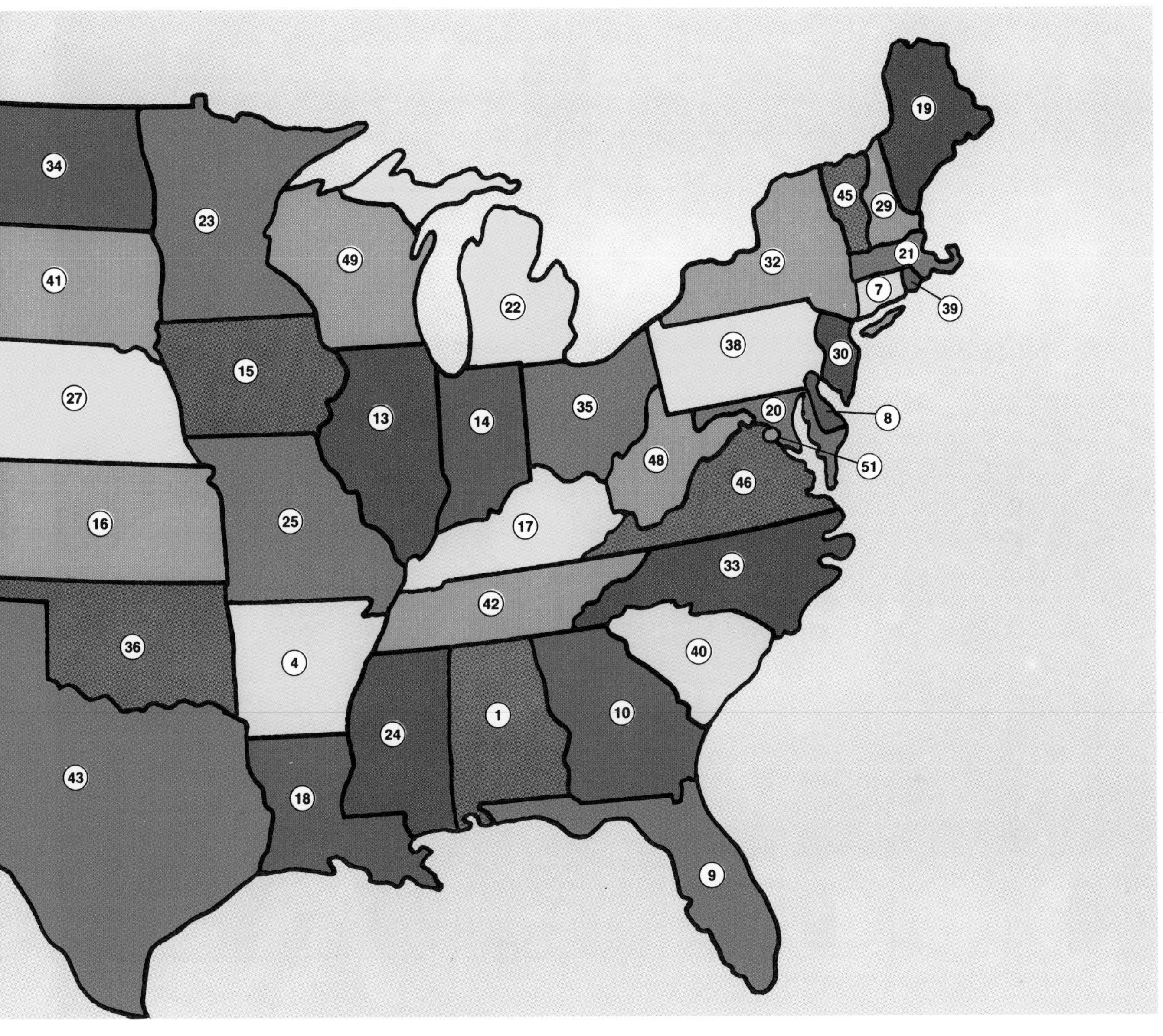

Миссури **25.** Missouri
Монтана **26.** Montana
Небраска **27.** Nebraska
Невада **28.** Nevada
Нью-Гемпшир **29.** New Hampshire
Нью-Джерси **30.** New Jersey
Нью-Мексико **31.** New Mexico
Нью-Йорк **32.** New York
Северная Каролина **33.** North Carolina
Северная Дакота **34.** North Dakota
Огайо **35.** Ohio
Оклахома **36.** Oklahoma
Орегон **37.** Oregon
Пенсильвания **38.** Pennsylvania
Род-Айленд **39.** Rhode Island

Южная Каролина **40.** South Carolina
Южная Дакота **41.** South Dakota
Теннесси **42.** Tennessee
Техас **43.** Texas
Юта **44.** Utah
Вермонт **45.** Vermont
Виргиния **46.** Virginia
Вашингтон **47.** Washington
Западная Виргиния **48.** West Virginia
Висконсин **49.** Wisconsin
Вайоминг **50.** Wyoming

округ Колумбия **51.** District of Columbia

Вселенная

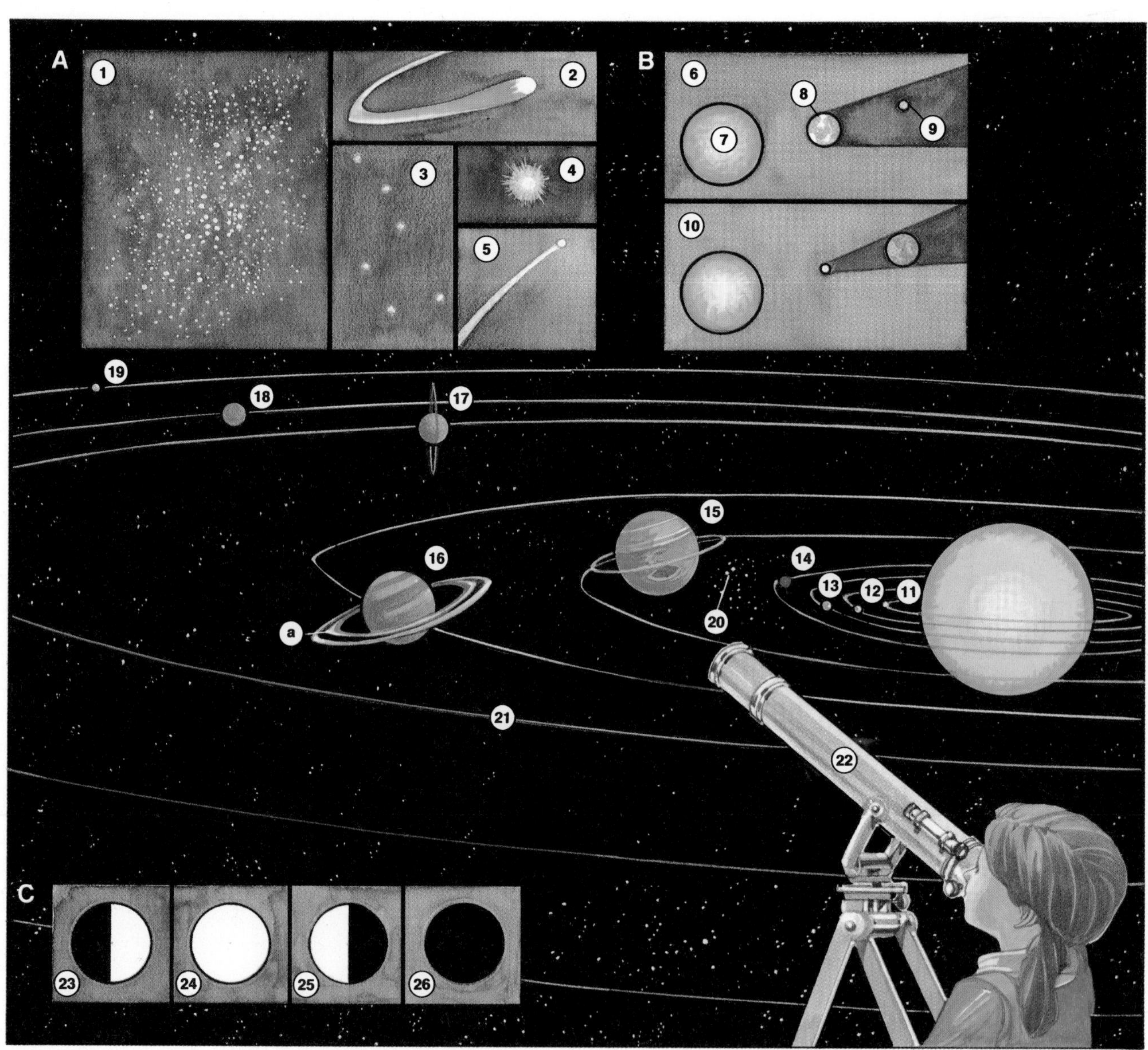

Космическое пространство	**A. Outer Space**
галактика	**1.** galaxy
комета	**2.** comet
(Большая Медведица) созвездие	**3.** (Big Dipper) constellation
звезда	**4.** star
метеор	**5.** meteor
Солнечная система	**B. The Solar System**
лунное затмение	**6.** lunar eclipse
Солнце	**7.** Sun
Земля	**8.** Earth
Луна	**9.** Moon
солнечное затмение	**10.** solar eclipse
Планеты	***The Planets***
Меркурий	**11.** Mercury
Венера	**12.** Venus
Земля	**13.** Earth
Марс	**14.** Mars
Юпитер	**15.** Jupiter
Сатурн	**16.** Saturn
кольцо	**a.** ring
Уран	**17.** Uranus
Нептун	**18.** Neptune
Плутон	**19.** Pluto
астероид	**20.** asteroid
орбита	**21.** orbit
телескоп	**22.** telescope
фазы луны	**C. Phases of the Moon**
первая четверть луны	**23.** first quarter
полнолуние	**24.** full moon
последняя четверть луны	**25.** last quarter
новолуние	**26.** new moon

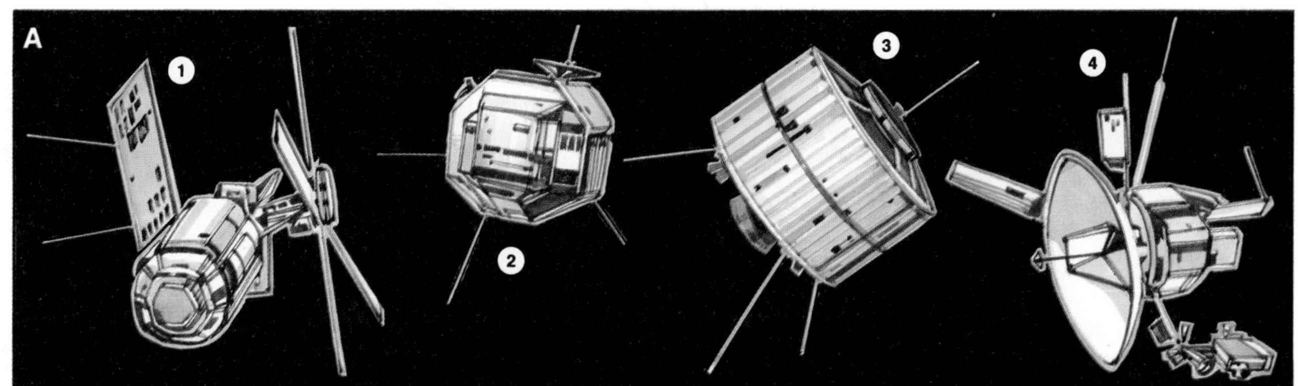

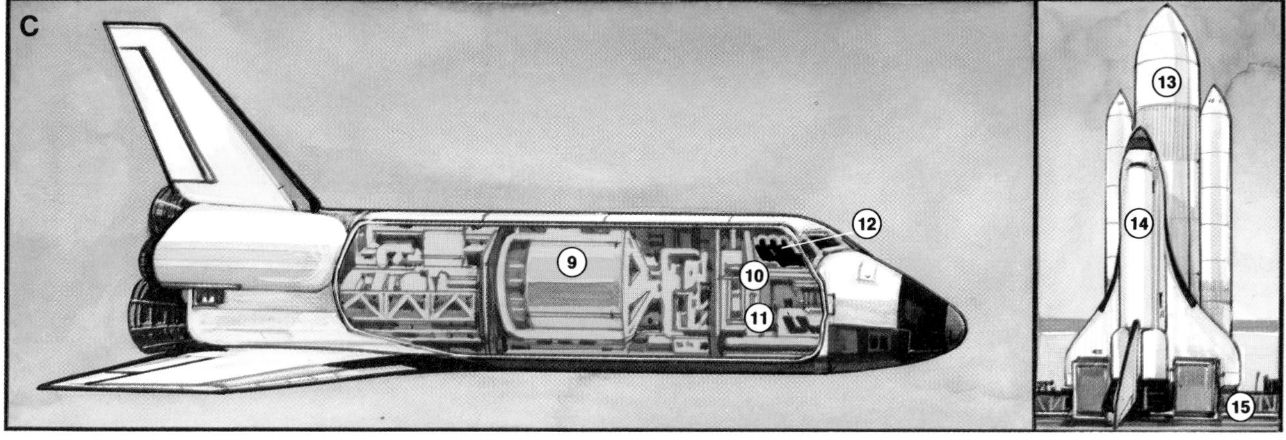

Космические летательные аппараты	**A. Spacecraft**
космическая станция	**1.** space station
спутник связи	**2.** communication satellite
метеорологический спутник	**3.** weather satellite
космический зонд	**4.** space probe
Посадка на Луне	**B. Landing on the Moon**
космонавт	**5.** astronaut
скафандр космонавта	**6.** space suit
лунный модуль	**7.** lunar module
командный отсек	**8.** command module
Космический челнок «Шаттл»	**C. The Space Shuttle**
грузовой отсек	**9.** cargo bay
открытая кабина	**10.** flight deck
жилой отсек	**11.** living quarters
экипаж	**12.** crew
ракета	**13.** rocket
космический челнок	**14.** space shuttle
стартовая площадка	**15.** launchpad

A Classroom

В классе

флаг	**1.**	flag
часы	**2.**	clock
громкоговоритель	**3.**	loudspeaker
учительница	**4.**	teacher
доска	**5.**	chalkboard
запирающийся шкафчик	**6.**	locker
доска объявления	**7.**	bulletin board
компьютер	**8.**	computer
полочка для мела	**9.**	chalk tray
мел	**10.**	chalk
губка	**11.**	eraser
коридор	**12.**	hall
вставные листы, бумаги	**13.**	(loose-leaf) paper
скоросшиватель	**14.**	ring binder
тетрадь	**15.**	spiral notebook
письменный стол	**16.**	desk
клей	**17.**	glue
кисточка	**18.**	brush
ученик	**19.**	student
точилка	**20.**	pencil sharpener
резинка	**21.**	pencil eraser
шариковая ручка	**22.**	ballpoint pen
линейка	**23.**	ruler
карандаш	**24.**	pencil
чертежная кнопка	**25.**	thumbtack
учебник	**26.**	(text)book
проектор	**27.**	overhead projector

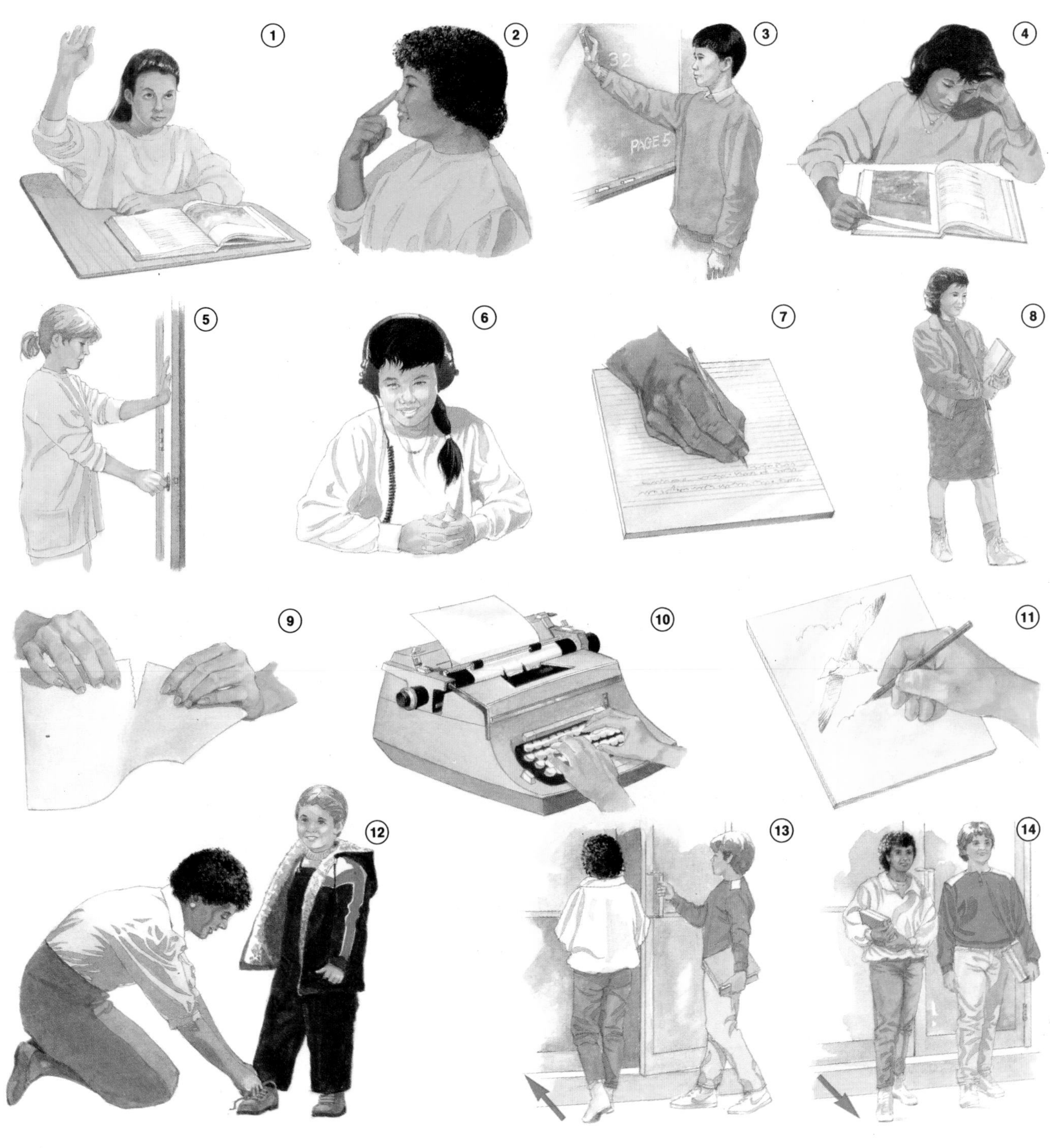

поднимать (руку)	**1.** raise (one's hand)
трогать	**2.** touch
вытирать, стирать	**3.** erase
читать	**4.** read
закрывать	**5.** close
слушать	**6.** listen
писать	**7.** write
ходить	**8.** walk
рвать	**9.** tear
печатать на машинке	**10.** type
рисовать	**11.** draw
завязывать	**12.** tie
выходить	**13.** leave
входить	**14.** enter

A Science Lab

Научная Лаборатория

призма	**1.** prism
коническая колба	**2.** flask
чашка Петри	**3.** petri dish
весы	**4.** scale
противовесы	**5.** weights
проволочная сетка	**6.** wire mesh screen
зажим	**7.** clamp
штатив для пробирок	**8.** rack
пробирка	**9.** test tube
пробка	**10.** stopper
миллиметровка	**11.** graph paper
защитные очки	**12.** safety glasses
таймер	**13.** timer
пипетка	**14.** pipette
увеличительное стекло	**15.** magnifying glass
фильтровальная бумага	**16.** filter paper
воронка	**17.** funnel
резиновая трубка	**18.** rubber tubing
штатив	**19.** ring stand
бунзеновская горелка	**20.** Bunsen burner
пламя	**21.** flame
термометр	**22.** thermometer
лабораторный стакан	**23.** beaker
лабораторный стол	**24.** bench
градуированный цилиндр	**25.** graduated cylinder
глазная пипетка	**26.** medicine dropper
магнит	**27.** magnet
щипцы	**28.** forceps
щипцы	**29.** tongs
микроскоп	**30.** microscope
предметное стекло	**31.** slide
пинцет	**32.** tweezers
набор инструментов для препарирования животных	**33.** dissection kit
табурет	**34.** stool

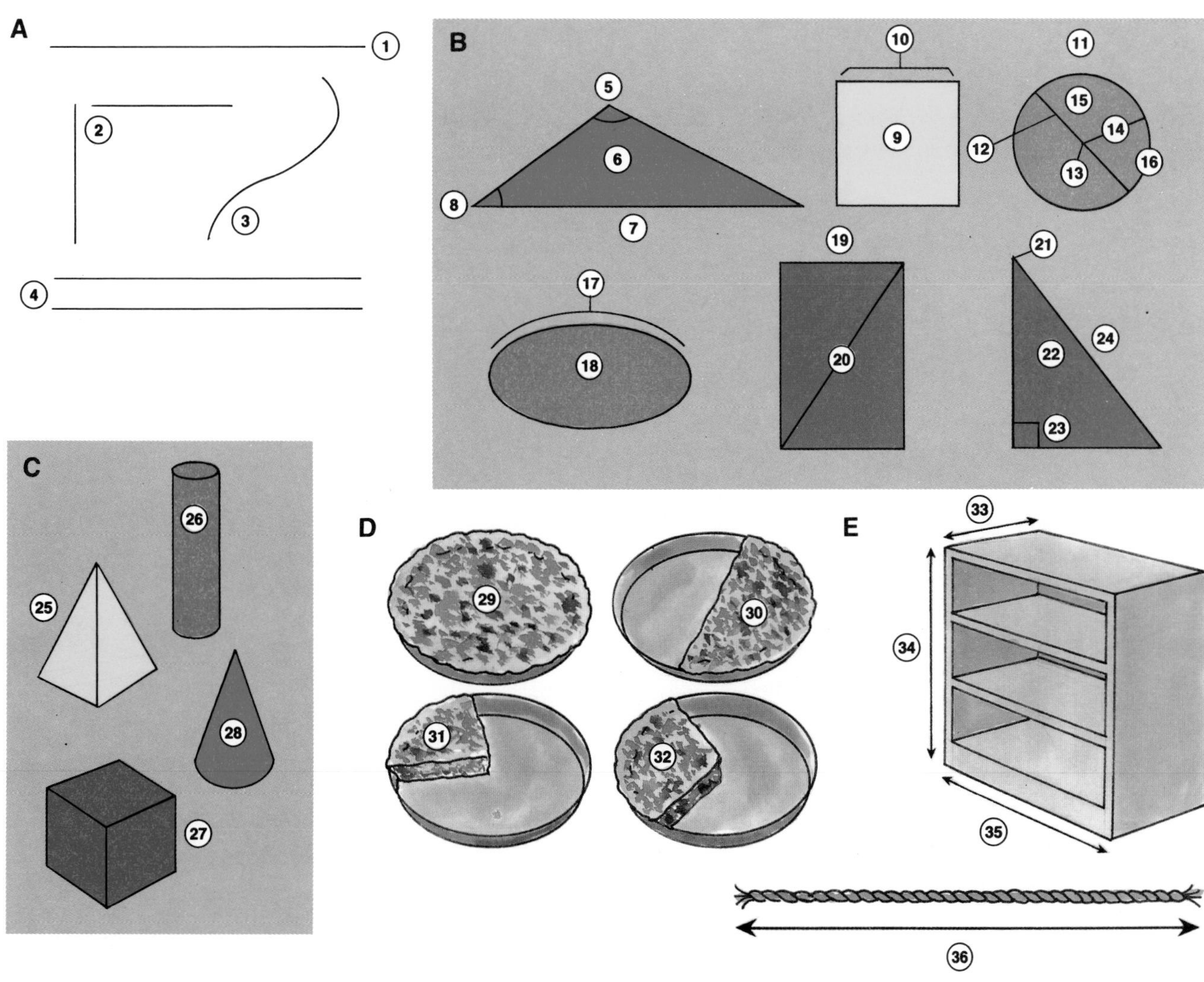

Линии	**A. Lines**
прямая линия	**1.** straight line
перпендикулярные линии	**2.** perpendicular lines
кривая линия	**3.** curve
параллельные линии	**4.** parallel lines
Геометрические фигуры	**B. Geometrical Figures**
тупой угол	**5.** obtuse angle
треугольник	**6.** triangle
основание	**7.** base
острый угол	**8.** acute angle
квадрат	**9.** square
сторона	**10.** side
круг	**11.** circle
диаметр	**12.** diameter
центр	**13.** center
радиус	**14.** radius
секция	**15.** section
дуга	**16.** arc
окружность	**17.** circumference
овал	**18.** oval
прямоугольник	**19.** rectangle
диагональ	**20.** diagonal
вершина	**21.** apex
прямоугольный треугольник	**22.** right triangle
прямой угол	**23.** right angle
гипотенуза	**24.** hypotenuse
Фигуры	**C. Solid Figures**
пирамида	**25.** pyramid
цилиндр	**26.** cylinder
куб	**27.** cube
конус	**28.** cone
Дроби	**D. Fractions**
целое	**29.** whole
половина (1/2)	**30.** a half (1/2)
четверть (1/4)	**31.** a quarter (1/4)
треть (1/3)	**32.** a third (1/3)
Измерение	**E. Measurement**
глубина	**33.** depth
высота	**34.** height
ширина	**35.** width
длина	**36.** length

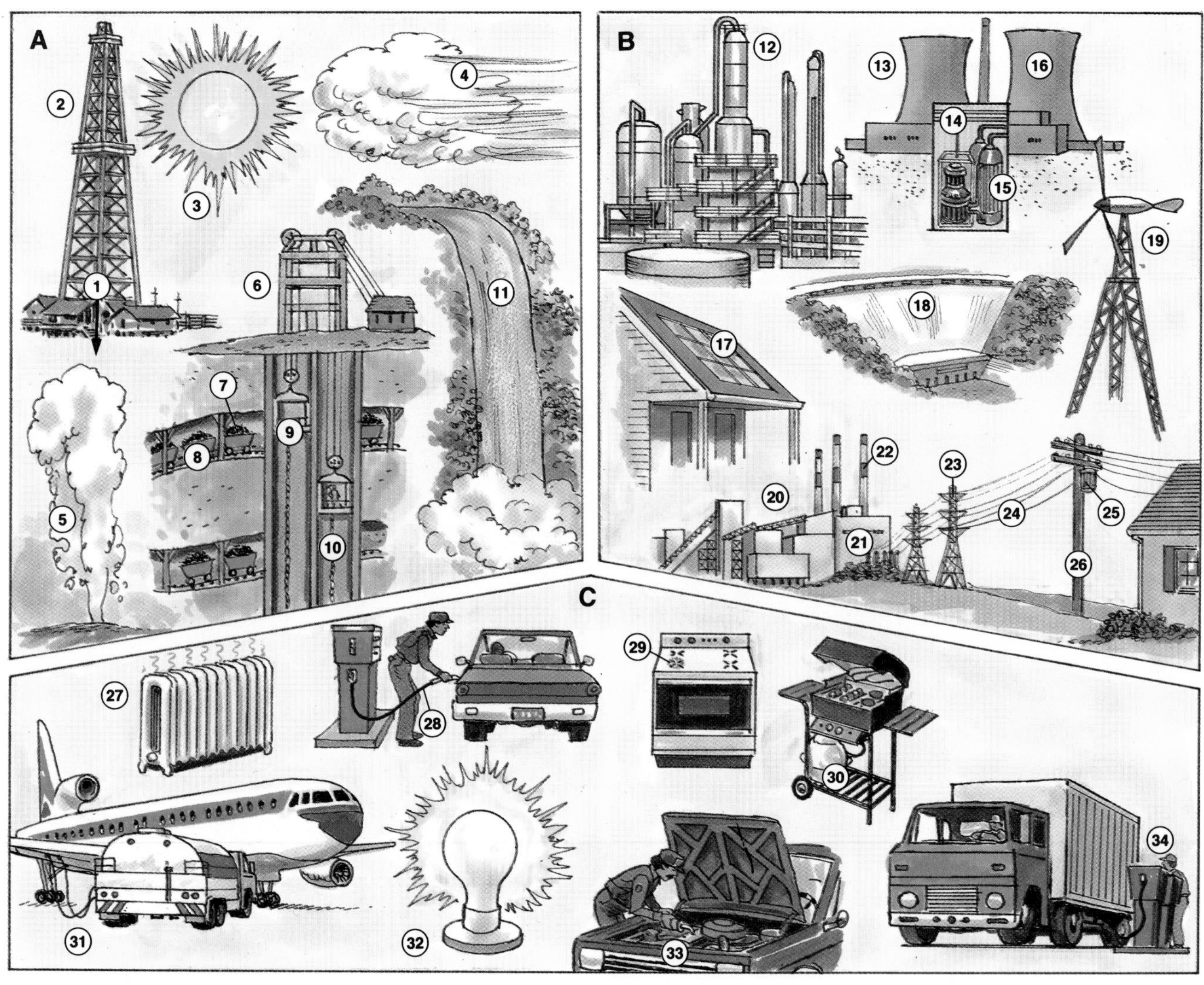

Источники энергии	**A. Sources of Power**
нефтяная скважина	**1.** oil well
буровая вышка	**2.** derrick
солнце	**3.** sun
ветер	**4.** wind
гейзер	**5.** geyser
угольная шахта	**6.** coal mine
уголь	**7.** coal
вагонетка	**8.** shuttle car
лифт	**9.** elevator
шахтный ствол	**10.** shaft
водопад	**11.** waterfall
Производство энергии	**B. Generation of Power**
нефтоочистительный завод	**12.** refinery
ядерный реактор	**13.** nuclear reactor
активная зона, ядро реактора	**14.** core
урановые стержни	**15.** uranium rods
охладительная башня, градирня	**16.** cooling tower
солнечный элемент	**17.** solar collector
плотина	**18.** dam
ветряная мельница	**19.** windmill
электростанция	**20.** power station
электрический генератор	**21.** electrical generator
дымовая труба	**22.** smokestack
вышка высоковольтной передачи	**23.** transmission towers
линии высоковольтной передачи	**24.** power lines
трансформатор	**25.** transformer
телеграфный столб	**26.** utility pole
Энергопродукты	**C. Uses and Products**
тепло	**27.** heat
бензин	**28.** gas(oline)
природный газ	**29.** natural gas
пропан	**30.** propane gas
топливо для реактивных двигателей	**31.** jet fuel
электроэнергия	**32.** electricity
машинное масло	**33.** motor oil
дизельное топливо	**34.** diesel fuel

Молочная ферма	**A. Dairy Farm**
фруктовый сад	**1.** orchard
плодовое дерево	**2.** fruit tree
жилой дом на ферме	**3.** farmhouse
силос (зерновой)	**4.** silo
сарай	**5.** barn
выгон, пастбище	**6.** pasture
фермер	**7.** farmer
гумно	**8.** barnyard
ограда	**9.** fence
баран, овца	**10.** sheep
корова	**11.** dairy cow
Зерновая ферма	**B. Wheat Farm**
домашний скот	**12.** livestock
стог сена	**13.** (bale of) hay
вилы	**14.** pitchfork
трактор	**15.** tractor
поле (пшеницы)	**16.** (wheat) field
комбайн	**17.** combine
ряд	**18.** row
пугало	**19.** scarecrow
Крупное фермерское хозяйство «ранчо»	**C. Ranch**
стадо (коров)	**20.** (herd of) cattle
пастух, ковбой	**21.** cowboy
пастушка	**22.** cowgirl
лошади	**23.** horses
загон для скота	**24.** corral
корыто	**25.** trough

Строительство

Строительная площадка	**A. Construction Site**
балки	**1.** rafters
кровельная дранка	**2.** shingle
нивелир	**3.** level
шлем, каска	**4.** hard hat
строитель	**5.** builder
план, «синька»	**6.** blueprints
леса	**7.** scaffolding
лестница	**8.** ladder
ступенька лестницы	**9.** rung
цемент	**10.** cement
фундамент	**11.** foundation
кирпичи	**12.** bricks
кирка	**13.** pickax
строительный рабочий	**14.** construction worker
лопата	**15.** shovel
доска	**16.** board
линейный монтер	**17.** linesman
подъемник	**18.** cherry picker

Дорожные работы	**B. Road Work**
конус для перекрытия дороги	**19.** cone
флажок	**20.** flag
баррикада	**21.** barricade
пневматический молот	**22.** jackhammer
тачка	**23.** wheelbarrow
дорожный барьер	**24.** center divider
бетономешалка	**25.** cement mixer
экскаватор	**26.** backhoe
бульдозер	**27.** bulldozer

- телефонистка — **1.** switchboard operator
- телефон с наушниками — **2.** headset
- распределительный щит, коммутатор — **3.** switchboard
- печатное устройство, принтер — **4.** printer
- бокс, кабина — **5.** cubicle
- машинистка — **6.** typist
- компьютер, текстовой редактор — **7.** word processor
- распечатка — **8.** printout
- календарь — **9.** calendar
- пишущая машинка — **10.** typewriter
- секретарша — **11.** secretary
- корзина для входящей работы, корреспонденции — **12.** in-box
- письменный стол — **13.** desk
- справочник адресов (на ролике) — **14.** rolodex
- телефон — **15.** telephone
- компьютер, ЭВМ — **16.** computer
- стул для машинистки — **17.** typing chair
- руководитель, управляющий — **18.** manager
- калькулятор — **19.** calculator
- книжные полки — **20.** bookcase
- ящик для хранения документов — **21.** file cabinet
- папка, подшивка — **22.** file folder
- канцелярский служащий, клерк — **23.** file clerk
- копировальная машина — **24.** photocopier
- маленький блокнот — **25.** message pad
- блокнот — **26.** (legal) pad
- сшиватель — **27.** stapler
- скрепки для бумаг — **28.** paper clips
- щипцы для удаления скобок — **29.** staple remover
- карандашная точилка — **30.** pencil sharpener
- конверт — **31.** envelope

Городские профессии 1

аптекарь	**1.** pharmacist
мастер, механик	**2.** mechanic
парикмахер	**3.** barber
агент (бюро путешествий)	**4.** travel agent
ремонтный мастер	**5.** repairperson
портниха (-ной)	**6.** tailor
продавец фруктов и овощей	**7.** greengrocer
пекарь	**8.** baker
оптик	**9.** optician
парикмахерша	**10.** hairdresser
продавец в цветочном магазине	**11.** florist
ювелир	**12.** jeweller
мясник	**13.** butcher

Ремонт — **A. Repair and Maintenance**

сантехник, водопроводник — **1.** plumber
плотник — **2.** carpenter
садовник — **3.** gardener
слесарь — **4.** locksmith
гент по продаже недвижимости — **5.** real estate agent
электрик — **6.** electrician
маляр — **7.** painter

Домашнее обслуживание — **B. Household Services**

экономика — **8.** housekeeper
уборщик, дворник — **9.** janitor
разносчик — **10.** delivery boy
швейцар — **11.** doorman

Работа на заводе — **C. Factory Work**

рабочий — **12.** shop worker
мастер, бригадир — **13.** foreman

A

Средства массовой информации — A. Media and Arts

1. метеоролог — weather forecaster
2. диктор последних известий — newscaster
3. художник — artist
4. фотограф — photographer
5. манекенщица — model
6. модельер — fashion designer
7. писатель — writer
8. архитектор — architect
9. «Диск-жоке», ведущий музыкальной радио-программы — disc jockey (DJ)
10. оператор — cameraperson
11. корреспондент, репортер — reporter
12. продавец — salesperson

Банк — B. Banking

13. служащий, должностное лицо — officer
14. охранник — security guard
15. кассир — teller

Канцелярские работники — C. Business Workers

16. программист — computer programmer
17. телефонистка — receptionist
18. бухгалтер — accountant
19. посыльный — messenger

зоопарк	**1.** zoo	урна	**11.** trash can
эстрада для оркестра	**2.** band shell	детская горка	**12.** slide
уличный торговец	**3.** vendor	песочница	**13.** sandbox
уличная тележка	**4.** hand truck	ороситель	**14.** sprinkler
карусель	**5.** merry-go-round	площадка для игр	**15.** playground
всадник	**6.** horseback rider	качели	**16.** swings
верховая тропа	**7.** bridle path	детские турники	**17.** jungle gym
пруд	**8.** (duck) pond	доска-качели	**18.** seesaw
беговая дорожка	**9.** jogging path	питьевой фонтан	**19.** water fountain
скамейка	**10.** bench		

Outdoor Activities

Отдых на открытом воздухе

плоскогорье **1.** plateau
туристы **2.** hikers
каньон **3.** canyon
холм **4.** hill
смотритель парка **5.** park ranger

Рыболовство **Fishing**

ручей **6.** stream
удилище, удочка **7.** fishing rod
леска **8.** fishing line
рыболовная сеть **9.** fishing net
болотные, речные сапоги **10.** waders
камни **11.** rocks

Место для пикника **Picnic Area**

гриль **12.** grill
корзина для пикника **13.** picnic basket
термос **14.** thermos
деревянный стол для пикника **15.** picnic table

Плавание на плотах		Rafting
плот	16.	raft
пороги	17.	rapids
водопад	18.	waterfall

Альпинизм		Mountain Climbing
гора	19.	mountain
вершина	20.	peak
отвесная скала	21.	cliff
мягкое крепление	22.	harness
веревка	23.	rope

Ночевка на открытом воздухе		Camping
палатка	24.	tent
походная плитка	25.	camp stove
спальный мешок	26.	sleeping bag
оборудование	27.	gear
рюкзак с рамой	28.	frame backpack
фонарь	29.	lantern
колышек	30.	stake
костер	31.	campfire
леса	32.	woods

На пляже

дощатый настил	**1.** boardwalk	песчаная дюна	**12.** sand dunes
буфет	**2.** refreshment stand	«фризби» (летающая тарелка)	**13.** Frisbee ™
мотель	**3.** motel	темные очки	**14.** sunglasses
велосипедист	**4.** biker	пляжное полотенце	**15.** beach towel
свисток	**5.** whistle	ведро	**16.** pail
спасатель (-ница)	**6.** lifeguard	детская лопатка	**17.** shovel
бинокль	**7.** binoculars	купальный костюм	**18.** bathing suit
вышка спасателя	**8.** lifeguard chair	загорающий	**19.** sunbather
спасательный круг	**9.** life preserver	шезлонг	**20.** beach chair
спасательная шлюпка	**10.** lifeboat	пляжный зонт	**21.** beach umbrella
детский надувной мяч	**11.** beach ball		

воздушный змей **22.** kite
бегуны **23.** runners
волна **24.** wave
доска для серфинга **25.** surfboard
надувной матрац **26.** air mattress
доска для плавания **27.** kickboard
пловец, пловчиха **28.** swimmer
камера **29.** tube
вода **30.** water
песок **31.** sand

песчаный замок **32.** sandcastle
плавки **33.** bathing trunks
трубка **34.** snorkel
маска для подводного плавания **35.** mask
ласты **36.** flippers
баллон с воздухом **37.** scuba tank
костюм аквалангиста **38.** wet suit
крем, лосьон для загара **39.** suntan lotion
ракушка **40.** shell
сумка-холодильник **41.** cooler

Спортивные соревнования между командами

Бейсбол	**Baseball**
судья	**1.** umpire
«кетчер» (захватывающий бейсбольного мяча)	**2.** catcher
маска кетчера	**3.** catcher's mask
рукавица кетчера	**4.** catcher's mitt
бита	**5.** bat
шлем отбивающего	**6.** batting helmet
отбивающий	**7.** batter
«Литтл Лиг» (соревнования по бейсболу для детей)	**Little League Baseball**
участник «Литтл Лиг»	**8.** Little Leaguer
форма	**9.** uniform
«Софтбол» (игра типа бейсбола с мягким мячом)	**Softball**
мяч	**10.** softball
фуражка	**11.** cap
рукавица	**12.** glove
Американский футбол	**Football**
мяч	**13.** football
шлем	**14.** helmet
«Лакросс» (Американская игра, изобретенная индейцами)	**Lacrosse**
защитная маска	**15.** face guard
клюшка с сеткой для захвата мяча	**16.** lacrosse stick
Хоккей с шайбой	**Ice Hockey**
шайба	**17.** puck
клюшка	**18.** hockey stick
Баскетбол	**Basketball**
щит	**19.** backboard
корзина	**20.** basket
мяч	**21.** basketball
Волейбол	**Volleyball**
мяч	**22.** volleyball
сетка	**23.** net
футбол	**Soccer**
вратарь	**24.** goalie
ворота	**25.** goal
мяч	**26.** soccer ball

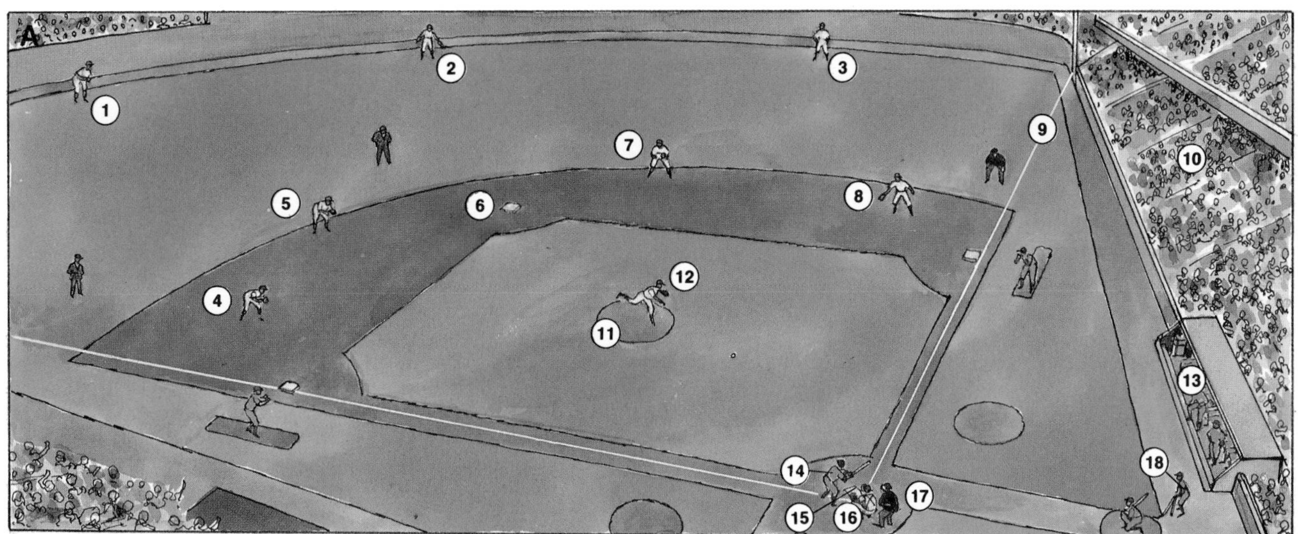

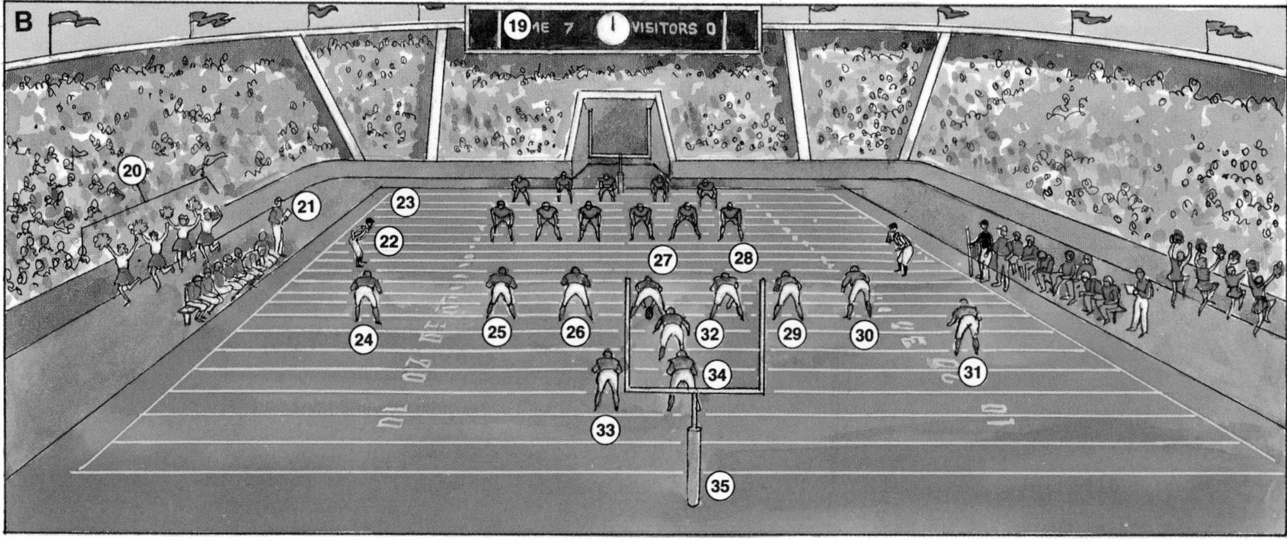

Поле бейсбола	A. Baseball Diamond
защитник левой стороны дальней части поля	1. left fielder
защитник середины дальней части поля	2. center fielder
защитник правой стороны дальней части поля	3. right fielder
защитник третьей базой	4. third baseman
щитник поля между 2-ой и 3-ей базой	5. shortstop
база	6. base
защитник второй базы	7. second baseman
защитник первой базы	8. first baseman
черта ограничения поля	9. foul line
трибуны для зрителей	10. stands
насыпь для питчера	11. pitcher's mound
«питчер» (игрок, бросающий мяч)	12. pitcher
скамья для команды	13. dugout
отбивающий	14. batter
финиш	15. home plate
«кетчер»	16. catcher
судья	17. umpire
носильщик бит	18. batboy

Поле американского футбола	B. Football Field
доска счета	19. scoreboard
девушки, подающие сигнал к овации	20. cheerleaders
тренер	21. coach
судья, арбитр	22. referee
конечная зона	23. end zone
крайний левый нападающий	24. split end
левый блокировщик	25. left tackle
левый полузащитник	26. left guard
центральный нападающий	27. center
правый полузащитник	28. right guard
правый блокировщик	29. right tackle
крайний правый нападающий	30. tight end
защитник флангов	31. flanker
«квортербек» (главный нападающий)	32. quarterback
средний нападающий	33. halfback
полусредний нападающий	34. fullback
стойка ворот	35. goalpost

Individual Sports
Индивидуальные спортивные игры

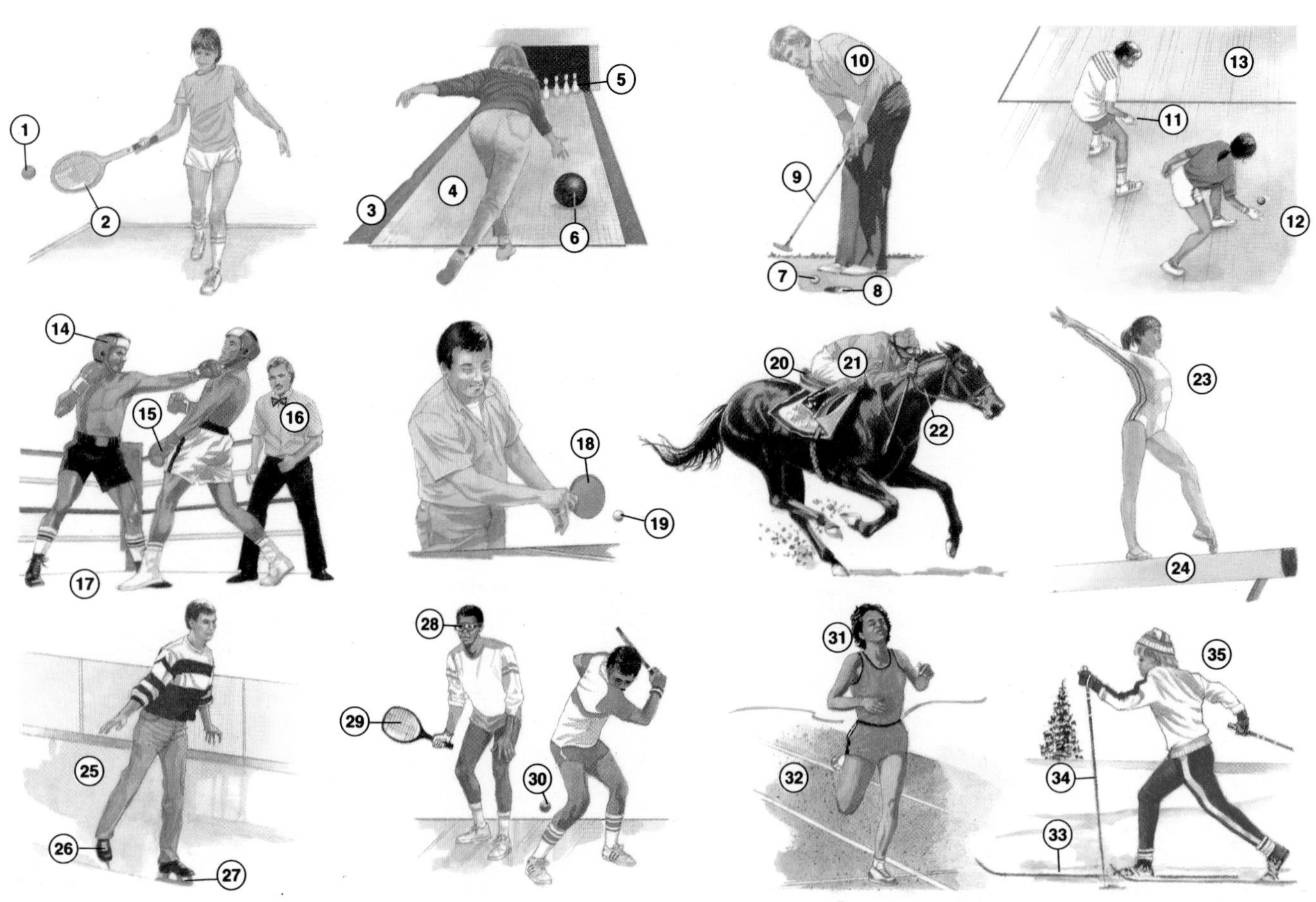

Теннис	**Tennis**
мяч	1. tennis ball
ракетка	2. racket
«Боулинг», игра в кегли	**Bowling**
желоб для возврата шара	3. gutter
кегельбан	4. lane
кегля	5. pin
шар	6. bowling ball
Гольф	**Golf**
мяч	7. golf ball
лунка	8. hole
короткая клюшка	9. putter
игрок в гольф	10. golfer
Гандбол	**Handball**
перчатка	11. glove
ручной мяч	12. handball
площадка	13. court
Бокс	**Boxing**
защитный шлем	14. head protector
боксерская перчатка	15. glove
судья, рефери	16. referee
ринг	17. ring
Пинг-понг	**Ping-Pong**
ракетка	18. paddle
мяч	19. ping-pong ball
Лошадиные бега	**Horse Racing**
седло	20. saddle
жокей	21. jockey
вожжи	22. reins
Гимнастика	**Gymnastics**
гимнастка	23. gymnast
гимнастическое бревно	24. balance beam
фигурное катание	**Ice Skating**
каток	25. rink
ботинок	26. skate
лезвие	27. blade
«Ракетбол»	**Racquetball**
защитные очки	28. safety goggles
ракетка	29. racquet
мяч	30. racquetball
Легкая атлетика	**Track and Field**
бегун	31. runner
беговая дорожка	32. track
Ходьба на лыжах	**Cross-Country Skiing**
лыжа	33. skis
палка	34. pole
лыжник	35. skier

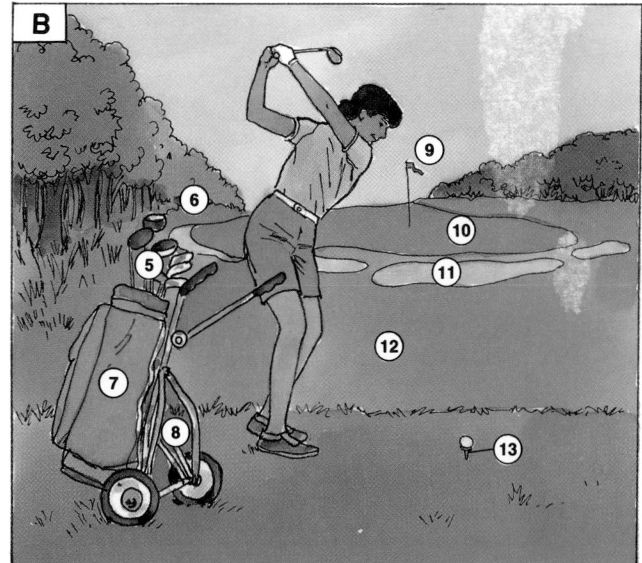

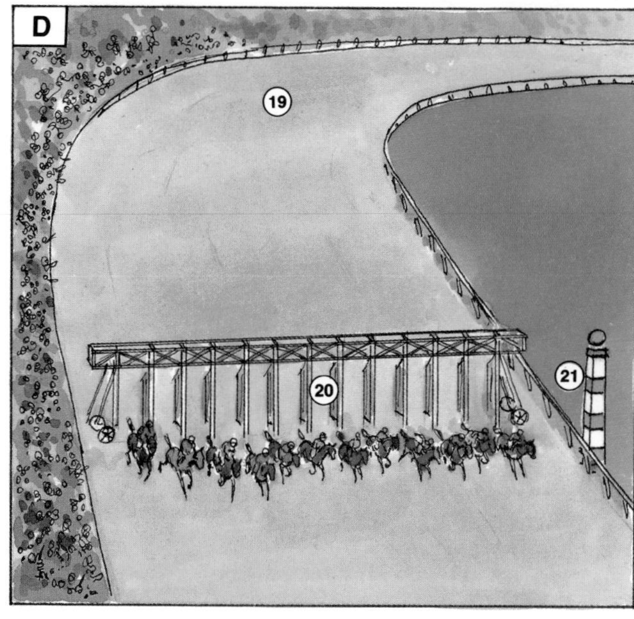

Теннисный корт	**A. Tennis Court**
место подачи	**1.** service court
сетка	**2.** net
линия подачи	**3.** service line
задняя линия	**4.** baseline
Поле гольфа	**B. Golf Course**
клюшки	**5.** clubs
«раф» (непостриженная трава на краю поля)	**6.** rough
сумка для клюшек	**7.** golf bag
ручная тележка	**8.** golf cart
флажок	**9.** flag
газон вокруг лунки на площадке гольфа	**10.** green
песчаное углубление вокруг лунки	**11.** sand trap
центр площадки	**12.** fairway
метка для мяча	**13.** tee

Лыжный склон	**C. Ski Slope**
палка	**14.** pole
лыжный ботинок	**15.** ski boot
крепление	**16.** binding
лыжа	**17.** ski
лыжный подъемник	**18.** ski lift
Ипподром	**D. Race Track**
финишная прямая	**19.** stretch
стартовые ворота	**20.** starting gate
финиш	**21.** finish line

Sports Verbs

Глаголы, относящиеся к спорту

ударять, бить	**1.** hit
подавать	**2.** serve
ударять ногой	**3.** kick
ловить, поймать	**4.** catch
передавать	**5.** pass
бежать, бегать	**6.** run
падать	**7.** fall
прыгать	**8.** jump

кататься (на коньках, роликах)	**9.** skate
бросать	**10.** throw
вести, бросать (мяч)	**11.** bounce
заниматься серфингом	**12.** surf
ездить (верхом, на велосипеде)	**13.** ride
прыгать (в воду), нырять, плавать под водой	**14.** dive
водить автомобиль	**15.** drive
бросать, стрелять	**16.** shoot

Musical Instruments

Музыкальные инструменты

Струнные инструменты		Strings
рояль	1.	piano
клавиатура		a. keyboard
ноты, партитура	2.	sheet music
гавайская гитара	3.	ukulele
мандолина	4.	mandolin
банджо	5.	banjo
арфа	6.	harp
скрипка	7.	violin
смычок		a. bow
альт	8.	viola
виолончель	9.	cello
контрабас	10.	bass
струна		a. string
гитара	11.	guitar
медиатор		a. pick

Духовые инструменты		Woodwinds
пикколо (миниатюрная флейта)	12.	piccolo
флейта	13.	flute
фагот	14.	bassoon
гобой	15.	oboe
кларнет	16.	clarinet

Ударные инструменты		Percussion
тамбурин	17.	tambourine
тарелки	18.	cymbals
барабан	19.	drum
барабанные палочки		a. drumsticks
барабан «конга»	20.	conga
литавра	21.	kettledrum
барабан «бонго»	22.	bongos

Медные инструменты		Brass
тромбон	23.	trombone
саксофон	24.	saxophone
труба	25.	trumpet
валторна	26.	French horn
туба	27.	tuba

Другие инструменты		Other Instruments
аккордеон	28.	accordion
орган	29.	organ
гармоника	30.	harmonica
ксилофон	31.	xylophone

Балет	**A. The Ballet**
занавес	**1.** curtain
декорация	**2.** scenery
балерина	**3.** dancer
прожектор	**4.** spotlight
сцена, эстрада	**5.** stage
оркестр	**6.** orchestra
дирижерский пульт	**7.** podium
дирижер	**8.** conductor
дирижерская палочка	**9.** baton
музыкант	**10.** musician
место в ложе	**11.** box seat
партер	**12.** orchestra seating
бельэтаж	**13.** mezzanine
балкон	**14.** balcony
зрители	**15.** audience
билетер	**16.** usher
театральная программа	**17.** programs

Музыкальная комедия	**B. Musical Comedy**
хор	**18.** chorus
актер	**19.** actor
актриса	**20.** actress

Роковая группа	**C. Rock Group**
синтезатор	**21.** synthesizer
пианист(-ка)	**22.** keyboard player
бас-гитарист	**23.** bass guitarist
солист(-ка), певец(-ица)	**24.** singer
гитарист	**25.** lead guitarist
электрическая гитара	**26.** electric guitar
барабанщик	**27.** drummer

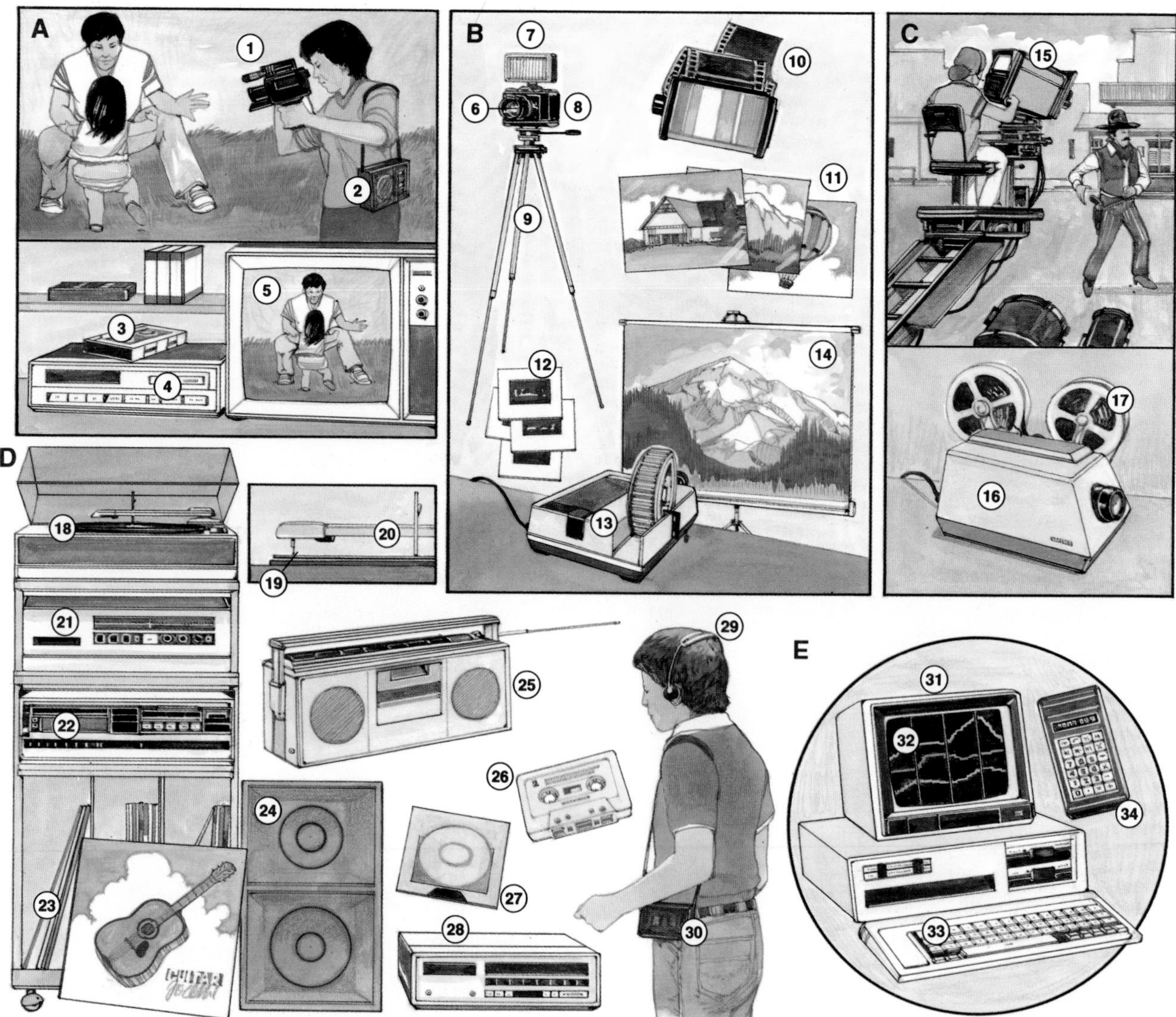

Вндео	**A. Video**
видеокамера	**1.** video camera
Миникам™ миникамера	**2.** Minicam ™
видеопленка	**3.** videocassette (tape)
видеомагнитофон	**4.** VCR (videocassette recorder)
телевизор	**5.** television
фотография	**B. Photography**
линза	**6.** lens
вспышка	**7.** flash
фотоаппарат	**8.** camera
штатив	**9.** tripod
кассета с фотопленкой	**10.** (roll of) film
отпечаток	**11.** prints
слайды, диапозитивы	**12.** slides
прожектор	**13.** slide projector
экран	**14.** screen
Кино	**C. Film**
кинокамера	**15.** movie camera
кинопроектор	**16.** projector
ролик, бобина кинопленки	**17.** (reel of) film

Звукозапись	**D. Audio**
проигрыватель	**18.** turntable
игла	**19.** cartridge needle
звукосниматель	**20.** arm
приемник	**21.** receiver
магнитофон	**22.** cassette deck
пластинки	**23.** records
громкоговоритель	**24.** speaker
стереомагнитофон	**25.** stereo cassette player
кассета	**26.** cassette
«Си-Ди» (компактный диск)	**27.** compact disc (CD)
проигрыватель для компактных дисков	**28.** compact disc player
наушники	**29.** headphones
плейер	**30.** Sony Walkman
Компьютеры	**E. Computers**
персональный компьютер	**31.** personal computer (PC)
экран	**32.** monitor
клавиатура	**33.** keyboard
калькулятор	**34.** calculator

Шитье	**A. Sewing**
швейная машина	**1.** sewing machine
шпулька	**2.** (spool of) thread
игольник	**3.** pincushion
ткань	**4.** material
фестонные ножницы	**5.** pinking shears
деталь, часть выкройки	**6.** pattern piece
выкройка	**7.** pattern
петля, петлица	**8.** buttonhole
пуговица	**9.** button
шов	**10.** seam
кайма, бейка, подшивка	**11.** hem
подрубочный шов	**12.** hem binding
кнопки	**13.** snap
крючок и петля	**14.** hook and eye
сантиметр	**15.** tape measure
застежка-молния	**16.** zipper
ножницы	**17.** (pair of) scissors
игла	**18.** needle
стежок	**19.** stitch
булавка	**20.** pin
наперсток	**21.** thimble
Рукоделие	**B. Other Needlecrafts**
вязание	**22.** knitting
шерсть	**23.** wool
моток	**24.** skein
вязальная игла	**25.** knitting needle
ручная вышивка гарусом по канве	**26.** needlepoint
вышивание	**27.** embroidery
вязание крючком	**28.** crochet
вязальный крючок	**29.** crochet hook
ткать	**30.** weaving
пряжа	**31.** yarn
сшивание лоскутов	**32.** quilting

Prepositions of Description

Предлоги описания

у (окна) **1.** at (the window)
над (черным котом) **2.** above (the black cat)
под (белым котом) **3.** below (the white cat)
между (подушками) **4.** between (the pillows)
на (ковре) **5.** on (the rug)

перед (камином) **6.** in front of (the fireplace)
в (выдвижном ящике) **7.** in (the drawer)
под (письменным столом) **8.** under (the desk)
за (креслом) **9.** behind (the chair)
на (столе) **10.** on top of (the table)
у, возле (телевизора) **11.** next to (the TV)

под (маяком)	**1.** through (the lighthouse)
вокруг (маяка)	**2.** around (the lighthouse)
с (горы)	**3.** down (the hill)
к (лунке)	**4.** toward (the hole)
от (лунки)	**5.** away from (the hole)
над (водой)	**6.** across (the water)
из (воды)	**7.** out of (the water)
по (мосту), через (мост)	**8.** over (the bridge)
на (площадку)	**9.** to (the course)
с (площадки)	**10.** from (the course)
подниматься (на холм)	**11.** up (the hill)
в (лунку)	**12.** into (the hole)

Дни недели	Days of the Week
воскресенье	Sunday
понедельник	Monday
вторник	Tuesday
среда	Wednesday
четверг	Thursday
пятница	Friday
суббота	Saturday

Месяцы	Months of the Year
январь	January
февраль	February
март	March
апрель	April
май	May
июнь	June
июль	July
август	August
сентябрь	September
октябрь	October
ноябрь	November
декабрь	December

Цифры		Numbers
ноль	0	zero
один	1	one
два	2	two
три	3	three
четыре	4	four
пять	5	five
шесть	6	six
семь	7	seven
восемь	8	eight
девять	9	nine
десять	10	ten
одиннадцать	11	eleven
двенадцать	12	twelve
тринадцать	13	thirteen
четырнадцать	14	fourteen
пятнадцать	15	fifteen
шестнадцать	16	sixteen
семнадцать	17	seventeen
восемнадцать	18	eighteen
девятнадцать	19	nineteen
двадцать	20	twenty
двадцать один	21	twenty-one
тридцать	30	thirty
сорок	40	forty
пятьдесят	50	fifty
шестьдесят	60	sixty
семьдесят	70	seventy
восемьдесят	80	eighty
девяносто	90	ninety
сто	100	a/one hundred
пятьсот	500	five hundred
шестьсот двадцать один	621	six hundred (and) twenty-one
тысяча	1,000	a/one thousand
миллион	1,000,000	a/one million

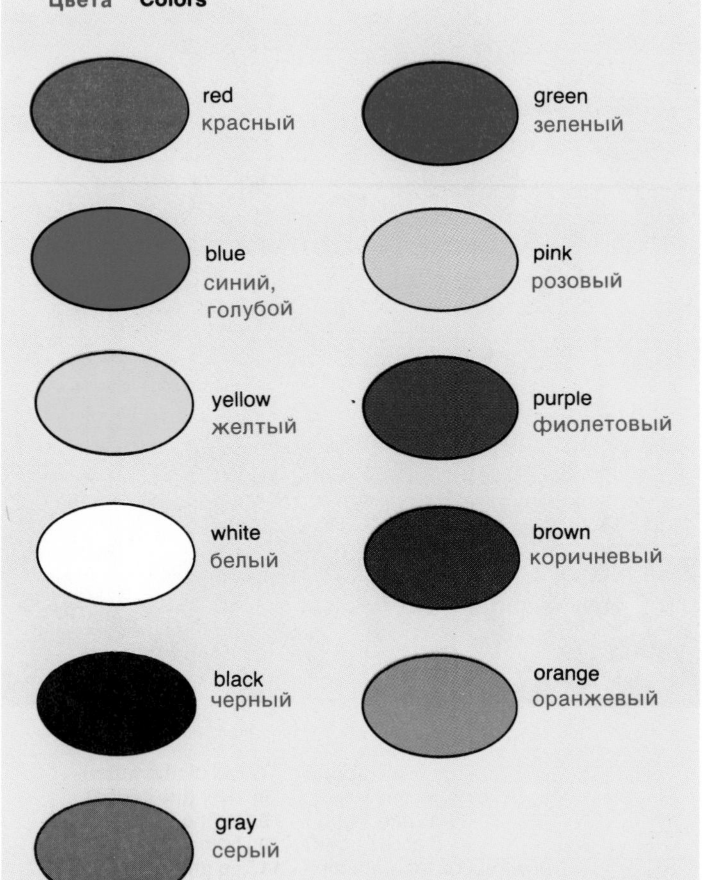

Two numbers occur after words in the index: the first refers to the page where the word is illustrated and the second to the item number of the word on that page. For example, above [ə bŭv/] **102** 2 means that the word *above* is the item numbered 2 on page 102. If only a bold number appears, then that word is part of the unit title or a subtitle.

The index includes a pronunciation guide for all the words illustrated in the book. This guide uses symbols commonly found in dictionaries for native speakers. These symbols, unlike those used in transcription systems such as the International Phonetic Alphabet, tend to preserve spelling and so should help you to become more aware of the connections between written English and spoken English.

Consonants

[b] as in **back** [băk]
[ch] as in **cheek** [chēk]
[d] as in **date** [dāt]
[dh] as in **the** [dh]
[f] as in **face** [fās]
[g] as in **gas** [găs]
[h] as in **half** [hăf]
[j] as in **jack** [jăk]
[k] as in **kite** [kīt]
[l] as in **leaf** [lēf]
[m] as in **man** [măn]
[n] as in **neck** [nĕk]
[ng] as in **ring** [rĭng]
[p] as in **pack** [păk]
[r] as in **rake** [rāk]
[s] as in **sand** [sănd]
[sh] as in **shell** [shĕl]
[t] as in **tape** [tāp]
[th] as in **three** [thrē]
[v] as in **vine** [vīn]
[w] as in **waist** [wāst]
[y] as in **yam** [yăm]
[z] as in **zoo** [zo͞o]
[zh] as in **measure** [mĕzh/ər]

Vowels

[ā] as in **bake** [bāk]
[ă] as in **back** [băk]
[ä] as in **bar** [bär]
[ē] as in **beat** [bēt]
[ĕ] as in **bed** [bĕd]
[ë] as in **bear** [bër]
[ī] as in **lime** [līm]
[ĭ] as in **lip** [lĭp]
[ï] as in **beer** [bïr]
[ō] as in **post** [pōst]
[ŏ] as in **box** [bŏks]
[ö] as in **claw** [klö]
or **for** [för]
[o͞o] as in **cool** [ko͞ol]
[o͝o] as in **book** [bo͝ok]
[ow] as in **cow** [kow]
[oy] as in **boy** [boy]
[ŭ] as in **cut** [kŭt]
[ü] as in **curb** [kürb]
[ə] as in **above** [ə bŭv/]

All pronunciation symbols used are alphabetical except for the schwa [ə], which is the most frequent vowel sound in English. If you use it appropriately in unstressed syllables, your pronunciation will sound more natural.

You should note that an umlaut ([¨]) calls attention to the special quality of vowels before [r]. (The sound [ö] can also represent a vowel not followed by [r] as in *claw.*) You should listen carefully to native speakers to discover how these vowels actually sound.

Stress

This guide also follows the system for marking stress used in many dictionaries for native speakers.

(1) Stress is not marked if a word consisting of a single syllable occurs in isolation.

(2) Where stress is marked, two levels are distinguished:
a bold accent [**/**] is placed after each syllable with primary stress,
a light accent [/] is placed after each syllable with secondary stress.

Syllable Boundaries

Syllable boundaries are indicated by a single space.

NOTE: The pronunciation used in this index is based on patterns of American English. There has been no attempt to represent all of the varieties of American English. Students should listen to native speakers to hear how the language actually sounds in a particular region.

above [ə bŭv/] **102** 2
abdomen [ăb/də mən] **4** 14
accelerator [ăk sĕl/ə rā/tər] **50** 27
accordion [ə kör/dē ən] **98** 28
accountant [ə kown/tənt] **86** 18
acorn [ā/körn] **61** 33b
acorn squash [ā/körn skwŏsh/] **7** 28
across [ə krös/] **103** 6
actor [ăk/tər] **99** 19
actress [ăk/trəs] **99** 20
acute angle [ə kyōōt/ăng/gəl] **79** 8
address [ă/drĕs] **46** 11
adjectives [ăj/ĭk tĭvz] **24, 25**
aerial tramway [ër/ē əl trăm/wā] **55** 31
Africa [ă/frĭ kə] **70** 4
after-shave lotion [ăf/tər shāv lō/shən] **23** 21
ailments [āl/mənts] **40**
air conditioner [ër/kən dĭ/shə nər] **32** 11
air filter [ër/fĭl/tər] **51** 52
Air Force [ër/förs/] **48** 19
air mattress [ër/mă/trəs] **91** 26
air pump [ër/ pŭmp/] **53** 13
air travel [ër/ tră/vəl] **56**
aircraft [ër/krăft/] **57**
aircraft carrier [ër/krăft kăr/yər] **48** 4
aircraft types [ër/krăft tīps/] **57**
(airmail) envelope [ër/māl ĕn/və lōp] **46** 16
airman [ër/mən] **48** 20
airport check-in [ër/pört chĕk/ĭn] **56**
aisle [ī/əl] **14** 10, **56** 23
Alabama [ăl/ə bă/mə] **72** 1
alarm clock [ə lärm/ klŏk] **32** 8
Alaska [ə lăs/kə] **72** 2
alcohol [ăl/kə höl/] **39** 22
alligator [ăl/ə gā/tər] **65** 8
almond(s) [ö/mənd(z)] **9** 31
Alps [ălps] **70** 44
Amazon River [ă/mə zŏn rĭv/ər] **71** 59
ambulance [ăm/byə ləns] **42** 6
amphibians [ăm fĭ/bē ənz] **65**
ammunition [ăm/yə nĭsh/ən] **48**
anchor [ăng/kər] **58** 24
Andes [ăn/dēz] **71** 43
ankle [ăng/kəl] **5** 49
animals [ăn/ə məlz] **62-69**
ant [ănt] **63** 12
Antarctic Ocean [ănt ärk/ tĭk ō/ shən] **70** 14
Antarctica [ănt ärk/tĭ kə] **70** 7
anteater [ănt/ē/tər] **66** 5
antenna [ăn tĕn/ə] **51** 46, **62** 1b
antler [ănt/lər] **67** 35a
apartment house [ə pärt/mənt hows/] **45** 23
apex [ā/pĕks] **79** 21
Appalachian Mountains [ăp/ə lā/chē ən mown/ tənz] **71** 41
apple [ă/pəl] **8** 2
apricot [ăp/rə kŏt/] **9** 25
apron [ā/prən] **16** 6
aquatic mammals [ə kwŏ/tĭk mă/məlz] **68**
Arabian Sea [ə rā/bē ən sē/] **70** 30
arc [ärk] **79** 16
architect [är/kə tĕkt/] **86** 8
Arctic [ärk/tĭk] **70** 8
Arizona [ăr/ə zō/nə] **72** 3
Arkansas [är/kən sö/] **72** 4
arm [ärm] **4** 6, **100** 20
armadillo [är/ mə dĭl/ō] **66** 2
armed forces [ärmd/ för/səz] **48**
armpit [ärm/pĭt/] **4** 10
armrest [ärm/rĕst/] **50** 3
Army [är/mē] **48** 15
around [ə rownd/] **103** 2
artery [är/tə rē] **5** 69
artichoke [är/tə chōk/] **6** 11
artist [är/təst] **86** 3
arts [ärts] **86**
ashtray [ăsh/trā/] **16** 29
Asia [ā/zhə] **70** 5
asparagus [ə spăr/ə gəs] **6** 18
asteroid [ăs/tə royd/] **74** 20
astronaut [ăs/trə nŏt/] **75** 5
at [ăt] **102** 1
Atacama Desert [ăt/ə kŏ/mə dĕz/ərt] **71** 50
athletic supporter [ăth lĕ/tĭk sə pör/tər] **22** 4
atlas [ăt/ləs] **47** 20
attachments [ə tăch/mənts] **35** 17
attendant [ə tĕn/dənt] **39** 8, **53** 12
audience [ö/dē əns] **99** 15
audio [ö/dē ō/] **100**
aunt [ănt] **3** 6
Australia [ö strāl/yə] **70** 6
author [ö/thər] **47** 8
automatic transmission [ö/ tə măt/ĭk trănz mĭ/shən] **50**
avocado [ăv/ə kŏ/dō] **9** 33
away from [ə wā/ frŭm] **103** 5
axe [ăks] **42** 14
baboon [bă bōōn/] **69** 19
baby [bā/ bē] **2** 5
baby carriage [bā/ bē kăr/ĭj] **45** 27
baby lotion [bā/ bē lō/shən] **33** 6
baby powder [bā/ bē pow/dər] **33** 7
baby wipes [bā/ bē wīps/] **33** 8
baby's room [bā/ bēz rōōm/] **33**
back [băk] **4** 11, **23** 19
backache [băk/āk/] **40** 8
backboard [băk/börd/] **92** 19
backhoe [băk/hō/] **82** 26
backpack [băk/păk/] **19** 4
backseat [băk/sēt/] **50** 32
backyard [băk/yärd/] **27**
back-up light [băk/əp līt/] **50** 30
bacon [bā/kən] **10** 11, **18,** 33
badge [băj] **43** 5
Baffin Bay [băf/ən bā/] **70** 16
bag [băg] **12** 8, **15** 25, **21** 35
baggage [băg/ĭj] **56** 8
bake [bāk] **31** 14
baked beans [bākt/ bēnz/] **18** 3
baked goods [bākt gŏŏdz/] **14** 11
baked potato [bākt/ pə tā/tō] **18** 20
baker [bā/kər] **84** 8
bakery [bā/kə rē] **44** 6
balance beam [băl/əns bēm/] **94** 24
balcony [băl/kə nē] **99** 14
(bale of) hay [bāl/ əv hā/] **81** 13
ball [böl] **5** 52
ballet [bă lā/] **99**
ballfields [böl/fēldz/] **93**
ballpoint pen [böl/poynt pĕn/] **76** 22
Baltic Sea [böl/tĭk sē/] **70** 22
bananas [bə nă/nəz] **9** 20
Band-Aid [bănd/ ād/] **39** 4
band shell [bănd/ shĕl/] **87** 2
bandage [băn/dĭj] **39** 24

banister [băn/ə stər] **28** 11
banjo [băn/jō/] **98** 5
banking [băng/kĭng] **86**
bar [bär] **13** 18, **16** 24
bar stool [bär/stōōl/] **16** 25
barber [bär/ bər] **84** 3
Barents Sea [băr/ənts sē/] **70** 23
barge [bärj] **58** 12
bark [bärk] **61** 35c
barn [bärn] **81** 5
barnyard [bärn/yärd/] **81** 8
barrel [băr/əl] **48** 23
barricade [băr/ ə kād/] **82** 21
bartender [bär/tĕn/dər] **16** 21
base [bās] **79** 7, **93** 6
baseball [bās/böl/] **92**
baseball diamond [bās/böl dī/mənd] **93**
baseline [bās/līn/] **95** 4
basin [bā/sən] **39** 16
basket [băs/kət] **92** 20
basketball [băs/kət böl/] **92**, **92** 21
bass [bās] **98** 10
bass guitarist [bās/gə tär/əst] **99** 23
bassoon [bă sōōn/] **98** 14
bat [băt] **66** 4, 92 5
batboy [băt/boy/] **93** 18
bath mat [băth/ măt/] **34** 12
bath towel [băth/ tow/əl] **34** 24
bathing suit [bā/dhĭng sōōt/] **90** 18
bathing trunks [bā/ dhĭng trŭngks/] **91** 33
bathrobe [băth/ rōb] **22** 20
bathroom [băth/ rōōm/] **34**
bathtub [băth/ tŭb/] **34** 11
baton [bə tŏn/] **99** 9
batter [băt/ ər] **92** 7, 93 14
battery [băt/ ə rē] **51** 54
batting helmet [băt/ĭng hĕl/mət] **92** 6
battleship [băt/ əl shĭp/] **48** 5
Bay of Bengal [bā/ əv bĕn göl/] **70** 32
bayonet [bā/ ə nĕt/] **48** 24
bays [bāz] **70**
beach [bēch] **90**
beach ball [bēch/ böl/] **90** 11
beach chair [bēch/ chĕr/] **90** 20
beach towel [bēch/ tow/ əl] **90** 15
beach umbrella [bēch/əm brĕl/ə] **90** 21
beads [bēdz] **23** 7
beak [bēk] **64** 3a
beaker [bē/kər] **78** 23
beard [bĭrd] **4** 39
bears [bërz] **69**
beat [bēt] **31** 8
Beaufort Sea [bō/ fərt sē/] **70** 15
beaver [bē/vər] **66** 12
bed [bĕd] **32** 21
bed rest [bĕd/ rĕst/] **41** 1
bedroom [bĕd/rōōm/] **32**
bedspread [bĕd/sprĕd/] **32** 23
bee [bē] **63** 19
beef [bēf] **10** 1
beef stew [bēf/ stōō/] **18** 14
beer [bĭr] **16** 23
beet(s) [bēts] **7** 33
beetle [bē/təl] **63** 10
behind [bə hīnd/] **102** 9
below [bə lō/] **102** 3
belt [bĕlt] **20** 16
bench [bĕnch] **43** 16, **44** 14, **78** 24, **87** 10
beret [bə rā/] **19** 22
Bering Sea [bër/ĭng sē/] **70** 34
berries [bër/ēz] 8
between [bə twēn/] **102** 4
beverages [bĕv/rə jəz] **14** 14
bib [bĭb] **33** 20
bicycle [bī/sĭ kəl] **52** 15
big [bĭg] **24** 8
(Big Dipper) constellation [bĭg/dĭ/pər kŏn stə lā/shən] **74** 3
big toe [bĭg/ tō/] **5** 53
bike stand [bīk/ stănd/] **52** 14
biker [bī/kər] **90** 4
bikes [bīks] **52**
(bikini) panties [bə kē/ nē păn/ tēz] **22** 11
bill [bĭl] **64** 24a
bin [bĭn] **15** 16
binding [bīn/ dĭng] **95** 16
binoculars [bə nŏk/ yə lərs] **90** 7
birch [bürch] **61** 32
birds [bürdz] **64**
biscuit [bĭs/ kət] **18** 27
bison [bī/sən] **67** 19
bit [bĭt] **37** 43a
black bear [blăk/ bër/] **69** 21
black bean(s) [blăk/ bēn(z)/] **6** 14
black eye [blăk/ ī/] **40** 5
Black Sea [blăk/ sē/] **70** 26
blackberries [blăk/ bër/ ēz] **8** 12
bladder [blă/ dər] **5** 72
blade [blād] **94** 27
blanket [blăng/ket] **32** 20
blazer [blā/zer] **20** 2
bleach [blēch] **35** 26
blender [blĕn/dər] **30** 12
blimp [blĭmp] **57** 5
blinds [blīndz] **32** 12
block [blŏk] **33** 32
blouse [blows] **21** 34
blue jay [blōō/ ja/] **64** 8
(blue) jeans [blōō/ jēnz/] **19** 6
blueberries [blōō/bër/ēz] **8** 14
blueprints [blōō/prĭnts/] **82** 6
blush [blŭsh] **23** 32
board [börd] **82** 16
boarding [bör/dĭng] **56**
boarding pass [bör/dĭng păs/] **56** 18
boardwalk [börd/wök/] **90** 1
body [bŏ/dē] **4**
boil [boyl] **31** 16
bollard [bŏl/ ərd] **58** 26
bolt [bōlt] **37** 38
bomb [bŏm] **48** 3
bomber [bŏm/ ər] **48** 2
bongos [bŏng/ gōz] **98** 22
book [bŏŏk] **13** 17
(book of) matches [bŏŏk/ əv mă/ chəz] **16** 28
bookcase [bŏŏk/ kās] **28** 22, **83** 20
bookstore [bŏŏk/ stör] **45** 18
boom [bōōm] **59** 7
booth [bōōth] **16** 9
boots [bōōts] **19** 21, **21** 32
bottle [bŏt/ əl] **12** 3, **33** 17
bottle opener [bŏt/ əl ō/ pə nər] **30** 6
bounce [bowns] **97** 11
bow [bō] **98** 7a
bow [bow] **58** 5
bowl [bōl] **13** 23
bowling [bōl/ĭng] **94**

bowling ball [bōlʹĭng bölʹ] **94** 6
box [bŏks] **13** 12
box seat [bŏksʹ sētʹ] **99** 11
box spring [bŏksʹ sprĭngʹ] **32** 18
boxer shorts [bŏkʹ sər shörtsʹ] **22** 2
boxing [bŏkʹ sĭng] **94**
boy's frame [boyzʹ frāmʹ] **52** 11
bra(ssiere) [brŏ]/[brə zïrʹ] **22** 13
brace [brās] **36** 9
bracelet [brāsʹlət] **23** 9
brain [brān] **5** 57
brake [brāk] **50** 26, **52** 17
brake light [brākʹlītʹ] **50** 29
branch [brănch] **61** 35a
brass [brăs] **98**
bread [brĕd] **14** 12
bread and butter plate [brĕdʹ ənd bŭtʹər plātʹ] **29** 11
break [brāk] **31** 7
breast [brĕst] **11** 21
bricks [brĭks] **82** 12
bridle path [brīdʹ əl păthʹ] **87** 7
briefcase [brēfʹkāsʹ] **21** 37
briefs [brēfs] **22** 12
broccoli [brŏkʹ ə lē] **6** 2
broil [broyl] **31** 13
broiler [broyʹlər] **30** 33
broken bone [brōʹkən bōnʹ] **40** 15
broom [broo͞m] **35** 7
brother [brŭdhʹər] **3** 9
brother-in-law [brŭdhʹ ər ən löʹ] **3** 11
bruise [broo͞z] **40** 17
brush [brŭsh] **76** 18
brussels sprouts [brŭsʹ əl sprowtsʹ] **6** 4
bucket [bŭkʹət] **35** 15
bucket seat [bŭkʹət sētʹ] **50** 16
buckle [bŭkʹ əl] **20** 17
bud [bŭd] **60** 18a
buffet [bə fāʹ] **29** 29
builder [bĭlʹdər] **82** 5
building number [bĭlʹdĭng nŭmʹ bər] **45** 24
bulb [bŭlb] **60** 8a
bull [bo͝ol] **67** 34
bulldozer [bo͝olʹdōʹ zər] **82** 27
bullet [bo͝olʹĭt] **48** 26
bulletin board [bo͝olʹĭ tən bördʹ] **76** 7
bumper [bŭmʹpər] **33** 5
bun [bŭn] **18** 7
bunch [bŭnch] **8** 1
Bunsen burner [bŭnʹsən bürʹ nər] **78** 20
buoy [bo͞oʹē]/[boy] **58** 16
bureau [byo͝orʹō] **32** 9
burn [bürn] **17** 14, **40** 18
burner [bürʹnər] **30** 29
bus [bŭs] **53** 20, **54**
bus driver [bŭsʹdrīʹvər] **54** 3
bus stop [bŭsʹstŏpʹ] **44** 13
busboy [bŭsʹboyʹ] **16** 3
bushes [bo͝oshʹ əz] **61** 41
business workers [bizʹnəs würʹkərz] **86**
butcher [bo͝oʹchər] **84** 13
butter [bŭtʹər] **18** 18
buttercup [bŭtʹər kŭpʹ] **60** 17
butterfly [bŭtʹ ər flīʹ] **63** 3
buttocks [bŭtʹəks] **4** 15
button [bŭtʹ ən] **20** 3, **101** 9
buttonhole [bŭtʹ ən hōlʹ] **101** 8
C-clamp [sēʹklămpʹ] **36** 2
cab driver [kăbʹdrīʹ vər] **55** 26
cabbage [kăbʹĭj] **6** 3
cabin [kăbʹĭn] **56** 19
cabin cruiser [kăbʹĭn kro͞oʹ zər] **59** 16
cabinet [kăbʹə nət] **30** 22
cable [kāʹbəl] **52** 23
cable car [kāʹbəl kärʹ] **55** 32
cactus [kăkʹtəs] **61** 40
calculator [kălʹkyə lāʹ tər] **83** 19, **100** 34
calendar [călʹən dər] **83** 9
calf [kăf] **4** 20, **67** 31
California [kălʹ ə förʹ nyə] **72** 5
call card [költkärdʹ] **47** 6
call number [kölʹnŭmʹ bər] **47** 6
call slip [kölʹslĭpʹ] **47** 12
camel [kămʹəl] **67** 33
camera [kămʹər ə] **100** 8
cameraperson [kămʹər ə pürʹ sən] **86** 10
camisole [kămʹə sōlʹ] **22** 9
camp stove [kămpʹstōvʹ] **89** 25
camper [kămʹpər] **53** 16
campfire [kămpʹfīrʹ] **89** 31
camping [kămʹpĭng] **89**
can [kăn] **12** 10
can opener [kănʹ ōʹ pə nər] **30** 4
canary [kə nërʹ ē] **64** 14
candle [kănʹdəl] **29** 27
candlestick [kănʹdəl stĭkʹ] **29** 28
canister [kănʹə stər] **30** 15
canned goods [kăndʹ go͝odzʹ] **14** 13
cannon [kănʹ ən] **48** 11
canoe [kə no͞oʹ] **59** 2
cantaloupe [kănʹ tə lōpʹ] **9** 36
canyon [kănʹ yən] **88** 3
cap [kăp] **19** 2, **21** 43, **92** 11
capsule [kăpʹ səl] **41** 5
car [kär] **54** 9
card catalog [kärdʹ kătʹ ə lög] **47** 4
cardigan [kärʹdĭ gən] **21** 26
cardinal [kärdʹnəl] **64** 11
cargo [kärʹgō] **58** 10
cargo area [kärʹgō ërʹ ē ə] **57** 12
cargo bay [kärʹgō bāʹ] **75** 9
cargo door [kärʹgō dörʹ] **57** 13
Caribbean Sea [kărʹ ə bēʹ ən sēʹ] **70** 20
carpenter [kärʹpən tər] **85** 2
carpenter's rule [kärʹ pən tərz ro͞olʹ] **36** 1
carrot(s) [kărʹ ət(s)] **7** 32
carry [kărʹē] **26** 16
carry-on bag [kărʹē ŏn băgʹ] **56** 2
cars [kärz] **50-51**
carton [kärʹtən] **12** 1
cartridge needle [kärʹtrĭj nēʹ dəl] **100** 19
carve [kärv] **31** 6
cash register [kăshʹrĕʹ jə stər] **15** 21
cashew(s) [kăshʹ o͞o(z)] **9** 27
cashier [kă shïrʹ] **15** 22
Caspian Sea [kăsʹpē ən sēʹ] **70** 27
casserole dish [kăsʹ ə rōl dĭshʹ] **30** 14
cassette [kə sĕtʹ] **100** 26
cassette deck [kə sĕtʹ dĕkʹ] **100** 22
cast [kăst] **39** 5
cat [kăt] **68** 4
catch [kăch] **96** 4
catcher [kăchʹ ər] **92** 2, **93** 16
catcher's mask [kăchʹərz măskʹ] **92** 3
catcher's mitt [kăchʹərz mĭtʹ] **92** 4
caterpillar [kătʹər pĭlʹər] **63** 1
cattle [kătʹ əl] **81** 20
Caucasus [köʹkə səs] **71** 45

cauliflower [kŏl/ ə flow/ ər] **6** 1
ceiling [sē/lĭng] **28** 2
ceiling fan [sē/lĭng făn/] **28** 1
celery [sĕl/ ə rē] **6** 10
cello [chĕl/o] **98** 9
cement [sə mĕnt/] **82** 10
cement mixer [sə mĕnt/ mĭk/ sər] **82** 25
cement truck [sə mĕnt/ trŭk/] **49** 13
center [sĕn/ tər] **79** 13, **93** 27
center divider [sĕn/ tər də vī/ dər] **53** 18, **82** 24
center fielder [sĕn/ tər fēl/dər] **93** 2
center lane [sĕn/ tər lān/] **53** 6
centerboard [sĕn/ tər börd/] **59** 6
centipede [sĕn/ tə pēd/] **63** 22
chain [chān] **23** 5, **52** 18
chair [chër] **29** 17
chalk [chök] **76** 10
chalk tray [chök/ trā/] **76** 9
chalkboard [chök/ börd/] **76** 5
chandelier [shăn/ də lïr/] **29** 3
change (the sheets) [chānj/ dhə shēts/] **38** 13
changing table [chān/ jĭng tā/ bəl] **33** 9
charcoal briquettes [chär/ kōl brĭ kĕts/] **27** 23
chart [chärt] **39** 10
check [chĕk] **15** 27, **16** 14
checked [chĕkt] **24** 18
checkout counter [chĕk/ owt kown/ tər] **15** 26
checkout desk [chĕk/ owt dĕsk/] **47** 2
cheerleaders [chïr/ lē/ dərz] **93** 20
cheek [chēk] **4** 35
cherries [chër/ ēz] **9** 19
cherry picker [chër/ ē pĭk/ ər] **82** 18
chest [chĕst] **4** 12
chest of drawers [chĕst/ əv drörz/] **32** 30
chestnut(s) [chĕs/ nŭt(s)] **9** 32
chick [chĭk] **64** 22
chicken [chĭk/ ən] **11** 24, **64** 23
child's seat [chīldz/ sēt/] **50** 33
children [chĭl/ drən] **2** 7
chills [chĭlz] **40** 4
chimney [chĭm/ nē] **27** 9
chimpanzee [chĭm păn/ zē] **69** 16
chin [chĭn] **4** 3
china [chī/ nə] **29** 1
china closet [chī/ nə klŏz/ ət] **29** 2
chipmunk [chĭp/ mŭnk] **66** 6
chop [chŏp] **26** 11, **31** 11
chops [chŏps] **10** 9, **10** 15
chorus [kör/ əs] **99** 18
(chrysanthe)mum [krə săn/ thə məm]/[mŭm] **60** 4
cigarette [sĭg/ ə rĕt/] **16** 31
circle [sür/ kəl] **79** 11
circuit breaker [sür/ kət brā/ kər] **35** 5
circular saw [sür/ kyə lər sö/] **36** 20
circumference [sür kŭm/ fə rəns] **79** 17
citrus fruits [sĭ/ trəs fro͞ots/] **8**
city [sĭt/ ē] **44-45**
clam(s) [klăm(z)] **11** 32
clamp [klămp] **78** 7
clarinet [klăr/ ə nĕt/] **98** 16
clasp [klăsp] **23** 17
classroom [klăs/ ro͞om/] **76**
claw [klö] **62** 13a, **68** 2a
clean [klēn] **24** 6, **26** 2
cleanser [klĕn/ zər] **35** 9
clear [klïr] **17** 6
cliff [klĭf] **89** 21
clip-on earring [klĭp/ ŏn ïr/ ĭng] **23** 15
clock [klŏk] **76** 2
close (*v*) [klōz] **77** 5
closed [klōzd] **24** 16
closet [klŏz/ ət] **32** 3
cloth diaper [klöth/ dī/ pər] **33** 13
clothes [klōz] **19-24**
clothesline [klōz/ līn/] **35** 19
clothespins [klōz/ pĭnz/] **35** 20
cloudy [klow/ dē] **25** 2
clove [klōv] **7** 25a
cloverleaf [klō/ vər lēf/] **53** 4
clubs [klŭbz] **95** 5
clutch [klŭch] **50** 25
coach [kōch] **93** 21
coal [kōl] **80** 7
coal mine [kōl/ mīn] **80** 6
coaster [kō/ stər] **16** 27
coat [kōt] **19** 24, **42** 13
cob [kŏb] **6** 12a
cobra [kō/ brə] **65** 11
cockpit [kŏk/pĭt/] **56** 13
cockroach [kŏk/ rōch/] **63** 9
cocktail lounge [kŏk/ tāl lownj/] **16**
cocktail waitress [kŏk/ tāl wā/ trəs] **16** 32
cocoon [kə ko͞on/] **63** 2
coconut [kō/ kə nŭt/] **8** 3
coffee [kö/ fē] **18** 35
coffeemaker [kö/ fē mā/ kər] **30** 31
coffeepot [kö/ fē pŏt/] **29** 18
coffee table [kö/ fē tā/ bəl] **28** 26
coins [koynz] **13** 26
colander [kŏl/ ən dər] **30** 7
cold [kōld] **25** 10, **40** 11
cold water faucet [kōld/ wŏ tər fö/ sət] **34** 18
collar [kŏl/ ər] **20** 20
colonial-style house [kə lō/ nē əl stīl hows/] **27**
Colorado [kŏl/ ə rŏd/ ō] **72** 6
column [kŏl/ əm] **50** 13
comb [kōm] **32** 6
combine (*n*) [kŏm/ bīn] **81** 17
comet [kŏm/ ət] **74** 2
comforter [kŭm/ fər tər] **32** 22
command module [kə mănd/ mŏj/ o͞ol] **75** 8
communication satellite [kə myo͞o/ nə kā shən săt/ ə līt] **75** 2
commuter [kə myo͞o/ tər] **55** 17
commuter train [kə myo͞o/ tər trān/] **55** 14
compact disc (CD) [kŏm/ păkt dĭsk/]/[sē/ dē/] **100** 27
compact disc player [kŏm/ păkt dĭsk/ plā/ ər] **100** 28
computer [kəm pyo͞o/ tər] **76** 8, **83** 16, **100**
computer programmer [kəm pyo͞o/ tər prō/ grăm ər] **86** 16
conductor [kən dŭk/ tər] **54** 7, **99** 8
cone [kōn] **61** 34b, **79** 28, **82** 19
conga [kŏng/ gə] **98** 20
Congo River [kŏng/ gō rĭv/ ər] **71** 62
Connecticut [kə nĕ/ tĭ kət] **72** 7
constellation [kŏn/ stə lā/ shən] **74** 3
construction [kən strŭk/ shən] **82**
(construction) boots [kən strŭk/ shən bo͞ots/] **21** 32

construction site [kən strŭk′ shən sīt′] **82**
construction worker [kən strŭk′ shən wür′ kər] **82** 14
container [kən tā′nər] **12** 2, **58** 7
(container)ship [kən tā′ nər shĭp′] **58** 9
containers [kən tā′ nərz] **12**
continents [kŏn′ tə nənts] **70**
control tower [kən trōl′ tow′ər] **57** 20
conveyor belt [kən vā′ər bĕlt] **15** 23, **56** 12
cook (*n*) [ko͝ok] **17** 4
cook (*v*) [ko͝ok] **17** 4
cookie [ko͝ok′ ē] **18** 22
cool [ko͞ol] **25** 9
cooler [ko͞o′ lər] **91** 41
cooling tower [ko͞o′lĭng tow′ər] **80** 16
copilot [kō′pī lət] **56** 16
cord [körd] **32** 26a, **54** 1
(corduroy) pants [kör′ də roy pănts′] **21** 27
core [kör] **8** 2b, **80** 14
cork [körk] **16** 18
corkscrew [körk′ skro͞o′] **16** 17
corn [körn] **6** 12, **60** 24
corner [kör′ nər] **44** 3
corral [kə răl′] **81** 24
cosmetics [kŏz mĕt′ ĭks] **23**
cotton balls [kŏt′ ən bölz′] **39** 23
cotton swab [kŏt′ ən swŏb′] **33** 10
counter [kown′ tər] **30** 27
court [kört] **43**, **94** 13
court officer [kört′ ö′ fə sər] **43** 19
court reporter [kört′ rə pör′ tər] **43** 14
cousin [kŭz′ən] **3** 7
cow [kow] **67** 32
cowboy [kow′ boy′] **81** 21
cowgirl [kow′ gürl′] **81** 22
crab(s) [kră b(z)] **11** 36, **62** 9
cradle [krā′ dəl] **33** 26
cranberries [krăn′ bër′ ēz] **8** 13
crane [krān] **58** 6
creamer [krē′ mər] **29** 24
crew [kro͞o] **75** 12
(crewneck) sweater [kro͞o′ nĕk swĕt′ ər] **19** 7
crib [krĭb] **33** 4
criket [krĭk′ ət] **63** 5
crime [krīm] **43**
crochet [krō shā′] **101** 28
crochet hook [krō′ shā′ ho͝ok′] **101** 29
crocus [krō′ kəs] **60** 9
cross-country skiing [krös′ kŭn trē skē′ ĭng] **94**
crosswalk [krös′ wök′] **44** 4
crow [krō] **64** 3
crutch [krŭch] **39** 7
cube [kyo͞ob] **79** 27
cubicle [kyo͞o′ bə kəl] **83** 5
cucumber(s) [kyo͞o′ kŭm bər(z)] **7** 20
cuff links [kŭf′ lĭnks′] **23** 12
cup [kŭp] **13** 19, **29** 20
curb [kürb] **45** 26
curtain [kür′ tən] **32** 10, **99** 1
curtain rings [kür′ tən rĭngz′] **34** 2
curtain rod [kür′ tən rŏd′] **34** 1
curve [kürv] **79** 3
cushion [ko͝osh′ ən] **28** 24
customer [kŭs′ tə mər] **15** 17
cut (*v*) [kŭt] **31** 9
cut (*n*) [kŭt] **40** 16
cutting board [kŭt′ ĭng börd′] **30** 26
cylinder [sĭl′ ĭn dər] **79** 26
cymbals [sĭm′ bəlz] **98** 18
daffodil [dăf′ ə dĭl] **60** 8
dairy cow [dër′ ē kow′] **81** 11
dairy farm [dër′ ē färm′] **81**
dairy products [dër′ ē prŏd′ ŭkts] **14** 4
daisy [dā′ zē] **60** 5
dam [dăm] **80** 18
dance [dăns] **99**
dancer [dăn′ sər] **99** 3
dark [därk] **24** 10
dashboard [dăsh′ börd′] **50** 19
date [dāt] **9** 23
daughter [dö′ tər] **3** 15
deck [dĕk] **27** 5, **58** 22
deer [dïr] **67** 26
defendant [də fĕn′ dənt] **43** 23
defense attorney [də fĕns′ ə tür′ nē] **43** 22
Delaware [dĕl′ ə wăr′] **72** 8
deli counter [dĕl′ ē kown′ tər] **14** 1
delivery boy [də lĭv′ ə rē boy′] **85** 10
delivery person [də lĭv′ ə rē pür′ sən] **49** 10
dental care [dĕn′ təl kër′] **39**
dentist [dĕn′ tĭst] **39** 17
department store [də pärt′ mənt stör′] **44** 5
depth [dĕpth] **79** 33
derrick [dĕr′ ĭk] **80** 2
deserts [dĕz′ ərts] **71**
desk [dĕsk] **28** 14, **76** 16, **83** 13
detective [də tĕk′ tĭv] **43** 2
diagonal [dī ăg′ ə nəl] **79** 20
diameter [dī ăm′ ə tər] **79** 12
dictionary [dĭk′ shə nër′ ē] **47** 24
diesel fuel [dē′ zəl fyo͞o′ əl] **80** 34
dig [dĭg] **26** 3
dime [dīm] **13** 29
dinghy [dĭng′ ē] **59** 18
dining room [dī′ nĭng ro͞om′] **29**
dipstick [dĭp′ stĭk′] **51** 58
dirt bike [dürt′ bīk′] **52** 8
disc jockey (DJ) [dĭsk′ jŏk′ ē]/[dē′ jā] **86** 9
dirty [dür′ tē] **24** 5
dish drainer [dĭsh′ drā′ nər] **30** 2
dish towel [dĭsh′ tow′ əl] **30** 18
dishwasher [dĭsh′ wŏsh′ ər] **30** 1
dishwashing liquid [dĭsh′ wŏsh ĭng lĭ′ kwĭd] **30** 10
disposable diaper [dĭs pō′ zə bəl dī′ pər] **33** 12
dissection kit [dĭ sĕk′ shən kĭt′] **78** 33
dive [dīv] **97** 14
dock [dŏk] **58** 28
doctor [dŏk′ tər] **39** 11
dogs [dögz] **69**
dogwood [dög′ wo͝od′] **61** 28
doll [dŏl] **33** 28
doll house [dŏl′ hows′] **33** 25
dollar bills [dŏl′ər bĭlz′] **13** 25
dolly [dŏl′ ē] **56** 6
dolphin [dŏl′ fĭn] **68** 13
donkey [dŏng′ kē] **67** 23
door handle [dör′ hăn′ dəl] **50** 4
door lock [dör′ lŏk′] **50** 1
doorman [dör′ mən] **85** 11
down [down] **103** 3
down vest [down′ vĕst′] **19** 12
dragonfly [drăg′ ən flī′] **63** 4
drain [drān] **34** 9
drainpipe [drān′ pīp′] **27** 18

drapes [drāps] **28** 23
draw [drö] **77** 11
drawer [drör] **47** 5
dress [drĕs] **20** 22
dried fruits [drīd′ froōts′] **9**
drill [drĭl] **39** 15
drink [drĭngk] **17** 2
drive [drīv] **97** 15
driveway [drīv′ wā′] **27** 1
drugstore [drŭg′ stör′] **45** 22
drum [drŭm] **98** 19
drummer [drŭm′ər] **99** 27
drumsticks [drŭm′ stĭks′] **98** 19a
dry [drī] **25** 14, **38** 9
dryer [drī′ər] **35** 24
duck [dŭk] **11** 25, **64** 25
(duck) pond [dŭk′ pŏnd′] **87** 8
dugout [dŭg′ owt′] **93** 13
dump truck [dŭmp′ trŭk′] **49** 14
dust [dŭst] **38** 15
dustpan [dŭst′ păn′] **35** 8
eagle [ē′ gəl] **64** 5
ear [ïr] **4** 34
(ear of) corn [ïr′ əv körn′] **6** 12
earmuffs [ïr′ mŭfs′] **19** 10
earrings [ïr′ ĭngz] **23** 1
Earth [ürth] **74** 8, **13**
east [ēst] **71** 73
East China Sea [ēst′ chī′ nə sē′] **70** 38
eat [ēt] **17** 1
eel [ēl] **65** 4
egg [ĕg] **18** 32, **64** 13
egg roll [ĕg′ rōl′] **18** 25
eggplant [ĕg′ plănt′] **7** 21
elbow [ĕl′ bō] **4** 8
electric drill [ĭ lĕk′ trĭk drĭl′] **37** 43
electric guitar [ĭ lĕk′ trĭk gĭ tär′] **99** 26
electric generator [ĭ lĕk′ trĭk gĕn′ ə rā tər] **80** 21
electrical tape [ĭ lĕk′ trĭ kəl tāp′] **37** 34
electrician [ĭ lĕk trĭ′ shən] **85** 6
electricity [ĭ lĕk trĭs′ ĭ tē] **80** 32
electronics [ĭ lĕk trŏn′ ĭks] **100**
elephant [ĕl′ ə fənt] **66** 17
elevator [ĕl′ ə vā′ tər] **45** 17, **80** 9
elm [ĕlm] **61** 36
embroidery [ĕm broi′ də rē] **101** 27
emergency brake [ĭ mür′ jən sē brāk′] **50** 15
emery board [ĕm′ ə rē börd′] **23** 24
encyclopedia [ĕn sī′ klə pē′ dē ə] **47** 25
end table [ĕnd′ tā′ bəl] **28** 29
end zone [ĕnd′ zōn′] **93** 23
energy [ĕn′ər jē] **80**
engagement ring [ĕn gāj′ mənt rĭng′] **23** 3
engine [ĕn′ jən] **51, 52** 32
engineer [ĕn′ jə nïr′] **55** 15
enter [ĕn′ tər] **77** 14
entrance ramp [ĕn′ trəns rămp′] **53** 21
envelope [ĕn′ və lōp′] **46** 16, **83** 31
equator [ĭ kwā′ tər] **71** 70
erase [ĭ rās′] **77** 3
eraser [ĭ rā′ sər] **76** 11
escarole [ĕs′ kə rōl′] **6** 7
esophagus [ĭ sŏf′ ə gəs] **5** 61
eucalyptus [yoō′ kə lĭp′ təs] **61** 27
Europe [yoŏr′ əp] **70** 3
examining table [ĭg zăm′ ə nĭng tā′ bəl] **39** 6
exhaust pipe [ĭg zöst′ pīp′] **52** 33
exit ramp [ĕg′ zĭt rămp′] **53** 2
exit sign [ĕg′ zĭt sīn′] **53** 24
Express Mail (package) [ĭk sprĕs′ māl păk′ ĭj] **46** 23
extension cord [ĭk stĕn′ shən körd′] **36** 5
eye [ī] **5**
eye drops [ī′ drŏps′] **41** 10
eye shadow [ī′ shă′ dō] **23** 30
eyebrow [ī′ brow′] **5** 44
eyebrow pencil [ī′ brow pĕn′ səl] **23** 26
eyelashes [ī′ lăsh′ əz] **5** 46
eyelid [ī′ lĭd′] **5** 45
eyeliner [ī′ lī′ nər] **23** 33
fabric softener [făb′ rĭk sö′ fə nər] **35** 27
face [fās] **4** 1
face guard [fās′ gärd′] **92** 15
factory work [făk′ tə rē würk′] **85**
fairway [fĕr′ wā′] **95** 12
fall [föl] **96** 7
Fall [föl] **26**
family [făm′ ə lē] **3**
family restaurant [făm′ ə lē rĕs′ tər ənt] **16**
fan belt [făn′ bĕlt′] **51** 53
fare [fĕr] **55** 21
fare box [fĕr′ bŏks′] **54** 5
farmhouse [färm′ hows′] **81** 3
farmer [fär′ mər] **81** 7
farming [fär′ mĭng] **81**
fashion designer [făsh′ ən də zī′ nər] **86** 6
father [fŏdh′ ər] **3** 5
faucet [fö′ sĭt] **34** 17, 18
fawn [fön] **67** 27
feather [fĕdh′ər] **64** 7a
feather duster [fĕdh′ ər dŭs′ tər] **35** 2
fence [fĕns] **81** 9
fender [fĕn′ dər] **52** 10
ferry [fĕr′ ē] **58** 17
fever [fē′ vər] **40** 2
field [fēld] **81** 16
fields and courses [fēldz′ ənd kör′ səz] **95**
fig [fĭg] **9** 21
fighter plane [fī′ tər plān′] **48** 1
file cabinet [fīl′ kăb′ ə nət] **83** 21
file clerk [fīl′ klürk′] **83** 23
file folder [fīl′ fōl′ dər] **83** 22
filet [fĭ lā′] **11** 28
fill [fĭl] **26** 9
film [fĭlm] **100** 10, **100** 17
filter paper [fĭl′ tər pā′ pər] **78** 16
fin [fĭn] **65** 3b
finger [fĭng′ gər] **4** 25
fingernail [fĭng′ gər nāl′] **4** 23
fingerprints [fĭng′ gər prĭnts′] **43** 24
finish line [fĭn′ ĭsh līn′] **95** 21
fire [fīr] **28** 9, **42** 5
fire engine [fīr′ ĕn′ jən] **42** 2
fire escape [fīr′ ə skāp′] **42** 4
fire extinguisher [fīr′ ĭk stĭng′ gwĭ shər] **42** 11
fire fighter [fīr′ fī′ tər] **42** 10
fire hydrant [fīr′ hī′ drənt] **42** 9
fire truck [fīr′ trŭk′] **42** 3
firefighting [fīr′ fī′ tĭng] **42**
firefly [fīr′ flī′] **63** 17

fireplace [fīr′ plās'] **28** 8
first baseman [fürst′ bās′ mən] **93** 8
first quarter [fürst′ kwör′ tər] **74** 23
fish [fĭsh] **11** 26, **65**
fisherman [fĭsh′ ər mən] **58** 2
fishing [fĭsh′ ĭng] **88**
fishing boat [fĭsh′ ĭng bōt'] **58** 1
fishing line [fĭsh′ ĭng līn'] **88** 8
fishing net [fĭsh′ ĭng nĕt'] **88** 9
fishing rod [fĭsh′ ĭng rŏd'] **88** 7
flag [flăg] **76** 1, **82** 20, **95** 9
flame [flām] **29** 26, **78** 21
flamingo [flə mĭng′ gō] **64** 29
flanker [flăng′ kər] **93** 31
flannel shirt [flăn′ əl shürt′] **19** 3
flare [flër] **51** 41
flash [flăsh] **100** 7
flashlight [flăsh′ līt'] **35** 3
flask [flăsk] **78** 2
(flat) sheet [flăt′ shēt'] **32** 19
flatbed [flăt′ bĕd'] **49** 18
flight attendant [flīt′ ə tĕn' dənt] **56** 20
flight deck [flīt′ dĕk'] **75** 10
flight engineer [flīt′ ĕn jə nïr'] **56** 17
flipper [flĭp′ ər] **68** 12a
flippers [flĭp′ ərz] **91** 36
floor [flör] **32** 29
Florida [flör′ ə də] **72** 9
florist [flör′ ĭst] **84** 11
flounder [flown′ dər] **65** 7
flowers [flow′ ərz] **60**
flute [flo͞ot] **99** 13
fly [flī] **63** 18
flying mammal [flī′ ĭng mă′ məlz] **66**
foal [fōl] **67** 22
foggy [fög′ ē] **25** 12
fold [fōld] **38** 1
food [fo͞od] **6-18**
foot [fo͝ot] **5**
football [fo͝ot′ böl'] **92, 92** 13
football field [fo͝ot′ böl fēld'] **93**
forceps [för′ səps] **78** 28
forearm [för′ ärm'] **4** 9
forehead [för′ hĕd'] **4** 32
forelegs [för′ lĕgz'] **66** 3d
foreman [för′ mən] **85** 13
fork [förk] **29** 12
forklift [förk′ lĭft'] **58** 4
foul line [fowl′ līn'] **93** 9
foundation [fown dā′ shən] **82** 11
four-door hatchback [för′ dör hăch′ băk] **51**
fox [fŏks] **68** 6
fractions [frăk′ shənz] **79**
frame [frām] **28** 4
frame backpack [frām′ băk′ păk] **89** 28
freezer [frē′ zər] **14** 3, **30** 20
freezing [frē′ zĭng] **25** 11
french fries [frĕnch′ frīz'] **18** 28
French horn [frĕnch′ hörn′] **98** 26
fried chicken [frīd′ chĭk′ ən] **18** 29
Frisbee™ [frĭz′ bē] **90** 13
frog [frŏg] **65** 17
from [frŭm] **103** 10
front bumper [frŭnt′ bŭm' pər] **51** 51
frozen foods [frō′zən fo͞odz′] **14** 2
fruit and vegetable market [fro͞ot′ ənd vĕj′ tə bəl mär' kət] **44** 28
fruit tree [fro͞ot′ trē'] **81** 2
fruits [fro͞ots] **8**
fry [frī] **31** 15
frying pan [frī′ ĭng păn'] **30** 5
fuel truck [fyo͞o′ əl trŭk'] **49** 3
full moon [fo͝ol′ mo͞on′] **74** 24
full slip [fo͝ol′ slĭp'] **22** 10
fullback [fo͝ol′ băk'] **93** 34
funnel [fŭn′ əl] **78** 17
fuselage [fyo͞o′ sə lŏj'] **57** 14
galaxy [găl′ək sē] **74** 1
Ganges River [găn′ jēz rĭv′ər] **71** 67
gangway [găng′ wā'] **58** 20
garage [gə rŏj′] **27** 2
garbage can [gär′ bĭj kăn'] **35** 31
garbage truck [gär′ bĭj trŭk'] **49** 6
garden hose [gär′ dən hōs'] **27** 14
gardenia [gär dēn′ yə] **60** 14
gardener [gärd′ nər] **85** 3
garlic [gär′ lĭk] **7** 25
garment bag [gär′ mənt băg'] **56** 1
garter belt [gär′ tər bĕlt'] **22** 14
(garter) snake [gär′ tər snāk'] **65** 9
gas gauge [găs′ gāj'] **50** 9
gas pump [găs′ pŭmp'] **53** 14
gas tank [găs′ tănk'] **50** 34
gas(oline) [găs′ ə lēn'] **80** 28
(gauze) bandage [göz′ băn′ dĭj] **39** 24
gauze pads [göz′ pădz'] **39** 25
gavel [găv′ əl] **43** 12
gear [gïr] **89** 27
gear changer [gïr′ chān' jər] **52** 22
gearshift [gïr′ shĭft'] **50** 17
geometrical figures [jē' ə mĕ′ trĭ kəl fĭg' yərz] **79**
Georgia [jör′ jə] **72** 10
geyser [gī′ zər] **80** 5
gibbon [gĭb′ ən] **69** 15
gill [gĭl] **65** 3c
giraffe [jə răf′] **67** 29
girdle [gür′ dəl] **22** 15
girl [gürl] **2** 9
girl's frame [gürlz′ frām'] **52** 3
give [gĭv] **17** 9
glass [glăs] **12** 20
glasses [glăs′ əz] **21** 44
glider [glī′ dər] **57** 4
globe [glōb] **47** 19
glove [glŭv] **92** 12, **94** 11, **94** 15
glove compartment [glŭv′ kəm pärt' mənt] **50** 20
gloves [glŭvz] **19** 1
glue [glo͞o] **36** 33, **76** 17
goal [gōl] **92** 25
goalie [gōl′ ē] **92** 24
goalpost [gōl′ pōst'] **93** 35
goat [gōt] **67** 28
Gobi Desert [gō′ bē dĕz′ ərt] **71** 54
golf [gŏlf] **94**
golf bag [gŏlf′ băg'] **95** 7
golf ball [gŏlf′ böl'] **94** 7
golf cart [gŏlf′ kärt'] **95** 8
golf course [gŏlf′ körs'] **95**
golfer [gŏl′ fər] **94** 10
goose [go͞os] **64** 26
gooseberries [go͞os′ bër' ēz] **8** 11
gopher [gō′ fər] **66** 8
gorilla [gə rĭl′ ə] **69** 17
graduated cylinder [grăj′ o͞o ā tĭd sĭl' ən dər] **78** 25
grains [grānz] **60**
granddaughter [grănd′ dö' tər] **2** 11
grandfather [grănd′ fŏ' dhər] **3** 2
grandmother [grănd′ mŭ' dhər] **3** 1
grandparents [grănd păr′ ənts] **2** 10
grandson [grănd′ sŭn'] **2** 12

grapefruit [grăp/ froot/] **8** 7
grapes [grāps] **8** 1
graph paper [grăf/ pā/ pər] **78** 11
grass [grăs] **27** 15
grasses [grăs/ əz] **60**
grasshopper [grăs/ hŏp/ ər] **63** 6
grate [grāt] **31** 2
Great Sandy Desert
[grāt/ săn/ dē dĕz/ ərt] **71** 55
green [grēn] **95** 10
greengrocer [grēn/ grō/ sər] **84** 7
grill [grĭl] **27** 22, **88** 12
grizzly bear [grĭz/ lē bër/] **69** 23
groceries [grō/ sə rēz] **15** 24
ground beef [grownd/ bēf/] **10** 2
grounding plug [grown/ dĭng plŭg/]
36 7
guitar [gĭ tär/] **98** 11
Gulf of Alaska [gŭlf/ əv ə lăs/kə]
70 17
Gulf of Guinea [gŭlf/ əv gĭn/ ē] **70** 25
Gulf of Mexico [gŭlf/ əv mĕk sə kō]
70 19
gulfs [gŭlfs] **70**
gun [gŭn] **43** 7
gun turret [gŭn/ tür/ ət] **48** 12
gutter [gŭt/ ər] **27** 10, **94** 3
gymnast [jĭm/ nəst] **94** 23
gymnastics [jĭm năs/ tĭks] **94**
hacksaw [hăk/ sö/] **36** 18
hair [hër] **4** 30
hair dryer [hër/ drī/ ər] **34** 26
hairbrush [hër/ brŭsh/] **32** 7
hairdresser [hër/ drĕs/ ər] **84** 10
half (1/2) [hăf] **79** 30
half slip [hăf/ slĭp/] **22** 8
halfback [hăf/ băk/] **93** 33
hall [höl] **76** 12
ham [hăm] **10** 12
hamburger [hăm/bür/ gər] **18** 9
hammer [hăm/ ər] **36** 13
hammock [hăm/ ək] **27** 11
hamper [hăm/ pər] **34** 28
hand [hănd] **4**
hand brake [hănd/ brāk/] **52** 24
hand grenade [hănd/ grə nād/] **48** 29
hand towel [hănd/ tow/ əl] **34** 23
hand truck [hănd/ trŭk/] **87** 4
handball [hănd/ böl/] **94**, **94** 12
handcuffs [hănd/ kŭfs/] **43** 4
handicrafts [hăn/ dē krăfts/] **101**
handlebars [hăn/ dəl bärz/] **52** 2
hang [hăng] **38** 6
hang glider [hăng/ glī/ dər] **57** 6
hangar [hăng/ ər] **57** 17
hanger [hăng/ ər] **32** 2
hard hat [härd/ hăt/] **21** 28, **82** 4
harmonica [här mŏn/ə kə] **98** 30
harness [här/ nəs] **89** 22
harp [härp] **98** 6
hat [hăt] **19** 18
hatchback [hăch/ băk/] **51** 43
hatchet [hăch/ ət] **36** 17
Hawaii [hə wŏ/ ē] **72** 11
hawk [hök] **64** 7
hay [hā] **81** 13
hazelnut(s) [hā/ zəl nŭt(s)/] **9** 30
head [hĕd] **4**, **36** 42a
(head of) cauliflower
[hĕd/ əv kŏl ə flow/ ər] **6** 1
head protector [hĕd prə tĕk/ tər] **94** 14
headache [hĕd/ āk/] **40** 6
headboard [hĕd/ börd/] **32** 14
headlights [hĕd/ līts/] **51** 48
headphones [hĕd/ fōnz/] **100** 29
headrest [hĕd/ rĕst/] **50** 35
headset [hĕd/ sĕt/] **83** 2
heart [härt] **5** 64
heat [hēt] **80** 27
heating pad [hē/ tĭng păd/] **41** 3
hedge clippers [hĕj/ klĭp/ ərz] **27** 29
heel [hēl] **5** 50, **20** 5
heels [hēlz] **20** 25
height [hīt] **79** 34
helicopter [hĕl/ə kŏp/ tər] **57** 2
helmet [hĕl/ mət] **42** 12, **52** 7, **92** 14
hem [hĕm] **101** 11
hem binding [hĕm/ bīn/ dĭng] **101** 12
herb(s) [ürb(z)] **6** 9
(herd of) cattle [hürd/ əv kăt/ əl] **81** 20
high [hī] **24** 11
high blood pressure [hī/ blŭd prĕsh/ ər]
40 10
high chair [hī/ chër/] **16** 8
high heels [hī/ hēlz/] **20** 25
highway travel [hī/ wā trăv/ əl] **53**
hikers [hī/ kərz] **88** 2
hiking boots [hī/ kĭng boots/] **19** 9
hill [hĭl] **88** 4
Himalayas [hĭm/ ə lā/ əz] **70** 47
hind legs [hīnd/ lĕgz/] **66** 3b
hip [hĭp] **4** 16
hippopotamus [hĭp/ ə pŏt/ə məs]
66 14
hit [hĭt] **96** 1
hitchhiker [hĭch/ hī/ kər] **53** 9
hockey stick [hŏk/ ē stĭk/] **92** 18
hog [hög] **66** 30
hold [hōld] **17** 12, **58** 8
hole [hōl] **94** 8
holly [hŏl/ ē] **61** 37
holster [hōl/ stər] **43** 8
home plate [hōm/ plāt/] **93** 15
honeydew melon
[hŭn/ ē doo mĕl/ ən] **9** 35
hood [hood] **51** 47
hoof [hoof] **66** 35b
hoofed mammals [hooft/ măm/ əlz] **66**
hook [hook] **32** 1, **36** 16
hook and eye [hook/ ənd ī/] **101** 14
horn [hörn] **50** 12, **52** 5, **66** 16a
horse [hörs] **66** 21
horse racing [hörs/ rā/ sĭng] **94**
horse-drawn carriage
[hörs/ drön kăr/ ĭj] **54** 33
horseback rider [hörs/ băk rī/ dər]
87 6
horses [hörs/ əz] **81** 23
hose [hōz] **42** 8, **50** 57
hot [hŏt] **25** 7
hot air balloon [hŏt/ ër bə loon/] **57** 1
hot dog [hŏt/ dög/] **18** 2
hot water faucet [hŏt/ wŏt ər fö/ sət]
34 17
house plants [hows/ plănts/] **60** 39
household items [hows/ hōld ī/ təmz]
15 15
household services
[hows/ hōld sür/ və səz] **85**
housekeeper [hows/ kē/ pər] **85** 8
houses [how/ zəz] **27**
housework [hows/ würk/] **38**
Huang River [hwŏng/ riv/ər] **71** 68
hubcap [hŭb/ kăp/] **50** 36

Hudson Bay [hŭd′ sən bā′] **70** 18
human body [hyōō′ mən bŏd′ ē] **4**
hummingbird [hŭm′ ĭng bürd′] **64** 2
hump [hŭmp] **67** 33a
husband [hŭz′ bənd] **2** 3, **3** 12
hyacinth [hī′ə sĭnth] **60** 10
hyena [hī ē′ nə] **68** 30
hypotenuse [hī pŏt′ə nōōs′] **79** 24
ice cream cone [īs′ krēm cōn′] **18** 36
ice hockey [īs′ hŏk′ ē] **92**
ice pack [īs′ păk′] **41** 4
ice skates [īs′ skāts′] **19** 15
ice skating [īs′ skā′ tĭng] **94**
ice tray [īs′ trā′] **30** 21
icy [ī′ sē] **25** 16
Idaho [ī′ də hō′] **72** 12
ignition [ĭg nĭsh′ ən] **50** 14
iguana [ĭ gwŏ′ nə] **65** 13
Illinois [ĭl′ ə noy′] **72** 13
in [ĭn] **102** 7
in front of [ĭn frŭnt′ əv] **102** 6
in-box [ĭn′ bŏks] **83** 12
(index) finger [ĭn′ dĕks fing′ gər] **4** 25
Indian Ocean [ĭn′ dē ən ō′ shən′] **70** 13
Indiana [ĭn′ dē ăn′ ə] **72** 14
individual sports [ĭn′ də vĭj′ ōō əl spörts′] **94**
infection [ĭn fĕk′ shən] **40** 14
inflatable raft [ĭn flā′ tə bəl răft′] **59** 20
information desk [ĭn′ fər mā′ shən dĕsk′] **47** 22
injection [ĭn jĕk′ shən] **41** 8
injuries [ĭn′ jə rēz] **40**
insect bite [ĭn′ sĕkt bīt′] **40** 3
insects [ĭn′ sĕkts] **63**
instep [ĭn′ stĕp′] **5** 51
instruments [ĭn′ strə mənts] **39** 13, **56** 14, **98**
internal organs [ĭn tür′ nəl ör′ gənz] **5**
intersection [ĭn′ tər sĕk′ shən] **44** 11
interstate highway [ĭn′ tər stāt hī′ wā] **53** 1
intestines [ĭn tĕs′ tənz] **5** 67
into [ĭn′ tōō] **103** 12
Iowa [ī′ə wə] **72** 15
iris [ī′ rəs] **5** 47, **60** 11
iron (*n*) [ī′ ərn] **35** 12
iron (*v*) [ī′ ərn] **38** 11
ironing board [ī′ər nĭng börd′] **35** 13
jack [jăk] **32** 26b, **50** 38
jacket [jăk′ ət] **19** 17, **21** 33
jackhammer [jăk′ hăm′ər] **82** 22
jail [jāl] **43** 1
janitor [jăn′ə tər] **85** 9
jar [jär] **12** 9
jaw [jö] **4** 38
jeans [jēnz] **19** 6
jeep [jēp] **48** 9
jelly [jĕl′ ē] **18** 31
jellyfish [jĕl′ ē fĭsh′] **62** 12
jet engine [jĕt′ ĕn′ jən] **57** 11
jet fuel [jĕt′ fyōō′ əl] **80** 31
(jet) plane [jĕt′ plān′] **57** 18
jeweller [jōō′ə lər] **84** 12
jewelry [jōō′ əl rē] **23**
jewelry box [jōō′ əl rē bŏks′] **32** 4
jigsaw [jĭg′ sö] **36** 3
jockey [jŏk′ ē] **94** 21
jogging path [jŏg′ ĭng păth′] **87** 9
judge [jŭj] **43** 10
jukebox [jōōk′ bŏks′] **16** 12
jump [jŭmp] **96** 8
jungle gym [jŭng′ əl jĭm′] **87** 17
Jupiter [jōō′ pə tər] **74** 15
jury [jŏŏr′ ē] **43** 21
jury box [joor′ ē bŏks′] **43** 20
kangaroo [kăng′ gə rōō′] **66** 3
Kansas [kăn′ zəs] **72** 16
Kara Sea [kär′ ə sē′] **70** 31
kayak [kī′ ăk] **59** 17
Kentucky [kĕn tŭk′ ē] **72** 17
ketchup [kĕch′ əp] **16** 4
kettledrum [kĕt′ əl drŭm′] **98** 21
keyboard [kē′ börd′] **98** 1a, **100** 33
keyboard player [kē′ börd plā′ ər] **99** 22
kickstand [kĭk′ stănd′] **52** 9
kidney [kĭd′ nē] **5** 70
kidney bean(s) [kĭd′ nē bēn(z)′] **6** 13
kitchen [kĭch′ ən] **30**
kite [kīt] **91** 22
kitten [kĭt′ ən] **68** 5
knee [nē] **4** 19
knee socks [nē′ sŏks′] **22** 16
knife [nīf] **29** 15
knitting [nĭt′ ĭng] **101** 22
knitting needle [nĭt′ ĭng nē′ dəl] **101** 25
knuckle [nŭk′ əl] **4** 22
koala [kō ŏl′ ə] **66** 1
label [lā′ bəl] **46** 21
lacrosse [lə krös′] **92**
lacrosse stick [lə krös′ stĭk′] **92** 16
ladder [lăd′ ər] **42** 1, **82** 8
ladybug [lā′ dē bŭg′] **63** 14
lamb [lăm] **10** 13, **67** 24
lamp [lămp] **28** 28
lampshade [lămp′ shād′] **28** 27
landing gear [lăn′ dĭng gïr′] **57** 15
lane [lān] **94** 4
lantern [lăn′ tərn] **88** 29
lapel [lə pĕl′] **20** 1
Laptev Sea [lăp′ tĕv sē′] **70** 33
last quarter [lăst′ kwör′ tər] **74** 25
launchpad [lönch′ păd′] **75** 15
laundry [lön′ drē] **35** 28
laundry basket [lön′ drē băs′ kət] **35** 29
laundry detergent [lön′ drē də tür′ jənt] **35** 25
lawn mower [lön′ mō′ ər] **27** 12
lead guitarist [lēd′ gĭ tär′ ĭst] **99** 25
leaf [lēf] **60** 36a
leave [lēv] **77** 13
left fielder [lĕft′ fēl′ dər] **93** 1
left guard [lĕft′ gärd′] **93** 26
left lane [lĕft′ lān′] **53** 5
left tackle [lĕft′ tăk′ əl] **93** 25
leg [lĕg] **4** 17, **10** 14, **11** 20
(legal) pad [lē′ gəl păd′] **83** 26
lemon [lĕm′ ən] **8** 9
Lena River [lē′ nə rĭv′ər] **71** 66
length [lĕngth] **79** 36
lens [lĕnz] **100** 6
leopard [lĕp′ərd] **68** 1
letter [lĕt′ər] **46** 7
letter carrier [lĕt′ər kăr′ yər] **46** 3
lettuce [lĕt′əs] **6** 6
level [lĕv′əl] **82** 3
librarian [lī brër′ ē ən] **47** 23
library card [lī′ brër ē kärd′] **47** 3
library clerk [lī′ brër ē klürk′] **47** 1
license plate [lī′ səns plāt′] **50** 28
lid [lĭd] **30** 9
life jacket [līf′ jăk′ ət] **59** 1
life preserver [līf′ prə zür′ vər] **90** 9
lifeboat [līf′ bōt′] **58** 19, **90** 10

lifeguard [līf′ gärd′] **90** 6
lifeguard chair [līf′ gärd chër′] **90** 8
light (*v*) [līt] **17** 13
light (*adj*) [līt] **24** 9
light switch [līt′ swĭch′] **32** 25
lightbulb [līt′ bŭlb′] **35** 22
lighter [lī′ tər] **16** 30
lighthouse [līt′ hows′] **58** 14
lily [lĭl′ ē] **60** 3
lima bean(s) [lī′ mə bēn(z)′] **6** 16
lime [līm] **8** 10
line [līn] **58** 25
lines [līnz] **79**
linesman [līnz′ mən] **82** 17
lion [lī′ ən] **68** 3
lip [lĭp] **4** 43
lipstick [lĭp′ stĭk′] **23** 29
liquor (bottle) [lĭk′ər bŏt′ əl] **16** 22
listen [lĭs′ ən] **77** 6
little finger [lĭt′ əl fĭng′ gər] **4** 28
little league baseball [lĭt′əl lēg bās′ böl] **92**
Little Leaguer [lĭt′ əl lēg′ ər] **92** 8
little toe [lĭt′ əl tō′] **5** 55
liver [lĭv′ ər] **5** 65
livestock [līv′ stŏk′] **81** 12
living quarters [lĭv′ ĭng kwör′ tərz] **75** 11
living room [lĭv′ ĭng rōōm′] **28**
lizard [lĭz′ ərd] **65** 15
llama [lŏm′ ə] **66** 15
loaf [lōf] **12** 7
loafer [lō′ fər] **21** 42
lobby [lŏb′ ē] **44** 2
lobster [lŏb′ stər] **10** 30, **62** 13
lock [lŏk] **52** 13
locker [lŏk′ ər] **76** 6
locksmith [lŏk′ smĭth′] **85** 4
log [lög] **28** 10
long [löng] **24** 2
long johns [löng′ jŏnz′] **22** 7
long sleeve [löng′ slēv′] **20** 15
loose [lōōs] **24** 4
(loose-leaf) paper [lōōs′ lēf pā′ pər] **76** 13
loudspeaker [lowd′ spē′ kər] **76** 3
Louisiana [lōō ē′ zē ăn′ ə] **72** 18
lounge chair [lownj′ chër′] **27** 24
low [lō] **24** 12
lunar eclipse [lōō′ nər ĭ klĭps′] **74** 6
lunar module [lōō′ nər mŏj′ ōōl] **75** 7
lunch box [lŭnch′ bŏks′] **20** 31
lunch truck [lŭnch′ trŭk′] **49** 8
lung [lŭng] **5** 63
machine gun [mə shēn′ gŭn′] **48** 25
magazine [măg′ ə zēn′] **47** 16
magnet [măg′ nət] **78** 27
magnifying glass [măg′ nə fī ĭng glăs′] **78** 15
magnolia [măg nōl′ yə] **61** 29
mail [māl] **46** 2
mail slot [māl′ slŏt′] **46** 13
mail truck [māl′ trŭk′] **46** 5
mailbag [māl′ băg′] **46** 4
mailbox [māl′ bŏks′] **46** 1
Maine [mān] **72** 19
maintenance [mān′ tə nəns] **95**
make (the bed) [māk′ dhə bĕd′] **38** 8
makeup [māk′ ŭp′] **23**
mallet [măl′ ĭt] **36** 11
mammals [măm′ əlz] **66-69**
man [măn] **2** 2
manager [măn′ ĭ jər] **83** 18
mandolin [măn′ də lĭn′] **98** 4
mane [mān] **66** 21a
mango [măng′ gō] **8** 5
manhole [măn′ hōl′] **45** 32
mantel [măn′ təl] **28** 7
mantis [măn′ tĭs] **63** 7
manual transmission [măn′ yōō əl trănz mĭsh′ ən] **50**
map [măp] **70**
maple [mā′ pəl] **61** 38
marigold [măr′ ə gōld′] **60** 6
marine [mə rēn′] **48** 18
Marines [mə rēnz′] **48** 17
Mars [märz] **74** 14
Maryland [mër′ ə lənd] **72** 20
mascara [mă skăr′ ə] **23** 28
mashed potatoes [măsht′ pə tā tōz] **18** 17
mask [măsk] **91** 35
Massachusetts [măs′ ə chōō′ sĭts] **72** 21
mast [măst] **59** 8
mat [măt] **50** 22
matches [măch′ əz] **16** 28
material [mə tĭr′ ē əl] **101** 4
math [măth] **79**
mattress [mă′ trəs] **32** 17
measurement [mĕzh′ ər mənt] **79**
meat [mēt] **10**
meatballs [mēt′ bölz′] **18** 11
mechanic [mə kăn′ ĭk] **84** 2
media [mē′ dē ə] **86**
medical care [mĕd′ ə kəl kër′] **39**
medicine [mĕd′ ə sən] **41**
medicine chest [mĕd′ ə sən chĕst′] **34** 14
medicine dropper [mĕd′ ə sən drŏp′ ər] **78** 26
Mediterranean Sea [mĕd′ ĭ tə rā′ nē ən sē′] **70** 24
melon [mĕl′ ən] **9** 35
menu [mĕn′ yōō] **16** 7
Mercury [mür′ kyə rē] **74** 11
merry-go-round [mër′ ē gō rownd′] **87** 5
message pad [mĕs′ ĭj păd′] **83** 25
messenger [mĕs′ən jər] **86** 19
metal detector [mĕt′ əl də tĕk′ tər] **56** 10
meteor [mē′ tē ər] **74** 5
meter [mē′ tər] **55** 23
mezzanine [mĕz′ ə nēn′] **99** 13
Michigan [mĭsh′ ə gən] **72** 22
microfilm [mī′ krə fĭlm′] **47** 13
microfilm reader [mī′ krə fĭlm rē′ dər] **47** 14
microscope [mī′ krə skōp′] **78** 30
microwave oven [mī′ krə wāv ŭv′ ən] **30** 23
middle finger [mĭd′ əl fĭng′ gər] **4** 26
milk [mĭlk] **14** 5
Minicam™ [mĭn′ ē kăm′] **100** 2
Minnesota [mĭn′ ə sō′ tə] **72** 23
mirror [mïr′ ər] **32** 5
Mississippi [mĭs′ ə sĭp′ ē] **72** 24
Mississippi River [mĭs′ ə sĭp′ ē rĭv′ ər] **71** 58
Missouri [mĭ zŏŏr′ ē] **73** 25
mitt [mĭt] **27** 20
mittens [mĭt′ ənz] **19** 11

mixed vegetables [mĭkst/ vĕj/ tə bəlz] **18** 16
mixing bowl [mĭk/ sĭng bōl/] **30** 24
mobile [mō/ bēl] **33** 2
model [mŏd/ əl] **86** 5
Mojave Desert [mō hŏv/ ē dĕz/ ərt] **71** 48
money [mŭn/ ē] **12**
money order [mŭn/ ē ör/ dər] **46** 18
monitor [mŏn/ ə tər] **100** 32
monkey [mŭng/ ke] **69** 14
monkey wrench [mŭng/ kē rĕnch/] **36** 12
monorail [mŏn/ ə rāl/] **55** 29
Montana [mŏn tăn/ ə] **73** 26
Moon [mo͞on] **74** 9
mooring [mo͝or/ ĭng] **59** 19
moose [mo͞os] **67** 35
mop [mŏp] **35** 6
(mop) refill [mŏp/ rē/ fĭl] **35** 11
mortar [mör/ tər] **48** 28
mosquito [mə skē/ tō] **63** 13
motel [mō tĕl/] **90** 3
moth [mŏth] **63** 21
mother [mŭdh/ ər] **3** 4
motor oil [mōt/ər oyl/] **80** 33
motor scooter [mōt/ ər sko͞o/ tər] **52** 29
motorboat [mōt/ ər bōt/] **59** 13
motorcycle [mōt/ər sī/ kəl] **52** 30, **53** 19
mountain [mown/ tən] **89** 19
mountain climbing [mown/ tən klīm/ ĭng] **89**
mountain ranges [mown/ tən rān/ jəz] **71**
mouse [mows] **66** 9
mousetrap [mows/ trăp/] **35** 32
mouth [mowth] **4** 2
mover [mo͞o/ vər] **49** 12
movie camera [mo͞o/ vē kăm/ ə rə] **100** 15
moving van [mo͞o/ vĭng văn/] **49** 11
mow [mō] **26** 6
mum [mŭm] **60** 4
muscle [mŭs/ əl] **5** 62
mushroom(s) [mŭsh/ ro͞om(z)] **7** 30
music [myo͞o/ zĭk] **99**
musical comedy [myo͞o/ zə kəl kŏm/ ə dē] **99**
musical instruments [myo͞o/ zə kəl ĭn/ strə mənts] **98**
musician [myo͞o zĭsh/ ən] **99** 10
mussel(s) [mŭs/ əl(z)] **11** 34, **62** 3
mustache [mŭs/ tăsh] **4** 40
mustard [mŭs/ tərd] **18** 1
nail [nāl] **37** 41
nail clippers [nāl/ klĭp/ ərz] **23** 31
nail polish [nāl/ pŏl/ ĭsh] **23** 25
nailbrush [nāl/ brŭsh/] **34** 20
napkin [năp/ kĭn] **29** 14
natural gas [năch/ ər əl găs/] **80** 29
Navy [nā/ vē] **48** 13
Nebraska [nə brăs/ kə] **73** 27
neck [nĕk] **4** 4
necklace [nĕk/ lĭs] **23** 6
nectarine [nĕk/ tə rēn/] **8** 17
needle [nē/ dəl] **39** 26, **60** 34a, **101** 18
needlecrafts [nē/ dəl krăfts/] **101**
needlepoint [nē/ dəl poynt/] **101** 26
neighborhood parks [nā/ bər ho͝od pärks/] **87**
nephew [nĕf/ yo͞o] **3** 13
Neptune [nĕp/ to͞on] **74** 18
nest [nĕst] **64** 31
net [nĕt] **92** 23
Nevada [nə văd/ ə] **73** 28
new [no͞o] **24** 13
New Hampshire [no͞o/ hămp/ shər] **72** 29
New Jersey [no͞o/ jür/ ze] **73** 30
New Mexico [no͞o/ mĕk/ sə kō] **73** 31
new moon [no͞o/ mo͞on/] **74** 26
New York [no͞o/ yörk/] **73** 32
newscaster [no͞oz/ kăs/ tər] **86** 2
newspaper [no͞oz/ pā/ pər] **21** 48
newsstand [no͞oz/ stănd/] **45** 30
next to [nĕkst/ to͞o] **102** 11
nickel [nĭk/ əl] **13** 28
niece [nēs] **3** 14
Niger River [nī/ jər rĭv/ ər] **71** 61
night table [nīt/ tā/ bəl] **32** 27
nightgown [nīt/ gown/] **22** 21
nightstick [nīt/ stĭk/] **43** 9
Nile River [nīl/ rĭv/ ər] **71** 63
nipple [nĭp/ əl] **33** 18
north [nörth] **71** 71
North America [nörth/ə mër/ ə kə] **70** 1
North Atlantic [nörth/ ăt lăn/ tĭk] 70 11
North Carolina [nörth/ kăr ə lī/ nə] **73** 33
North Dakota [nörth/ də kō/ tə] **73** 34
North Pacific [nörth/ pə sĭf/ ĭk] **70** 9
North Sea [nörth/ sē/] **70** 21
nose [nōz] **4** 36, **57** 8
nostril [nŏs/ trĭl] **4** 37
nozzle [nŏz/ əl] **42** 17
nuclear reactor [no͞o/ klē ər rē ăk/ tər] **80** 13
nurse [nürs] **39** 19
nut [nŭt] **37** 39
nuts [nŭts] **9**
oak [ōk] **61** 33
oar [ör] **59** 22
oarlock [ör/ lŏk/] **59** 21
oats [ōts] **60** 23
Ob River [ŏb/ rĭv/ ər] **71** 64
oboe [ō /bō] **98** 15
obtuse angle [ŏb to͞os/ ăng/ gəl] **79** 5
occupations [ŏk/ yə pā/ shənz] **84-86**
ocean liner [ō/ shən lī/ nər] **58** 27
oceans [ō/ shənz] **70**
octopus [ŏk/ tə pəs] **62** 6
office [ö/ fĭs] **83**
office building [ö/ fĭs bĭl/ dĭng] **44** 1
officer [ö/ fĭ sər] **86** 13
Ohio [ō hī/ ō] **73** 35
oil [oyl] **38** 12
oil well [oyl/ wĕl/] **80** 1
ointment [oynt/ mənt] **41** 9
Oklahoma [ō/ klə hō/ mə] **73** 36
old [ōld] **24** 14
on [ŏn] **102** 5
on top of [ŏn tŏp/ əv] **102** 10
onion(s) [ŭn/ yən(z)] **7** 31
open [ō/ pən] **24** 15, **31** 3
optician [ŏp tĭsh/ ən] **84** 9
oral hygienist [ör/ əl hī jē/ nĭst] **39** 14
orange [ör/ ĭnj] **8** 8
orangutan [ə răng/ ə tăn/] **69** 18
orbit [ör/ bĭt] **74** 21
orchard [ör/ chərd] **81** 1
orchestra [ör/ kə strə] **99** 6

orchestra seating [ör′ kə strə sēt′ ĭng] **99** 12
orchid [ör′ kĭd] **60** 12
order [ör′ dər] **17** 5
Oregon [ör′ ə gən] **73** 37
organ [ör′ gən] **98** 29
ostrich [ŏs′ trĭch] **64** 12
otter [ŏt′ ər] **68** 10
out of [owt′ əv] **103** 7
outboard motor [owt′ börd mō′ tər] **59** 12
outer space [owt′ər spās′] **74**
outlet [owt′ lət] **36** 6
oval [ō′ vəl] **79** 18
oven [ŭv′ ən] **30** 32
over [ō′ vər] **103** 8
overalls [ō′ vər ölz′] **21** 30
overcoat [ō′ vər kōt′] **19** 20
overhead projector [ō′ vər hĕd prə jĕk′ tər] **76** 27
overpass [ō′ vər păs′] **53** 3
owl [owl] **64** 6
oyster(s) [oy′ stər(z)] **11** 33, **62** 2
pacifier [păs′ ə fī′ ər] **33** 22
pack [păk] **13** 16
package [păk′ ĭj] **12** 4, **46** 19
pad [păd] **83** 26
paddle [păd′ əl] **59** 3, **94** 18
pail [pāl] **90** 16
paint (*v*) [pānt] **26** 1
paint (*n*) [pānt] **37** 31
paintbrush [pānt′ brŭsh′] **37** 30
Painted Desert [pān′ təd dez′ ərt] **71** 49
painter [pān′ tər] **85** 7
painting [pān′ tĭng] **28** 5
(pair of) scissors [pĕr′ əv sĭz′ ərz] **101** 17
pajamas [pə jŏm′ əz] **22** 19
palm [pŏm] **4** 29, **61** 26
pan [păn] **37** 28
pancakes [păn′ kāks′] **18** 5
pancreas [pang′ krē əs] **5** 71
panda [păn də] **69** 20
panel truck [păn′ əl trŭk′] **49** 9
pansy [păn′ zē] **60** 2
panties [păn′ tēz] **22** 11
pants [pănts] **21** 27
pantyhose [păn′ tē hōz′] **22** 5
papaya [pə pī′ yə] **8** 6
paper [pā′ pər] **76** 13
paper clips [pā′ pər klĭps′] **83** 28
paper towels [pā′ pər tow′əlz] **35** 23
parachute [păr′ ə shōōt′] **48** 6
parakeet [păr′ ə kēt] **64** 15
parallel lines [păr′ə lĕl līnz′] **79** 4
paramedic [păr′ ə mĕd′ ĭk] **42** 7
Parana River [păr′ ə nŏ′ rĭv′ ər] **71** 60
parents [păr′ ənts] **2** 6
park [pärk] **87**
park ranger [pärk′ rān′ jər] **88** 5
parka [pär′ kə] **19** 8
parking lights [pär′ kĭng līts′] **51** 49
parking garage [pär′ kĭng gə rŏj′] **45** 19
parking meter [pär′ kĭng mē′ tər] **45** 20
parrot [păr′ ət] **64** 16
part [pärt] **4** 31
pass [păs] **96** 5
passenger [păs′ ĭn jər] **55** 25
passenger car [păs′ ĭn jər kär′] **53** 15
pasture [păs′ chər] **81** 6
patient [pā ′shənt] **39** 20
patio [păt′ ē ō′] **27** 17
pattern [păt ′ ərn] **101** 7
pattern piece [păt′ ərn pēs′] **101** 6
paw [pö] **69** 29a
pay [pā] **17** 7
pea(s) [pē(z)] **6** 17
peach [pēch] **9** 37
peacock [pē′ kŏk′] **64** 18
peak [pēk] **89** 20
peanut(s) [pē′ nŭt(s)′] **9** 28
pear [pĕr] **8** 18
pedal [pĕd′ əl] **39** 18, **52** 19
pedestrian [pə dĕs′ trē ən] **44** 12
peel (*n*) [pēl] **9** 20a
peel (*v*) [pēl] **31** 5
pegboard [pĕg′ börd′] **36** 15
pelican [pĕl′ ə kən] **64** 24
pencil [pĕn′ səl] **76** 24
pencil eraser [pĕn′ səl ə rā′ sər] **76** 21
pencil sharpener [pĕn′ səl shär′ pə nər] **76** 20, **83** 30
Pennsylvania [pĕn səl vān′ yə] **73** 38
penny [pĕn′ ē] **13** 27
penguin [pĕn′ gwĭn] **64** 27
people [pē′ pəl] **2**
pepper shaker [pĕp′ ər shā′ kər] **29** 9
pepper(s) [pĕp′ ər(z)] **7** 22
percussion [pər kŭsh′ ən] **98**
perfume [pür′ fyōōm] **23** 27
periodicals section [pĭr′ ē ŏd′ ə kəlz sĕk′ shən] **47** 15
periscope [pĕr′ə skōp′] **48** 8
perpendicular lines [pür′ pən dĭk′ yə lər līnz′] **79** 2
Persian Gulf [pür′ zhən gŭlf′] **70** 28
personal computer (PC) [pür′ sə nəl kŭm pyōō′ tər]/[pē′ sē′] **100** 31
personnel [pür′ sə nĕl′] **48**
petal [pĕt′ əl] **60** 18b
petri dish [pēt′ rē dĭsh′] **78** 3
petunia [pə tōōn′ yə] **60** 7
pharmacist [fär′ mə sĭst] **84** 1
phases of the moon [fā′ zəz əv dhə mōōn′] **74**
pheasant [fĕz′ ənt] **64** 19
Phillips screwdriver [fĭl′ ĭps skrōō′ drī vər] **37** 25
phone [fōn] **32** 26
photocopier [fō′ tə kŏp′ ē ər] **83** 24
photocopy machine [fō tə kŏp ē mə shēn′] **47** 18
photographer [fə tŏg′ rə fər] **86** 4
photography [fə tŏg′ rə fē] **100**
piano [pē ăn′ ō] **98** 1
piccolo [pĭk′ ə lō′] **98** 12
pick (*v*) [pĭk] **26** 7
pick (*n*) [pĭk] **98** 11a
pickup truck [pĭk′ ŭp trŭk′] **49** 4
pickax [pĭk′ ăks′] **82** 13
pickle [pĭk′ əl] **18** 8
picnic area [pĭk′nĭk ĕr′ ē ə] **88**
picnic basket [pĭk′ nĭk băs′ kət] **88** 13
picnic table [pĭk′ nĭk tā′ bəl] **88** 15
piece [pēs] **12** 22
pier [pĭr] **58** 3
pierced earring [pĭrst′ ĭr′ ĭng] **23** 16
pigeon [pĭj′ ən] **64** 1
pill [pĭl] **41** 7
pillow [pĭl′ ō] **32** 16
pillowcase [pĭl′ ō kās′] **32** 15

pilot [pī′ lət] **56** 15
pin [pĭn] **23** 8, **94** 5, **101** 20
pincushion [pĭn′ ko͝osh′ ən] **101** 3
pine [pīn] **60** 34
pineapple [pīn′ ăp′ əl] **8** 4
ping-pong [pĭng′ pŏng′] **94**
ping-pong ball [pĭng′ pŏng böl′] **94** 19
pinking shears [pĭng′ kĭng shïrz′] **101** 5
pipe [pīp] **16** 26, **35** 18
pipette [pī pĕt′] **78** 14
pit [pĭt] **8** 37a
pitcher [pĭch′ ər] **29** 4, **93** 12
pitcher's mound [pĭch′ ərz mownd′] **93** 11
pitchfork [pĭch′ förk′] **81** 14
pizza [pēt′ sə] **18** 30
plaid [plăd] **24** 22
plane [plān] **57** 18
planets [plăn′ əts] **74**
plant (*v*) [plănt] **26** 4
plants (*n*) [plănts] **60**
plate [plāt] **29** 13
plateau [plă tō′] **88** 1
platform [plăt′ förm′] **54** 11
playground [plā′ grownd′] **87** 15
playpen [plā′ pĕn′] **33** 30
pleasure boating [plĕzh′ ər bō′ tĭng] **59**
pliers [plī′ ərz] **36** 19
plug [plŭg] **37** 43d
plum [plŭm] **9** 34
plumber [plŭm′ ər] **85** 1
plunger [plŭn′ jər] **35** 14
Pluto [ploo′ tō] **74** 19
pocket [pŏk′ ət] **21** 41
pod [pŏd] **6** 17a
podium [pō′ dē əm] **99** 7
poinsettia [poyn sĕt′ē ə] **60** 15
poison ivy [poy′ zən ī′ vē] **61** 45
poison oak [poy′ zən ōk′] **61** 43
poison sumac [poy′ zən so͞o′ măk] **61** 44
poisonous plants [poy′ zə nəs plănts′] **61**
polar bear [pōl′ ər bër′] **69** 22
pole [pōl] **94** 34, **95** 14
police officer [pə lēs′ öf′ ə sər] **43** 6
police station [pə lēs′ stā′ shən] **43**
polish [pŏl′ ĭsh] **38** 3
polka dot [pō′ kə dŏt′] **24** 19
pond [pŏnd] **87** 8
pony [pō′ nē] **67** 20
poplar [pŏp′ lər] **61** 30
porch [pörch] **27** 6
porcupine [pör′ kyə pīn′] **66** 11
pork [pörk] **10** 6
pork chops [pörk′ chŏps′] **18** 15
port [pört] **58**
porter [pör′ tər] **56** 5
porthole [pört′ hōl′] **58** 21
post [pōst] **23** 18
post office [pōst′ öf′ ĭs] **44** 9, **46**
postal worker [pōs′ təl wür′ kər] **46** 14
postcard [pōst′ kärd′] **46** 17
postmark [pōst′ märk′] **46** 9
pot [pŏt] **30** 13
pot holder [pŏt′ hōl′ dər] **30** 34
potato chips [pə tā′ tō chĭps′] **18** 4
potato(es) [pə tā′ tō(z)] **7** 23
potty [pŏt′ ē] **33** 33
pouch [powch] **66** 3c
pouched mammals [powcht′ măm′ əlz] **66**
poultry [pōl′ trē] **10**
pour [pör] **31** 4
power lines [pow′ ər līnz′] **80** 24
power sander [pow′ ər săn′ dər] **37** 26
power saw [pow′ ər sö′] **27** 25
power station [pow′ ər stā′ shən] **80** 20
prepositions [prep′ ə zĭ′ shənz] **102**, **103**
primates [prī′ māts] **69**
print [prĭnt] **24** 21
printer [prĭn′ tər] **83** 4
printout [prĭnt′ owt′] **83** 8
prints [prĭnts] **100** 11
prism [prĭz′ əm] **78** 1
private jet [prī′ vət jĕt′] **57** 3
produce [prŏd′ o͞os] **14** 9
programs [prō′ grămz] **99** 17
projector [prə jĕk′ tər] **100** 16
propane gas [prō′ pān găs′] **80** 30
propeller plane [prə pĕl′ ər plān′] **57** 7
prosecuting attorney [prŏ′ sə kyo͞o tĭng ə tür′ nē] **43** 17
prune [pro͞on] **9** 22
public library [pŭb′ lĭk lī′ brër ē] **47**
public transportation [pŭb′ lĭk trăns pər tā′ shən] **54**
public telephone [pŭb′ lĭk tĕl′ ə fōn] **44** 7
puck [pŭk] **92** 17
pump [pŭmp] **13** 14, **52** 21
pumpkin [pŭmp′ kĭn] **7** 26
punishment [pŭn′ ĭsh mənt] **43**
pupil [pyo͞o′ pəl] **5** 48
puppy [pŭp′ ē] **69** 27
purse [pürs] **20** 23
push [po͝osh] **26** 12
putter [pŭt′ ər] **94** 9
puzzle [pŭz′ əl] **33** 31
pyramid [pïr′ ə mĭd′] **79** 25
quantities [kwŏn′ tə tēz] **12**
quarter [kwör′ tər] **11** 18, **13** 30, **79** 31
quarterback [kwör′ tər băk′] **93** 32
quill [kwĭl] **66** 11a
quilting [kwĭl′ tĭng] **101** 32
rabbit [răb′ ĭt] **66** 13
raccoon [ră ko͞on′] **68** 7
race track [rās′ trăk′] **95**
(racing) handlebars [rā′ sĭng hăn′ dəl bärz] **52** 2
rack [răk] **47** 17, **78** 8
racket [răk′ ĭt] **94** 2
racquet [răk′ ĭt] **94** 29
racquetball [răk′ ĭt böl′] **94** 30
radiator [rā′ dē āt′ ər] **51** 56
radio [rā′ dē ō′] **50** 18
radish(es) [răd′ ĭsh (əz)] **7** 29
radius [rā′ dē əs] **79** 14
raft [răft] **89** 16
rafters [răf′ tərz] **82** 1
rafting [răf′ tĭng] **89**
rags [răgz] **35** 4
rain boots [rān′ bo͞ots′] **19** 25
raincoat [rān′ kōt′] **21** 38
rainy [rān′ ē] **25** 1
raise (one's hand) [rāz′ wŭnz hănd′] **77** 1
raisin(s) [rā′ zən(z)] **9** 24
rake (*v*) [rāk] **26** 10
rake (*n*) [rāk] **27** 30
ranch [rănch] **81**

ranch house [rănch/ hows/] **27**
ranching [rănch/ ĭng] **81**
rapids [răp/ ĭdz] **89** 17
rash [răsh] **40** 1
raspberries [răz/ bër/ ēz] **8** 16
rat [răt] **66** 7
rattle [răt/ əl] **33** 21
rattlesnake [răt/ əl snāk/] **65** 10
razor [rā/ zər] **23** 20
razor blades [rā/ zər blādz/] **23** 23
read [rēd] **77** 4
real estate agent [rēl/ ə stāt ā/ jənt] **85** 5
rear bumper [rïr/ bŭm/ pər] **50** 42
rearview mirror [rïr/ vyōō mïr/ ər] **50** 7
receipt [rə sēt/] **15** 20, **55** 24
receiver [rə sē/ vər] **100** 21
receptionist [rə sĕp/ shə nəst] **86** 17
recliner [rə klī/ nər] **28** 16
records [rĕk/ ərdz] **100** 23
rectangle [rĕk/ tăng/ gəl] **79** 19
Red Sea [rĕd/ sē/] **70** 29
redwood [rĕd/ wŏŏd/] **61** 25
(reel of) film [rēl/ əv fĭlm/] **100** 17
referee [rĕf/ ə rē/] **93** 22, **94** 16
reference section [rĕf/ ə rəns sĕk/ shən] **47** 21
(reference) librarian [rĕf/ ə rəns lī brër/ e ən] **47** 23
refill [rē/ fĭl/] **35** 11
refinery [rə fī/ nə rē] **80** 12
reflector [rə flĕk/ tər] **52** 25
refreshment stand [rə frĕsh/ mənt stănd/] **90** 2
refrigerator [rə frĭj/ ə rā/ tər] **30** 19
reins [rānz] **94** 22
relationshops [rə lā/ shən shĭps/] **2**
remedies [rĕm/ ə dēz] **41**
remote control [rə mōt/ kən trōl/] **28** 17
repair [rə për/] **38** 10
repairperson [rə për/ pür/ sən] **84** 5
reporter [rə pör/ tər] **86** 11
reptiles [rĕp/ tĭlz] **65**
rescue [rĕs/ kyōō] **42**
restaurant [rĕs/ tə rənt] **16**
retriever [rə trē/ vər] **69** 26
return address [rə türn/ ă drĕs/] **46** 8
rhinoceros [rī nŏs/ ə rəs] **66** 16
Rhode Island [rōd/ ī/ lənd] **73** 39
rice [rīs] **60** 21
ride [rīd] **97** 13
rider [rī/ dər] **54** 6
rifle [rī/ fəl] **48** 21
right angle [rīt/ ăng/ gəl] **79** 23
right fielder [rīt/ fēl/ dər] **93** 3
right guard [rīt/ gärd/] **93** 28
right lane [rīt/ lān/] **53** 7
right tackle [rīt/ tăk/ əl] **93** 29
right triangle [rīt/ trī/ ăng gəl] **79** 22
rind [rīnd] **8** 8b
ring(s) [rĭng(z)] **23** 2, **74** 16a, **94** 17
ring binder [rĭng/ bīn/ dər] **76** 14
ring finger [rĭng/ fĭng/ gər] **4** 27
ring stand [rĭng/ stănd/] **78** 19
rink [rĭngk] **94** 25
Rio Grande River [rē/ ō grănd/ rĭv/ ər] **71** 57
rivers [riv/ ərz] **71**
road sign [rōd/ sīn/] **53** 23
road work [rōd/ würk/] **82**
roadrunner [rōd/ rŭn/ ər] **64** 32
roast [rōst] **10** 3, **10** 8
roasting pan [rōs/ tĭng păn/] **30** 17
robes [rōbz] **43** 11
robin [rŏb/ in] **64** 9
rock group [rŏk/ grōōp/] **99**
rocket [rŏk/ ət] **75** 13
rocks [rŏks] **88** 11
rocking chair [rŏk/ ĭng chër/] **33** 16
Rocky Mountains [rŏk/ ē mown/ tənz] **71** 40
rodents [rō/ dənts] **66**
roll [rōl] **12** 11, **18** 19
(roll of) film [rōl/ əv fĭlm/] **100** 10
roller [rōl/ ər] **37** 29
rolling pin [rōl/ ĭng pĭn/] **30** 25
rolodex [rōl/ ə dĕks/] **83** 14
rooster [rōō/ stər] **64** 21
roof [rōōf] **27** 4
root [rōōt] **60** 35d
rope [rōp] **89** 23
rose [rōz] **60** 18
rotor [rō/ tər] **57** 2a
rough [rŭf] **95** 6
router [row/ tər] **37** 37
row [rō] **47** 11, **81** 18
rowboat [rō/ bōt/] **59** 23
Rub/al Khali Desert [rōōb/ ăl kŏl/ ē dĕz/ ərt] **71** 52
rubber tubing [rŭb/ ər tōōb/ ĭng] **78** 18
rudder [rŭd/ ər] **59** 5
rug [rŭg] **32** 28
ruler [rōō/ lər] **76** 23
run [rŭn] **96** 6
rung [rŭng] **82** 9
runner [rŭn/ ər] **91** 23, **94** 31
runway [rŭn/ wā/] **57** 19
saddle [săd/ əl] **94** 20
safety glasses [sāf/ tē glăs/ əz] **78** 12
safety goggles [sāf/ tē gŏg/ əlz] **94** 28
safety pin [sāf/ tē pĭn/] **33** 11
Sahara Desert [sə hër/ ə dĕz/ ərt] **71** 51
sail [sāl] **59** 9
sailboard [sāl/ börd/] **59** 15
sailboat [sāl/ bōt/] **59** 4
sailor [sāl/ ər] **48** 14
salad bowl [săl/ əd bōl/] **29** 25
salad dressing [săl/ əd drĕs/ ĭng] **18** 12
salamander [săl/ ə măn/ dər] **65** 14
salesperson [sālz/ pür/ sən] **86** 12
salt shaker [sölt/ shā/ kər] **29** 10
sand (*v*) [sănd] **26** 14
sand (*n*) [sănd] **90** 31
sand dunes [sănd/ dōōnz/] **90** 12
sand trap [sănd/ trăp/] **95** 11
sandal [săn/ dəl] **20** 19
sandbox [sănd/ bŏks/] **87** 13
sandcastle [sănd/ kăs/ əl] **91** 32
sandpaper [sănd/ pā/ pər] **37** 27
sandwich [sănd/ wĭch] **16** 16
sanitation worker [săn ə tā/ shən wür/ kər] **49** 7
Saturn [săt/ ərn] **74** 16
saucepan [sös/ păn/] **30** 8
saucer [sö/ sər] **29** 21
sausage [sö/ sĭj] **10** 7
saw [sö] **36** 8
saxophone [săk/ sə fōn/] **98** 24
scaffolding [skăf/ əl dĭng] **82** 7
scale [skāl] **14** 7, **34** 32, **78** 4
scallop(s) [skăl/ əp(s)] **11** 35, **62** 10

scarecrow [skër/ krō/] **81** 19
scarf [skärf] **19** 19
scenery [sē/ nə rē] **99** 2
school [sko͞ol] **76, 77**
science lab [sī/ əns lăb/] **78**
scissors [sĭz/ərz] **101** 17
scoreboard [skör/ börd/] **93** 19
scorpion [skör/ pē ən] **63** 8
scouring pad [skowr/ ĭng păd/] **30** 11
scrape [skrāp] **26** 15
scraper [skrāp/ ər] **36** 14
screen [skrēn] **27** 19, **100** 14
screw [skro͞o] **37** 42
screwdriver [skro͞o/ drī/ vər] **37** 24
scrub [skrŭb] **38** 2
scuba tank [sko͞o/ bə tăngk/] **91** 37
sea gull [sē/ gŭl/] **64** 4
sea horse [sē/ hörs/] **65** 1
Sea of Japan [sē/ əv jə păn/] **70** 36
Sea of Okhotsk [sē/əv ō kŏtsk/] **70** 35
seafood [sē/ fo͞od/] **10**
seal [sēl] **68** 12
seam [sēm] **101** 10
seas [sēz] **70**
seat [sēt] **52** 16, **54** 2
seat belt [sēt/ bĕlt] **50** 23
second baseman [sĕk/ ənd bās/ mən] **93** 7
secretary [sĕk/ rə tër/ ē] **83** 11
section [sĕk/ shən] **8** 8a, **79** 15
security [sə kyo͝or/ ə tē] **56**
security guard [sə kyo͝or/ ə tē gärd/] **56** 9, **86** 14
sedan [sə dăn/] **51**
seed [sēd] **8** 8c
seesaw [sē/ sö/] **87** 18
serve [sürv] **17** 3, **96** 2
service area [sür/ vəs ër/ ē ə] **53** 11
sevice court [sür/ vəs kört/] **95** 1
service line [sür/ vəs līn/] **95** 3
set (the table) [sĕt/ dhə tā/ bəl] **17** 8
sewing [sō/ ĭng] **101**
sewing machine [sō/ ĭng mə shēn/] **101** 1
shade [shād] **33** 1
shaft [shăft] **80** 10
shampoo [shăm po͞o/] **34** 8
shank [shănk] **36** 43b
shark [shärk] **65** 5
shaving cream [shā/ vĭng krēm/] **23** 22
sheep [shēp] **67** 25, **81** 10
sheet [shēt] **32** 19
sheet music [shēt/ myo͞o/ zĭk] **98** 2
shelf [shĕlf] **14** 6, **47** 26
shell [shĕl] **48** 27, **62** 1a, **65** 18a, **90** 40
shellfish [shĕl/ fĭsh/] **11**
shepherd [shĕp/ ərd] **69** 28
shingle [shĭng/ gəl] **82** 2
ship [shĭp] **58** 9
shirt [shürt] **21** 46
shock absorbers [shŏk/ əb zör/ bərz] **52** 31
shoe [sho͞o] **21** 49
shoelace [sho͞o/ lās/] **20** 7
shoot [sho͞ot] **97** 16
shop worker [shŏp/ wür/ kər] **85** 12
shopping bag [shŏp/ ĭng băg/] **20** 18
shopping basket [shŏp/ ĭng băs/ kət] **14** 8
shopping cart [shŏp/ ĭng kärt/] **15** 19
short [shört] **24** 1
short sleeve [shört/ slēv/] **20** 21
shorts [shörts] **20** 14
shortstop [shört/ stŏp/] **93** 5
shoulder [shōl/ dər] **4** 5, **53** 22
(shoulder) bag [shōl/ dər băg/] **21** 35
shovel (*n*) [shŭv/ əl] **27** 31, **82** 15, **90** 17
shovel (*v*) [shŭv/ əl] **26** 13
shower cap [show/ ər kăp/] **34** 3
shower curtain [show/ ər kŭr/ tən] **34** 5
shower head [show/ ər hĕd/] **34** 4
shrimp [shrĭmp] **11** 31, **62** 8
shutter [shŭt/ ər] **27** 8
shuttle car [shŭt/ əl kär/] **80** 8
side [sīd] **79** 10
side mirror [sīd/ mïr/ ər] **50** 2
sideburn [sīd/ bürn/] **4** 33
sidewalk [sīd/ wök/] **45** 25
Sierra Madre [sē ër/ ə mŏ/ drē] **71** 42
silo [sī/ lō] **81** 4
silverware [sĭl/ vər wër/] **29** 22
simple animals [sĭm/ pəl ăn/ ə məlz] **62**
singer [sĭng/ ər] **99** 24
sink [sĭngk] **34** 19
sister [sĭs/ tər] **3** 10
sister-in-law [sĭs/ tər ən lö/] **3** 8
six-pack [sĭks/ păk/] **13** 13
skate (*n*) [skāt] **94** 26
skate (*v*) [skāt] **97** 9
skein [skān] **101** 24
ski [skē] **95** 17
ski boot [skē/ bo͞ot/] **95** 15
ski cap [skē/ kăp/] **19** 16
ski lift [skē/ lĭft/] **95** 18
ski slope [skē/ slōp/] **95**
skier [skē/ ər] **94** 35
skis [skēz] **94** 33
skin [skĭn] **9** 37b
skirt [skürt] **21** 36
skunk [skŭngk] **68** 8
slacks [slăks] **20** 4
sleeping bag [slē/ pĭng băg/] **89** 26
sleepwear [slēp/ wër/] **22**
slice (*n*) [slīs] **13** 21
slice (*v*) [slīs] **31** 10
slide [slīd] **78** 31, **87** 12
slide projector [slīd/ prə jĕk/ tər] **100** 13
slides [slīdz] **100** 12
sling [slĭng] **39** 3
splippers [slĭp/ ərz] **22** 18
slug [slŭg] **62** 4
small [smöl] **24** 7
smoke [smōk] **42** 15
smoke detector [smōk/ də tĕk/ tər] **33** 15
smokestack [smōk/ stăk/] **58** 18, **80** 22
snacks [snăks] **14** 18
snail [snāl] **62** 1
snake [snāk] **65** 9
snap [snăp] **101** 13
sneakers [snē/ kərz] **20** 11
snorkel [snör/ kəl] **91** 34
snow plow [snō/ plow/] **49** 5
snowy [snō/ e] **25** 3
soap [sōp] **34** 15
soap dish [sōp/ dĭsh/] **34** 6
soccer [sŏk/ ər] **92**
soccer ball [sŏk/ ər böl/] **92** 26
socks [sŏks] **22** 17

sofa [sō′ fə] **28** 25
soft drink [söft′ drĭngk′] **16** 11
softball [söft′ böl′] **92**, **92** 10
solar collector [sō′ lər kə lĕk′ tər] **80** 17
solar eclipse [sō′ lər ĭ klĭps′] **74** 10
solar system [sō′ lər sĭs′ təm] **74**
soldier [sōl′ jər] **48** 16
sole [sōl] **20** 6
solid [sŏl′ əd] **24** 20
solid figures [sŏl′ əd fĭg′ yərz] **79**
son [sŭn] **3** 16
Sony Walkman [sō′ nē wök′ mən] **100** 30
sore throat [sör′ thrōt′] **40** 12
south [sowth] **71** 72
South America [sowth′ ə mër′ ə kə] **70** 2
South Atlantic [sowth′ ăt lăn′ tək] **70** 12
South Carolina [sowth′ kăr ə lī′ nə] **73** 40
South China Sea [sowth′ chī′ nə sē′] **70** 39
South Dakota [sowth′ də kō′ tə] **73** 41
South Pacific [sowth pə sĭf′ ək] **70** 10
space probe [spās′ prōb] **75** 4
space program [spās′ prō′ grăm] **75**
space shuttle [spās′ shŭt′ əl] **75** 14
space station [spās′ stā′ shən] **75** 1
space suit [spās′ sōōt′] **75** 6
spacecraft [spās′ krăft′] **75**
spaghetti [spə gĕt′ ē] **18** 10
spaniel [spăn′ yəl] **69** 24
spare ribs [spër′ rĭbz′] **10** 10
spare tire [spër′ tīr′] **51** 39
sparrow [spăr′ ō] **64** 10
spatula [spăch′ə lə] **27** 21
speaker [spē′ kər] **28** 21, **100** 24
speed limit sign [spēd′ lĭm ət sīn′] **53** 8
speedometer [spə dŏm′ ə tər] **50** 10
spider [spī′ dər] **63** 16
spinach [spĭn′ əch] **6** 8
spinal cord [spī′ nəl körd′] **5** 58
spiral notebook [spī′ rəl nōt′ bŏŏk] **76** 15
split [splĭt] **11** 17
split end [splĭt′ ĕnd′] **93** 24
spoke [spōk] **52** 26
sponge [spŭnj] **34** 7
(sponge) mop [spŭnj′ mŏp′] **35** 6
(spool of) thread [spōōl′ əv thrĕd′] **101** 2
spoon [spōōn] **29** 8
sports car [spörts′ kär′] **53** 17
sports [spörts] **92-97**
spotlight [spŏt′ līt′] **99** 4
sprain [sprān] **40** 13
spray can [sprā′ kăn′] **13** 24
spray starch [sprā′ stärch′] **35** 21
spread [sprĕd] **17** 11
Spring [sprĭng] **26**
sprinkler [sprĭng′ klər] **27** 13, **87** 14
sprocket [sprŏk′ ət] **52** 20
square [skwër] **79** 9
squid [skwĭd] **62** 5
squirrel [skwür′ əl] **66** 10
stage [stāj] **99** 5
staircase [stër′ kās] **28** 12
stake [stāk] **89** 30
stamp [stămp] **46** 10
stands [stăndz] **93** 10
staple remover [stāp′ əl rə moo′ vər] **83** 29
stapler [stāp′ lər] **83** 27
star [stär] **74** 4
starfish [stär′ fĭsh′] **62** 7
starting gate [stär′ tĭng gāt′] **95** 20
station [stā′ shən] **55** 18
station wagon [stā′ shən wăg′ ən] **50**
steak [stāk] **10** 5, **11** 29, **18** 21
steam [stēm] **31** 12
steamer [stēm′ ər] **30** 3
steering wheel [stïr′ ĭng wēl′] **50** 8
stem [stĕm] **8** 2a, **60** 1a
step [stĕp] **28** 13
stepladder [stĕp′ lăd′ ər] **35** 1
stereo cassette player [stĕr′ ē ō kə sĕt plā′ ər] **100** 25
stereo system [stĕr′ ē ō sĭs′ təm] **28** 20
stern [stürn] **58** 11
stethoscope [stĕth′ ə skōp′] **39** 9
stewing meat [stoo′ ĭng mēt] **10** 4
stick [stĭk] **12** 5
stick shift [stĭk′ shĭft′] **50** 24
sting [stĭng] **63** 8a
stingray [stĭng′ rā′] **65** 6
stir [stür] **31** 1
stitch [stĭch] **101** 19
stitches [stĭch′ əz] **39** 21
stockings [stŏk′ ĭngz] **22** 6
stomach [stŭm′ ək] **5** 66
stomachache [stŭm′ ək āk′] **40** 7
stool [stōōl] **78** 34
stopper [stŏp′ ər] **34** 10, **78** 10
stork [störk] **64** 30
stove [stōv] **30** 30
straight line [strāt′ līn′] **79** 1
(strand of) beads [strănd′ əv bēdz′] **23** 7
strap [străp] **54** 8
straw [strö] **16** 10
strawberry [strö′ bër′ ē] **8** 15
strawberry shortcake [strö′ bër ē shört′ kāk] **18** 26
stream [strēm] **88** 6
street [strēt] **45** 31
street cleaner [strēt′ klē′ nər] **49** 1
street sign [strēt′ sīn′] **44** 8
streetcar [strēt′ kär′] **55** 30
streetlight [strēt′ līt′] **45** 29
stretch [strĕch] **95** 19
stretch bandage [strĕch′ băn′ dĭj] **40** 13a
stretcher [strĕch′ ər] **39** 12
stretchie [strĕch′ ē] **33** 19
string [strĭng] **46** 20, **98** 10a
string bean(s) [strĭng′ bēn(z)′] **6** 15
strings [strĭngz] **98**
striped [strīpt] **24** 17
stroller [strō′ lər] **33** 14
student [stoo′ dənt] **76** 19
stuffed animal [stŭft′ ăn ə məl] **33** 27
subject [sŭb′ jəkt] **47** 10
submarine [sŭb′ mə rēn′] **48** 7
subway [sŭb′ wā′] **54**
subway station [sŭb′ wā stā′ shən] **44** 16
sugar (packet) [shŏŏg′ ər păk′ ət] **16** 13
sugar bowl [shŏŏg′ ər bōl′] **29** 23
sugarcane [shŏŏg′ ər kān′] **60** 20
suitcase [sōōt′ kās′] **56** 7
Summer [sŭm′ ər] **26**

sun [sŭn] **74** 7, **80** 3
sunbather [sŭn′ bā′ dhər] **90** 19
sundae [sŭn′ dē] **18** 23
sunflower [sŭn′ flŏw′ ər] **60** 19
sunglasses [sŭn′ glăs′ əz] **90** 14
sunny [sŭn′ ē] **25** 4
(sunnyside-up) egg
[sŭn′ ē sīd ŭp′ ĕg′] **18** 32
sunroof [sŭn′ ro͞of′] **51** 44
suntan lotion [sŭn′ tăn lō′ shən] **91** 39
supermarket [so͞o′ pər mär′ kət] **14**
surf [sürf] **97** 12
surfboard [sürf′ börd′] **91** 25
surgery [sŭr′ jə rē] **41** 2
suspect [sŭs′ pĕkt] **43** 3
swan [swŏn] **64** 28
sweatband [swĕt′ bănd′] **20** 12
sweater [swĕt′ ər] **19** 7, **19** 13, **19** 23
sweatpants [swĕt′ pănts′] **20** 10
sweatshirt [swĕt′ shürt′] **20** 8
sweep [swēp] **38** 7
swimmer [swĭm′ ər] **91** 28
swing [swĭng] **33** 24
swings [swĭngz] **87** 16
switch [swĭch] **37** 43c
switchboard [swĭch′ börd′] **83** 3
switchboard operator
[swĭch′ börd ŏp′ ə rā tər] **83** 1
swordfish [sörd′ fĭsh′] **65** 3
synthesizer [sĭn′ thə sī′ zər] **99** 21
syringe [sə rĭnj′] **39** 27
syrup [sĭr′ əp] **18** 6
T-shirt [tē′ shürt′] **21** 29
table [tā′ bəl] **29** 7
tablecloth [tā′ bəl klöth′] **29** 16
tablet [tăb′ lət] **41** 6
taco [tŏ′ kō] **18** 24
tadpole [tăd′ pōl′] **65** 16
tail [tāl] **57** 10, **65** 3a, **66** 3a
taillight [tāl′ līt′] **50** 31
tailor [tā′ lər] **84** 6
take [tāk] **17** 10
takeoff [tāk′ ŏf′] **57**
Takla Makan Desert
[tŏk′ lə mə kŏn′ dĕz′ ərt] **71** 53
tambourine [tăm′ bə rēn′] **98** 17
tank [tăngk] **48** 10
tank top [tăngk′ tŏp′] **20** 13
tanker [tăngk′ ər] **58** 15
tap [tăp] **16** 20
tape [tāp] **46** 22
tape measure [tāp′ mĕzh′ ər] **36** 21, **101** 15
taxi [tăk′ sē] **55**
taxi stand [tăk′ sē stănd′] **55** 28
taxicab [tăk′ sē kăb′] **55** 27
tea [tē] **16** 15
teacher [tē′ chər] **76** 4
teakettle [tē′ kĕt′ əl] **30** 28
team sports [tēm′ spörts′] **92**
teapot [tē′ pŏt′] **29** 19
tear [tër] **77** 9
teddy bear [tĕd′ ē bër′] **33** 3
tee [tē] **95** 13
telephone [tĕl′ ə fōn′] **83** 15
telescope [tĕl′ ə skōp′] **74** 22
television [tĕl′ ə vĭzh′ ən] **28** 18, **100** 5
teller [tĕl′ ər] **86** 15
temperature [tĕm′ pər ə chər] **25** 6
Tennessee [tĕn′ ə sē′] **73** 42
tennis [tĕn′ əs] **94**
tennis ball [tĕn′ əs böl′] **94** 1
tennis court [tĕn′ əs kört′] **95**
tent [tĕnt] **89** 24
tentacle [tĕn′ tə kəl] **62** 12a
terminal [türm′ ə nəl] **51** 55, **58** 29
terminal building [türm′ ə nəl bĭl′ dĭng] **57** 16
termite [tür′ mīt] **63** 11
terrier [tĕr′ ē ər] **69** 25
test tube [tĕst′ to͞ob′] **78** 9
Texas [tĕk′ səs] **73** 43
textbook [tĕkst′ bo͝ok′] **76** 26
theater [thē′ ə tər] **99**
thermometer
[thər mŏm′ ə tər] **25** 5, **78** 22
thermos [thür′ məs] **88** 14
thigh [thī] **4** 18, **11** 19
thimble [thĭm′ bəl] **101** 21
third (1/3) [thürd] **79** 32
third baseman [thürd′ bās′ mən] **93** 4
thorn [thörn] **60** 18c
thread [thrĕd] **37** 42b, **101** 2
three-piece suit [thrē′ pēs so͞ot] **21** 40
throat [thrōt] **5** 59
through [thro͞o] **103** 1
throw [thrō] **97** 10
thumb [thŭm] **4** 24
thumbtack [thŭm′ tăk′] **76** 25
ticket [tĭk′ ət] **55** 16, **56** 4
ticket window [tĭk′ ət wĭn′ dō] **55** 19
tie (*n*) [tī] **21** 47
tie (*v*) [tī] **77** 12
tie clip [tī′ klĭp′] **23** 14
tie pin [tī′ pĭn′] **23** 13
tiger [tī′ gər] **68** 2
tight [tīt] **24** 3
tighten [tī′ tən] **38** 4
tight end [tīt′ ĕnd′] **93** 30
tights [tīts] **19** 14
tile [tīl] **34** 27
timer [tī′ mər] **78** 13
timetable [tīm′ tă′ bəl] **55** 20
tip [tĭp] **55** 22
tire [tīr] **50** 37, **52** 28
tissues [tĭsh′ o͞oz] **32** 13
title [tī′ təl] **47** 9
to [to͞o] **103** 9
toast [tōst] **18** 34
toaster [tōs′ tər] **30** 16
toe [tō] **5** 54
toenail [tō′ nāl′] **5** 56
toilet [toy′ lət] **34** 29
toilet brush [toy′ lət brŭsh′] **34** 31
toilet paper [toy′ lət pā′ pər] **34** 30
toiletries [toy′ lə trēz] **23**
token booth [tō′kən bo͞oth′] **54** 13
tollbooth [tōl′ bo͞oth′] **53** 27
tomato(es) [tə mā′ tō(z)] **6** 19
tongs [tŏngz] **78** 29
tongue [tŭng] **4** 41
tongue depressor [tŭng′ də prĕs′ ər] **40** 12a
toolbox [to͞ol′ bŏks′] **36** 23
toolshed [to͞ol′ shĕd′] **27** 28
tooth [to͞oth] **4** 42
toothache [to͞oth′ āk′] **40** 9
toothbrush [to͞oth′ brŭsh′] **34** 21
toothless mammals [to͞oth′ ləs măm′ əlz] **66**
toothpaste [to͞oth′ pāst′] **34** 16
tortoise [tör′ təs] **65** 18
tossed salad [töst′ săl′ əd] **18** 13
touch [tŭch] **77** 2

touring handlebars
[tŏŏr′ ĭng hăn′ dəl bärz] **52** 12
tow truck [tō′ trŭk] **49** 2
toward [törd] **103** 4
towel rack [tow′ əl răk′] **34** 25
towrope [tō′ rōp′] **59** 11
toy chest [toy′ chĕst′] **33** 29
track [trăk] **54** 10, **94** 32
track and field [trăk′ənd fēld′] **94**
tractor [trăk′ tər] **81** 15
tractor trailer [trăk′ tər trā′ lər] **49** 15
traffic cop [trăf′ ək kŏp′] **44** 10
traffic light [trăf′ ək līt′] **45** 21
trailer [trā′ lər] **53** 10
train [trān] **55**
training wheels [trān′ ĭng wēlz′] **52** 1
transcript [trăn′ skrĭpt] **43** 15
transfer [trăns′ fər] **54** 4
transformer [trăns fôr′ mər] **80** 25
transmission towers
[trănz mĭsh′ ən tow′ ərz] **80** 23
transportation [trăns′ pər tā′ shən] **54**
transporter [trăns′ pör tər] **49** 17
trash basket [trăsh′ băs′ kət] **44** 15
trash can [trăsh′ kăn′] **87** 11
travel agent [trăv′ əl ā′ jənt] **84** 4
traveler [trăv′ ə lər] **56** 3
tray [trā] **16** 33
tray table [trā′ tā′ bəl] **56** 22
treatments [trēt′ mənts] **41**
tree [trē] **61** 35
trees [trēz] **60**
triangle [trī′ ăng′ gəl] **79** 6
tricycle [trī′ sĭ kəl] **52** 6
trigger [trĭg′ ər] **48** 22
tripod [trī′ pod] **100** 9
trim [trĭm] **26** 8
trombone [trŏm bōn′] **98** 23
trough [tröf] **81** 25
trout [trowt] **65** 2
trowel [trow′ əl] **27** 27
truck [trŭk] **49**, **53** 25
truck driver [trŭk′ drī′ vər] **49** 16
trumpet [trŭm′ pət] **98** 25
trunk [trŭngk] **51** 40, **61** 35b, **66** 17a
tub [tŭb] **12** 6
tuba [tōō′ bə] **98** 27
tube [tōōb] **13** 15, **91** 29
tugboat [tŭg′ bōt′] **58** 13
tulip [tōō′ ləp] **60** 1
turkey [tür′ kē] **10** 23, **64** 20
turnip [tür′ nəp] **6** 34
turn signal lever [türn′ sĭg nəl lĕ′ vər]
50 11
turn signal lights [türn′ sĭg nəl līts′]
51 50
turnstile [türn′ stīl′] **54** 12
turntable [türn′ tā′ bəl] **100** 18
turtle [tür′ təl] **65** 12
(turtleneck) sweater
[tür′ təl nĕk swĕ′ tər] **19** 13
tusk [tŭsk] **66** 17b
TV antenna [tē′ vē ăn tĕn′ ə] **27** 3
tweezers [twē′ zərz] **78** 32
twig [twĭg] **61** 33a
(two-door) sedan [tōō′ dör sə dăn′] **51**
type [tīp] **77** 10
typewriter [tīp′ rī′ tər] **83** 10
typing chair [tī′ pĭng chër′] **83** 17
typist [tī′ pəst] **83** 6
U.S. mailbox [yōō′ ĕs māl′ bŏks] **46** 6
U.S. Postal System
[yōō′ ĕs pōs′ təl sĭs təm] **46**
ukulele [yōō′ kə lā′ lē] **98** 3
umbrella [ŭm brĕl′ ə] **20** 24
umpire [ŭm′ pīr] **92** 1, **93** 17
uncle [ŭng′ kəl] **3** 3
under [ŭn′ dər] **102** 8
underpants [ŭn′ dər pănts′] **22** 3
undershirt [ŭn′ dər shürt′] **22** 1
underwear [ŭn′ dər wër′] **22**
uniform [yōō′ nə förm′] **21** 45, **92** 9
United States of America
[yōō nī′ təd stāts′ əv əmër′ ə kə] **72**
universe [yōō′ nə vürs′] **74**
up [ŭp] **103** 11
upper arm [ŭp′ ər ärm′] **4** 7
Urals [yŏŏr′ əlz] **71** 46
uranium rods [yōō rā′ nē əm rōdz′]
80 15
Uranus [yŏŏr′ ə nəs] **74** 17
usher [ŭsh′ ər] **99** 16
Utah [yōō′ tö] **73** 44
utility pole [yōō tĭl′ ə tē pōl′] **80** 26
utility room [yōō tĭl′ ə tē rōōm] **35**
(V-neck) sweater [vē′ nĕk swĕt′ ər]
19 23
vacuum [văk′ yōōm] **38** 14
vacuum cleaner [văk′ yōōm klē′ nər]
35 16
valve [vălv] **52** 27
van [văn] **53** 26
vase [vās] **28** 6
VCR (videocassette recorder)
[vē′ sē är′]/
[vĭd′ ē ō kə sĕt′ rə kör′ dər] **100** 4
vegetables [vĕj′ tə bəlz] **6**
vehicles and equipment
[vē′ ə kəlz ənd ə kwĭp′ mənt] **48**
vein [vān] **5** 68
vendor [vĕn′ dər] **87** 3
vent [vĕnt] **50** 21
Venus [vē′ nəs] **74** 12
verbs [vürbz] **17**, **26**, **31**, **38**, **77**, **96**
Vermont [vür mŏnt′] **73** 45
vest [vĕst] **21** 39
video [vĭd′ē ō] **100**
video camera [vĭd′ ē ō kăm′ ə rə]
100 1
videocassette (tape)
[vĭd′ ē ō kə sĕt′ tāp′] **100** 3
vine [vīn] **61** 42
viola [vē ōl′ ə] **98** 8
violet [vī′ ə lət] **60** 16
violin [vī ə lĭn′] **98** 7
Virginia [vər jĭn′ yə] **73** 46
vise [vīs] **37** 36
visor [vīz′ ər] **50** 5
volleyball [vŏl′ ē böl′] **92**, **92** 22
waders [wā′ dərz] **88** 10
waist [wāst] **4** 13
waiter [wā tər] **16** 5
waitress [wā′ trəs] **16** 2
walk [wök] **77** 8
walker [wök′ ər] **33** 23
wall [wöl] **28** 3
wall unit [wöl′ yōō′ nət] **28** 19
wall-to-wall carpeting
[wöl′ tə wöl kär′ pə tĭng] **28** 15
wallet [wöl′ ət] **20** 9
walnut(s) [wöl′ nət(s)] **8** 29
walrus [wöl′ rŭs] **68** 11
warm [wörm] **25** 8

wash [wŏsh] **38** 16
washcloth [wŏsh′ klöth′] **34** 22
washer [wŏsh′ ər] **37** 40
washing machine [wŏsh′ ĭng mə shēn′] **35** 30
Washington [wŏsh′ ĭng tən] **73** 47
wasp [wŏsp] **63** 20
wastepaper basket [wāst′ pā pər băs′ kət] **34** 13
watch [wŏch] **23** 10
watchband [wŏch′ bănd′] **23** 11
water (*n*) [wŏt′ ər] **42** 16, **91** 30
water (*v*) [wŏt′ ər] **26** 5
water fountain [wŏt′ ər fown′ tən] **87** 19
water glass [wŏt′ ər glăs′] **29** 6
waterfall [wŏt′ər föl] **80** 11, **89** 18
water-skier [wŏt′ər skē′ ər] **59** 10
watercress [wŏt′ər krĕs′] **6** 5
watering can [wŏt′ər ĭng kăn′] **27** 16
watermelon [wŏt′ər mĕl′ ən] **9** 26
wave [wāv] **91** 24
weapon [wĕp′ənz] **48**
weather [wĕdh′ər] **25**
weather forecaster [wĕdh′ər för′ kăst ər] **86** 1
weather satellite [wĕdh′ər săt′ ə līt] **75** 3
weaving [wē′ vĭng] **101** 30
web [wĕb] **63** 15
wedding ring [wĕd′ ĭng rĭng′] **23** 4
weights [wāts] **78** 5
west [wĕst] **71** 74
West Virginia [wĕst′ vər jĭn′ yə] **73** 48
wet [wĕt] **25** 15
wet suit [wĕt′ so͞ot′] **91** 38
whale [wāl] **68** 9
wheat [wēt] **60** 22
wheat farm [wēt′ färm′] **81**
(wheat) field [wēt′ fēld′] **81** 16
wheel [wēl] **52** 4
wheelbarrow [wēl′ băr′ ō] **27** 32, **82** 23
wheelchair [wēl′ chër′] **39** 2
whistle [wĭs′ əl] **90** 5
whole [hōl] **11** 27, **79** 29
whole (chicken) [hōl′ chĭk′ ən] **11** 16
width [wĭdth] **79** 35
wife [wīf] **2** 4
willow [wĭl′ ō] **61** 31
wind [wĭnd] **80** 4
windbreaker [wĭnd′ brā′ kər] **19** 5
windlass [wĭnd′ ləs] **58** 23
windmill [wĭnd′ mĭl′] **80** 19
window [wĭn′ dō] **27** 7, **46** 15
window cleaner [wĭn′ dō klē′ nər] **35** 10
windpipe [wĭnd′ pīp′] **5** 60
windshield [wĭnd′ shēld′] **51** 45
windshield wiper [wĭnd′ shēld wī′ pər] **50** 6
windsurfer [wĭnd′ sür′ fər] **59** 14
windy [wĭn′ dē] **25** 13
wine [wīn] **16** 19
wine glass [wīn′ glăs′] **29** 5
wing [wĭng] **11** 22, **57** 9, **63** 4a, **64** 1a
Winter [wĭn′ tər] **26**
wipe [wīp] **38** 5
wire [wīr] **37** 35
wire mesh screen [wīr′ mĕsh skrēn′] **78** 6
Wisconsin [wĭs kŏn′ sən] **73** 49
witness [wĭt′ nəs] **43** 13
witness stand [wĭt′ nəs stănd′] **43** 18
wolf [wo͝olf] **69** 29
woman [wo͝om′ən] **2** 1
wood [wo͝od] **36** 4
wood plane [wo͝od′ plān′] **37** 32
woodpecker [wo͝od′ pĕk′ ər] **64** 17
woods [wo͝odz] **89** 32
woodwinds [wo͝od′ wĭndz′] **98**
wool [wo͝ol] **101** 23
word processor [würd′ prŏ′ sĕs ər] **83** 7
work gloves [würk′ glŭvz′] **27** 26
workbench [würk′ bĕnch′] **36** 22
workshop [würk′ shŏp′] **36**
world [würld] **70**
worm [würm] **62** 11
wrench [rĕnch] **36** 10
wrist [rĭst] **4** 21
write [rīt] **77** 7
writer [rī′ tər] **86** 7
Wyoming [wī ō′ mĭng] **73** 50
X ray [ĕks′ rā′] **39** 1
X ray screener [ĕks′ rā skrē′ nər] **56** 11
xylophone [zī′ lə fōn′] **98** 31
yam [yăm] **7** 24
Yangtze River [yăng′ sē rĭv′ ər] **71** 69
yarn [yärn] **101** 31
Yellow Sea [yĕl′ ō sē′] **70** 37
Yenisey River [yĕn′ ə sā′ rĭv′ ər] **71** 65
Yukon River [yo͞o′ kŏn rĭv′ ər] **71** 56
zebra [zē′ brə] **66** 18
zinnia [zĭn′ ē ə] **60** 13
zip code [zĭp′ kōd′] **46** 12
zipper [zĭp′ ər] **101** 16
zoo [zo͞o] **87** 1
zucchini [zo͞o kē′ nē] **7** 27

абажур **28** 27
абрикос **9** 25
аварийный знак **51** 41
август **104**
авианосец **48** 4
авокадо **9** 33
Австралия **70** 6
автобус **53** 20; **54A**
автобусная остановка **44** 13
автоматический прерыватель **35** 5
автомобили **50–51**
автомобили с автоматической коробкой передач **50A**
автомобили с ручной коробкой передач **50B**
автопогрузчик **58** 4
автор **47** 8
автоуборщик **49** 1
автоцистерна **49** 3
агент (**бюро путешествий**) **84** 4
агент по продаже недвижимости **85** 5
адвокат **43** 22
адрес **46** 11
административное здание **44** 1
Азия **70** 5
аист **64** 30
Айдахо **72** 12
Айова **72** 15
аккордеон **98** 28
аккумулятор **51** 54
актер **99** 19
активная зона 80 14
актриса **99** 20
акула **65** 5
Алабама **72** 1
аллигатор **65** 8
альпинизм **89**
Альпы **71** 44
альт **98** 8
Аляска **72** 2
Амазонка **71** 59
американский лось **67** 35
американский футбол **92**
амортизаторы **52** 31
амфибии и пресмыкающиеся **65B**
ананас **8** 4
ангар **57** 17
Анды **71** 43
Антарктика **70** 7
Антарктический океан **70** 14
антенна **51** 46; **62** 1b
анютины глазки **60** 2
апельсин **8** 8
Аппалачи **71** 41
аппарат для чтения микрофильмов **47** 14
апрель **104**
аптека **45** 22
аптекарь **84** 1
аптечка **34** 14
Арабское море **70** 30
арахис **9** 28
арбитр **93** 22
арбуз **9** 26
Аризона **72** 3
Арканзас **72** 4
армия **48** 15
артерия **5** 69
артишок **6** 11
арфа **98** 6
архитектор **86** 8
астероид **74** 20
атлас **47** 20
Африка **70** 4
аэропорт **57** 16
бабочка **63** 3
бабуин **69** 19
бабушка **3** 1
багаж **56** 8
багажник **51** 40
багажное отделение **56** 21
база **93** 6
байдарка **59** 17
байдарочное весло **59** 3
бакалея **15** 24
бакенбарды **4** 33
баклажан **7** 21
балерина **99** 3
балет **99A**
балки **82** 1
балкон **99** 14
баллон с воздухом **91** 37
Балтийское море **70** 22
бананы (кисть бананов) **9** 20
банджо **98** 5
банк **86B**
банка **12** 6, (обычно стеклянная) 9, (металлическая) 10; **30** 15
баночка **12** 2
бар **16B**
барабан **98** 19
барабан «бонго» **98** 22
барабан «конга» **98** 20
барабанные палочки **98** 19a
барабанщик **99** 27
баран **81** 10
баранина **10** 13
бараньи отбивные **10** 15
Баренцево море **70** 23
баржа **58** 12
бармен **16** 21
баррикада **82** 21
бас-гитарист **99** 23
баскетбол **92**
батат **7** 24
батон **12** 7
бегать **96** 6
бегемот **66** 14
беговая дорожка **87** 9; **94** 32
бегун **94** 31
бегуны **91** 23
бедро **4** 16, 18; (курицы) **11** 19
бежать **96** 6
безалкогольный напиток **16** 11
беззубые млекопитающие **66**
безымянный палец **4** 27
бейка **101** 11
бейсбол **92**
бекон **10** 11; **18** 33
бельевая веревка **35** 19
белка **66** 10
бельэтаж **99** 13
белый **104**
белый медведь **69** 22
Бенгальский залив **70** 32

бензин **80** 28
бензобак **50** 34
бензовоз **49** 3
береза **61** 32
берет **19** 22
Берингово море **70** 34
бетоновоз **49** 13
бетономешалка **82** 25
библиотека **47**
библиотекарь **47** 1
библиотекарша **47** 23
библиотечный билет **47** 3
бивень **66** 17b
бизон **67** 19
билет **55** 16; **56** 4
билетер **99** 16
билетная касса **55** 19
бинокль **90** 7
бинт **39** 24
бита **92** 5
бить **96** 1
бифштекс **18** 21
бланк заказа **47** 12
блины **18** 5
блокнот **83** 26
блузка **21** 34
блюдце **29** 21
бобина кинопленк **100** 17
бобр **66** 12
бобы в томатном соусе **18** 3
богомол **63** 7
божья коровка **63** 14
бокал **29** 5
боковое зеркало **50** 2
бокс (кабина) **83** 5
бокс (спорт) **94**
боксерская перчатка **94** 15
болезни и (телесные) повреждения **40**
болотные **88** 10
болт **37** 38
боль в горле **40** 12
боль в желудке, животе **40** 7
боль в спине **40** 8
больной **39** 20
Большая Медведица **74** 3
Большая Песчаная пустыня **71** 55
большой **24** 8
большой палец **4** 24; **5** 53
бомба **48** 3
бомбардировщик **48** 2
бомбомет **48** 28
бор-машина **39** 15
боров **67** 30
борода **4** 39
бортпроводник **56** 20
босоножки **20** 19
ботинки **19** 9
ботинок **94** 26
«боулинг» **94**
брандспойт **42** 17
браслет **23** 9
брат **3** 9
брать **17** 10
бревно **28** 10
бригадир **85** 13
брикеты угля **27** 23
бритва **23** 20
бровь **5** 44
бройлер (нижняя часть плиты) **30** 33
брокколи **6** 2
броненосец **66** 2
бросать **97** 10, (мяч) 11, 16
брошь **23** 8
брюки **20** 4
брюссельская капуста **6** 4
брюшная полость **4** 14
будильник **32** 8
буй **58** 16
буксир **58** 13
буксирный трос **59** 11
буксировщик **49** 2
булавка (для галстука) **23** 11; **33** 11; **101** 20
булочка **18** 7, 19
булочная **44** 6
бульдозер **82** 27
бум **59** 7
бумаги **76** 13
бумажник **20** 9
бумажные полотенца **35** 23
бунзеновская горелка **78** 20
буровая вышка **80** 2
бурундук **66** 6
бусы **23** 7
бутерброд **16** 16
бутон розы **60** 18a
бутылка **12** 3; (для кормления ребенка) **33** 17
буфет **29** 29; **90** 2
буханка (хлеба) **12** 7
бухгалтер **86** 18
бухты **70**
бык **67** 34
бюстгальтер **22** 13
в (выдвижном ящике) **102** 7; (лунку) 103 12
в горошек **24** 19
в классе **76**
в порту **58**
вагон **54** 9
вагонетка **80** 8
ваза **28** 6
Вайоминг **73** 50
валторна **98** 26
ванна **34** 11
ванная **34**
ванное полотенце, (-ая) (простыня) **34** 24
вантуз **35** 14
варежки **19** 11
варить **17** 4; **31** 16
варить на пару **31** 12
ватные тампоны **39** 23
Вашингтон **73** 47
ведро **35** 15; **90** 16
веко **5** 45
волосипед **52** 15
велосипед-вездеход **52** 8
велосипедист **90** 4
велосипеды **52**
вельветовые брюки **21** 27
вена **5** 68
Венера **74** 12
вентилятор **28** 1; **50** 21
вентиляторный ремень **51** 53
веранда **27** 5, 17
верблюд **67** 33

веревка **46** 20; **89** 23
Вермонт **73** 45
верстак **36** 22
вертолет **57** 2
верхняя часть руки **4** 7
верховая тропа **87** 7
верфь **58** 28
вершина **79** 21; **89** 20
весло **59** 22
весна **26**
вести (мяч) **97** 11
вестибюль **44** 2
весы **14** 7; **34** 32; **78** 4
ветвь **61** 33а, 35а
ветер **80** 4
веточка **61** 33а
ветреный **25** 13
ветровое стекло **51** 45
ветряная мельница **80** 19
ветчина **10** 12
вешалка **32** 2
вешалка для подотенец **34** 25
вешать **38** 6
взбивать **31** 8
взлет **57B**
взлетно-посадочная полоса **57** 19
видео **100A**
видеокамера **100** 1
видеомагнитофон **100** 4
видеопленка **100** 3
виды почты **46C**
виды самолетов **57A**
вилка **29** 12
вилы **81** 14
вино **16** 19
винт **37** 42
винтовка **48** 21
виолончель **98** 9
Виргиния **73** 46
Висконсин **73** 49
вишня **9** 19
включатель **32** 25; **37** 43с
внук **2** 12
внутренние органы **5F**
внучка **2** 11
вода **42** 16; **91** 30
водитель **54** 3
водитель такси **55** 26
водить автомобиль **97** 15
воднолыжник **59** 10
водопад **80** 11; **89** 18
водопровод **35** 18
водопроводчик **85** 1
водосток **27** 18
водосточный желоб **27** 10
военно-воздушные силы **48** 20
военно-морской флот **48** 13
вожжи **94** 22
воздушный змей **91** 22
воздушный насос **53** 13
воздушный транспорт **56**
воздушный фильтр **51** 52
воздушный шар **57** 1
возле (телевизора) **102** 11
вокзал **55** 18
вокруг (маяка) **103** 2
волк **69** 29
воллейбол **92**
волна **91** 24
волосы **4** 30
вооруженные силы **48**
воробей **64** 10
ворона **64** 3
воронка **78** 17
ворота **92** 25
воротник **20** 20
восемнадцать **104**
восемь **104**
восемьдесят **104**
воскресенье **104**
восток **71** 73
Восточно-Китайское море **70** 38
вратарь **92** 24
врач **39** 11
всадник **87** 6
вселенная **74**
вспышка **100** 7
вставные листы **76** 13
вторник **104**
второй летчик **56** 16
входить **77** 14
въезд на шоссе **53** 21
выгон **81** 6
выдвижной ящик **47** 5
выдра **68** 10
выкройка **101** 6, 7
высокий **24** 11
высота **79** 34
вытирать **38** 5, 9, (пыль) 15
вытирать **77** 3
выхлопная труба **52** 33
выходить **77** 13
выход с шоссе **53** 2
вышивание **101** 27
вышка высоковольтной передачи **80** 23
вышка спасателя **90** 8
вьющееся, ползучее растение **61** 42
вяз **61** 36
вязальная игла **101** 25
вязальный крючок **101** 29
вязаная шапка **19** 16
вязание **101** 22
вязание крючком **101** 28
Гавайи **72** 11
гавайская гитара **98** 3
гаечный ключ **36** 10
газета **21** 48
газетный киоск **45** 30
газовая (электрическая) плита **30** 30
газон вокруг лунки на площадке гольфа **95** 10
гайка **37** 39
галактика **74** 1
галстук **21** 47
гамак **27** 11
«гамбургер» (булочка с бифштексом) **18** 9
Ганг **71** 67
гандбол **94**
гараж **27** 2
гардения **60** 14
гармоника **98** 30
гастроном **14–15**
гвардня **80** 16
Гвинейский залив **70** 25
гвоздь **37** 41
гейзер **80** 5

геометрические фигуры **79B**
гиацинт **60** 10
гиббон **69** 15
гидрант **42** 9
гиена **69** 30
Гималаи **71** 47
гимнастика **94**
гимнастическое бревно **94** 24
гимнастка **94** 23
гипертония **40** 10
гипотенуза **79** 24
гиппопотам **66** 14
гипсовая повязка (гипс) **39** 5
гитара **98** 11
гитарист **99** 25
глаголы, относящиеся к домашней работе и к ремонту **38**
глаголы, относящиеся к спорту **96**
глаголы, употребляемые в кухне **31**
глаголы, употребляемые в ресторане **17**
глаголы, употребляемые в соответствии с временем года **26**
глаголы, употребляемые в школе **77**
гладильная доска **35** 13
гладить **38** 11
глаз **5D**
глазная пипетка **78** 26
глазные капли **41** 10
глобус **47** 19
глубина **79** 33
глубокая тарелка **13** 23
гнездо **64** 31
гобой **98** 15
говядина **10** 1
голова **4C**
головастик **65** 16
головка **37** 42a
головная боль **40** 6
головоломка (игра) **33** 31
голубой **104**
голубь **64** 1
гольф **94**
гольфы **22** 16
гора **89** 19
горб **67** 33a
горилла **69** 17
горло **5** 59
горные хребты **71**
город **44–45**
городские парки **87**
городские профессии **84**
городской транспорт **54–55**
горох **6** 17
горчица **18** 1
гостиная **28**
готовить **17** 4
«гофер» **66** 8
грабли **27** 30
градирня **80** 16
градуированный цилиндр **78** 25
гребенка **32** 6
гребешок (-шки) **11** 35; **62** 10
гребная шлюпка **59** 23
грейпфрут **8** 7
грелка **41** 3
гремучая змея **65** 10
гренки **18** 34
грецкий(-е) орех(-и) **9** 29
грибы **7** 30
грива **67** 21a
гриль **27** 22; **88** 12
громкоговоритель **28** 21; **76** 3; **100** 24
грудинка **10** 11
грудь **4** 12
грудь (курицы) **11** 22
груз **58** 10
грузовая платформа **49** 18
грузовик **49** 11; **53** 25
грузовики **49**
грузовик-фургон **49** 9
грузовой отсек **57** 12; **58** 8; **75** 9
грузчик **49** 12
груша **8** 18
грызуны **66**
грязное белье **35** 28
грязный **24** 5
губа **4** 43
губка **34** 7; **76** 11
губная помада **23** 29
Гудзонов залив **70** 18
гумно **81** 8
гусеница **63** 1
гусь **64** 26
давать **17** 9
два **104**
двадцать **104**
двадцать один **104**
двадцать пять центов **13** 30
двенадцать **104**
дверная ручка **50** 4
дверь багажника **51** 43
дверь грузового отделения **57** 13
двигатель **51A**
двигать **26** 12
двор **27C**
дворник **50** 6; **85** 9
двоюродн(-ая) сестра, (-ый) брат **3** 7
двухдверный седан **51D**
двухэтажный дом **27B**
девочка **2** 9
девушки, подающие сигнал к овации **93** 20
девяносто **104**
девятнадцать **104**
девять **104**
дедушка **3** 2
дедушка и бабушка **2** 10
декабрь **104**
декорация **99** 2
Делавер **72** 8
дельтаплан **57** 6
дельфин **68** 13
денежный перевод **46** 18
деньги **12–13**
дерево **61** 35
деревья **60–61**
деревянный стол для пикника **88** 15
держать **17** 12
десять **104**
десять центов **13** 29
деталь выкройки **101** 6
детектив **43** 2
детектор металла **56** 10

дети **2** 7
детская горка **87** 12
детская комната **33**
детская кроватка **33** 4
детская лопатка **90** 17
детские качели **33** 24
детские салфетки **33** 8
детские турники **87** 17
детский горшок **33** 33
детский комбинезон **33** 19
детский лосьон **33** 6
детский манеж **33** 30
детский надувной мяч **90** 11
детский стул **16** 8
детское кресло **50** 33
джинсы **19** 6
джип **48** 9
Джорджия **72** 10
диагональ **79** 20
диаметр **79** 12
диапозитивы **100** 12
диван **28** 25
диванная подушка **28** 24
дизельное топливо **80** 34
дикобраз **66** 11
диктор последних известий **86** 2
дирижабль **57** 5
дирижер **99** 8
дирижерская полочка **99** 9
дирижерский пульт **99** 7
«Диск-жоке», ведущий музыкальной радио-программы **86** 9
дисковая пила **36** 20
дистанционное управление **28** 17
длина **79** 36
длиннохвостый попугай **64** 15
длинный **24** 2
длинный рукав **20** 15
дни недели **104**
дождевик **21** 38
дождливый **25** 1
док **58** 28
должностное лицо **86** 13
долларовые купюры **13** 25
долька **8** 8a
домашнего обихода **15** 15
домашнее обслуживание **85B**
домашний скот **81** 12
домашняя птица **10–11**, **11B**
домкрат **51** 38
дорожные работы **82B**
дорожный барьер **82** 24
дорожный знак **53** 23
доска **30** 26; **76** 5; **82** 16
доска для плавания **91** 27
доска для серфинга **91** 25
доска объявления **76** 7
доска с парусом **59** 15
доска счета **93** 19
доска-качели **87** 18
доставка почты **46A**
доставщик **49** 10
дочь **3** 15
дощатый настил **90** 1
древесина **36** 4
дренажная труба **27** 18
дроби **79D**
дрофа **64** 32
дуб **61** 33
дуб ядоносный **61** 43
дубинка **43** 9
дуга **79** 16
дуршлаг **30** 7
духи **23** 27
духовка **30** 32
духовые инструменты **98**
душ **34** 4
дым **42** 15
дымовая труба **58** 18; **80** 22
дыня **9** 35, 36
дыхательная трахея **5** 60
дядя **3** 3
дятел **64** 17
Европа **70** 3
ежевика **8** 12
ежедневный пассажир **55** 17
ездить (верхом, на велосипеде) **97** 13
Енисей **71** 65
енот **68** 7
есть **17** 1
жабры **65** 3c
жакет **21** 33
жало **63** 8a
жар **40** 2
жареная курица **18** 29
жарить **31** 15
жарить на открытом огне **31** 13
жаркий **25** 7
жаркое (из говядины) **18** 14
желе **18** 31
желоб для возврата шара **94** 3
Желтое море **70** 37
желтый **104**
желтый нарцисс **60** 8
желудевая тыква **7** 28
желудок **5** 66
желудь **61** 33b
жена **2** 4
женская рама **52** 3
женщина **2** 1
жеребенок **67** 22
жетон **43** 5
живот **41** 4
жидкое мыло (для посуды) **30** 10
жилет **21** 39
жилое здание **45** 23
жилой автофургон **53** 16
жилой дом на ферме **81** 3
жилой отсек **75** 11
жираф **67** 29
жокей **94** 21
жук **63** 10
журнал **47** 16
за (креслом) **102** 9
завязывать **77** 12
загон для скота **81** 24
загорающий **90** 19
загребать **26** 10
заднее сиденье **50** 32
задние габаритные огни **50** 31
задние ноги **66** 3b
задний бампер **51** 42
задняя линия **95** 4
задняя спинка **32** 24
зажигалка **16** 30
зажигание **50** 14
зажигать **17** 13
зажим **23** 19; **36** 2; **78** 7
зажим для галстука **23** 14

заземлительный
штепсель **36** 7
заказывать **17** 5
закрывать **77** 5
закрытый **24** 16
залив Аляска **70** 17
залив Баффина **70** 16
заливы **70**
замок **50** 1; **52** 13
занавес **32** 10; **99** 1
занавески **28** 23; **34** 5
заниматься серфингом **97** 12
запад **71** 74
Западная Виргиния **73** 48
запасная губка к швабре **35** 11
запасное колесо **51** 39
запирающийся шкафчик **76** 6
запонки **23** 12
заправка к салату **18** 12
запястье **4** 21
заражение **40** 14
застежка **23** 17
застежка-молния **101** 16
затягивать **38** 4
защитная маска **92** 15
защитник второй базы **93** 7
защитник левой стороны дальней
части поля **93** 1
защитник первой базы **93** 8
защитник поля между 2-ой и
3-ей базой **93** 5
защитник правой стороны
дальней части поля **93** 3
защитник середины дальней
части поля **93** 2
защитник третьей базой **93** 4
защитник флангов **93** 31
защитные очки **78** 12; **94** 28
защитный шлем **94** 14
звезда **74** 4
звездочка **52** 20
звонок **52** 5
звукозапись **100D**
звуковой сигнал **50** 12
звукосниматель **100** 20
зебра **66** 18
зеленый **104**
Земля **74** 8, 13
зеркало **32** 5
зеркало заднего обзора **50** 7
зерновая ферма **81B**
зернышко **8** 8c
зима **26**
зимний жакет **19** 24
зимняя одежда **19**
змея **65** 9
знак ограничения скорости **53** 8
знак съезда с шоссе **53** 24
значок **43** 5
зонт **20** 24
зоопарк **87** 1
зрачок **5** 48
зрители **99** 15
зуб **4** 42
зубная боль **40** 9
зубная паста **34** 16
зубная щетка **34** 21
зубной врач **39** 17
зубной врач-гигиенист **39** 14
зубоврачебное обслуживание **39**
зубоврачебные инструменты
39 13
зубок чесночной головки **7** 25a
зять **3** 11
ива **61** 31
игла **39** 26; **66** 11a; **101** 19
игольник **101** 3
игра в кегли **94**
игрок в гольф **94** 10
игуана **65** 13
из (воды) **103** 7
измерение **79E**
изоляционная лента **37** 34
изюм **9** 24
икра **4** 20
Иллинойс **72** 13
иллюминатор **58** 21
ильм **61** 36
инвалидная коляска **39** 2
Индиана **72** 14
индивидуальные спортивные
игры **94**
Индийский океан **70** 13
индюк **11** 23; **64** 20
инженер **56** 17
инжир **9** 21
инструменты **98**
инфекция **40** 14
инъекция **41** 8
ипподром **95D**
ирис **60** 11
история болезни **39** 10
источники энергии **80A**
истребитель **48** 1
июль **104**
июнь **104**
к (лунке) **103** 4
кабачок «цуккини» **7** 27
кабина **56** 19; **83** 5
кабина пилота **56** 13
каблук **20** 5
Кавказ **71** 45
кайма **101** 11
кактус **61** 40
календарь **83** 9
Калифорния **72** 5
калькулятор **83** 19; **100** 34
кальмар **62** 5
кальсоны **22** 7
камбала **65** 7
камера **91** 29
камин **28** 8
каминная полка **28** 7
камни **88** 11
канализационный колодец **45** 32
канарейка **64** 14
канат **58** 25
канатная дорога **55** 31
Канзас **72** 16
каноэ **59** 2
канцелярский служащий **83** 23
канцелярские работники **86C**
каньон **88** 3
капот **51** 47
капсула **41** 5
капуста **6** 3
карандаш **23** 33; **76** 24
карандаш для бровей **23** 26
карандашная точилка **83** 30
кардинал **64** 11
Карибское море **70** 20

карман **21** 41
карниз **34** 1
Карское море **70** 31
карта мира **70–71**
картина **28** 5
картонная коробка **12** 1
картотека **47** 4
картотечная карточка **47** 6
картофель **7** 25
картофель жареный (соломка) **18** 28
картофельное пюре **18** 17
карусель **87** 5
каска **42** 12; **82** 4
Каспийское море **70** 27
касса **15** 21, 26; **54** 5
касса для продажи жетонов **54** 13
кассета **100** 26
кассета с фотопленкой **100** 10
кассир **86** 15
кассирша **15** 22
кастрюля **30** (с ручкой) 8, 13
кататься (на коньках, роликах) **97** 9
катер **59** 16
каток **94** 25
кафельная плитка **34** 26
качели **87** 16
каштан **9** 32
каяк **59** 17
квадрат **79** 9
«квортербек» (главный нападающий **93** 32
кегельбан **94** 4
кегля **94** 5
кенгуру **66** 3
Кентукки **72** 17
кепка **19** 2
«кетчер» **92** 3; **93** 16
кетчуп **16** 4
кизил **61** 28
кино **100C**
кинокамера **100** 15
кинопроектор **100** 16
киоск (будка) по сбору платы за пользование дорогой **53** 27
кипятить (воду) **31** 16
кирка **82** 13
кирпичи **82** 12
кисточка **76** 18
кисть **37** 30
кисть бананов **9** 20
кисть винограда **8** 1
кит **68** 9
кишечник **5** 67
клавиатура **98** 1a; **100** 33
клаксон **52** 5
кларнет **98** 16
клей **37** 33; **76** 17
клен **61** 38
клерк **83** 23
клетка **24** 22
клетчатый **24** 18
клешня **62** 13a
клипсы **23** 15
клубника **8** 15
клык **66** 17b
клюв **64** 3a, 24a
клюква **8** 13
клюшка **92** 18
клюшка с сеткой для захвата мяча **92** 16
клюшки **95** 5
кнехт **58** 26
книжечка **13** 17
книжечка спичек **16** 28
книжная полка **28** 22
книжные полки **83** 20
книжный магазин **45** 18
кнопки **101** 13
коала **66** 1
кобачок «цуккини» **7** 27
кобра **65** 11
кобура **43** 8
ковбой **81** 21
ковер **28** 15; **32** 28
коврик **34** 12; **50** 22
коготь **68** 2a
кожаный ботинок типа мокасина **21** 42
кожица **9** 37a
кожура **8** 8b; **9** 20a, 37a
коза **67** 28
козел **67** 28
кокон **63** 2
кокосовый орех **8** 3
колбаса **10** 7
колготки **19** 14; **22** 5
колено **4** 19
колесо **52** 4
колибри **64** 2
количества **12–13**
колонка **53** 14
Колорадо **72** 6
колпак **50** 36
колыбель **33** 26
колышек **89** 30
кольцо (-а) **23** 2; **74** 16a
кольцо невесты **23** 3
колючка **60** 18c
командный отсек **75** 8
комар **63** 13
комбайн **81** 17
комбинация **22** 10
комбинезон (рабочий) **21** 5
комета **74** 2
коммутатор **83** 3
комнатные растения **61** 39
комод **32** 9, 30
компьютер **76** 8; **83** 7, 16
конвейерная лента **15** 23
конверт **83** 31; (дляавиапочты) **46** 16
Конго **71** 62
кондиционер **32** 11
кондуктор **54** 7
конечная зона **93** 23
коническая колба **78** 2
Коннектикут **72** 7
консервный нож **30** 4
консервы **14** 13
контейнер **58** 7
контейнеровоз **58** 9
контора **83**
контрабас **98** 10
контрольная башня **57** 20
контрольный стол **47** 2
конус **79** 28

конус для перекрытия
дороги **82** 19
конфорка **30** 29
коньки **19** 15
копать **26** 3
копировальная машина
47 18; **83** 24
копытные млекопитающие **66**
копыто **67** 35b
кора **61** 35c
корень **61** 35d
корзина **14** 8; **92** 20
корзина для белья **35** 29
корзина для входящей работы,
корреспонденции **83** 12
корзина для грязного белья
34 28
корзина для мусора **34** 13
корзина для пикника **88** 13
коридор **76** 12
коричневый **104**
корма **58** 11
коробка (картонная) **13** 12
корова **67** 32; **81** 11
короткая клюшка **94** 9
короткий **24** 1
короткий рукав **20** 21
корреспондент **86** 11
корыто **81** 25
корыто для краски **37** 28
косилка (для травы) **27** 12
косить **26** 6
косметика **23**
косметические салфетки **32** 13
космическая станция **75** 1
космические летательные
аппараты **75A**
космический зонд **75** 4
космический челнок **75** 14
космический челнок «Шаттл» **75C**
космическое пространство **74A**
космонавт **75** 5
костер **89** 31
косточка **9** 37b
костыль **39** 7
костюм аквалангиста **91** 38
кот **68** 4
котенок **68** 5
кофе **18** 35
кофейник **29** 18; **30** 31
кофейный стол **28** 26
кочан цветной капусты **6** 1
кочерыжка кукурузного початка
6 12a
кошелек **20** 23
краб(-ы) **11** 36; **62** 9
крайний левый нападающий
93 24
крайний правый нападающий
93 30
кран **16** 20; **58** 6
кран горячей воды **34** 17
кран холодной воды **34** 18
красить **26** 1
краска **37** 31
красное дерево **61** 25
Красное море **70** 29
красный **104**
крахмал **35** 21
креветка **11** 31; **62** 8
крепление **95** 16
крем для бритья **23** 22
крем для загара **91** 39
крес водяной (жеруха) **6** 5
кресло на колесах **39** 2
кресло с откидной спинкой
28 16
кресло-качалка **33** 16
кривая линия **79** 3
кризантема **60** 4
кровать **32** 21
кровельная дранка **82** 2
крокус **60** 9
кролик **66** 13
кроссовки **20** 11
крошить **31** 11
круг **79** 11
крупное фермерское хозяйство
«ранчо» **81C**
крыжовник **8** 11
крыло **52** 10; **57** 9; **63** 4a;
64 1a
крыло (курицы) **11** 22
крыльцо **27** 6
крыса **66** 7
крыша **27** 4
крышка **30** 9
крючки для занавески **34** 2
крючок **32** 1; **36** 16
крючок и петля **101** 14
ксилофон **98** 31
куб **79** 27
кубик **33** 32
кувшин **29** 4
кувшинчик для сливок **29** 24
кузнечик **63** 6
кукла **33** 28
кукольный домик **33** 25
кукуруза **60** 24
кулек (бумажный) **15** 25
кулинарно-гастрономический
отдел **14** 1
купальный костюм **90** 18
купальный халат **22** 20
курица **11** 24; **64** 23
куртка **19** 17
куртка с капюшоном **19** 8
кусок **13** 18, 21, 22
кусок говядины для жаренья **10** 3
кусок мяса для жаренья **10** 5
кусок рыбы для жаренья **11** 29
кусок свинины для жаренья **10** 8
кусты **61** 41
кухня **30**
кухонный стол **30** 27
кушетка (для медицинского
осмотра) **39** 6
лабораторный стакан **78** 23
лабораторный стол **78** 24
ладонь **4** 29
лайм **8** 10
лак для ногтей **23** 25
«лакросс» (Американская игра,
изобретенная индейцами) **92**
лама **66** 15
лампа **28** 28
лампочка **35** 22
лапа **69** 29a

ларь **15** 16
ласт **68** 12f
ласты **68** 10a; **91** 36
латук **6** 6
лебедка **58** 23
лебедь **64** 28
лев **68** 3
левый блокировщик **93** 25
левый полузащитник **93** 26
левый ряд **53** 5
легкая атлетика **94**
легкие закуски **15** 18
легкое **5** 63
ледяная (дорога) **25** 16
ледяной **25** 16
ледяной компресс **41** 4
лезвие **94** 27
лезвия для бритья **23** 23
лейка **27** 16
лейкопластырь **39** 4
лекарство **41**
Лена **71** 66
леопард **68** 1
лепесток **60** 18b
леса **82** 7; **89** 32
леска **88** 8
лесной орех **9** 30
лестница **28** 12; **35** 1; **42** 1; **82** 8
летающие млекопитающие **66**
лето **26**
летучая мышь **66** 4
летччк **56** 15
лечения и лекарства **41**
лилия **60** 3
лимон **8** 9
лимская фасоль **6** 16
линейка **76** 23
линейный корабль **48** 5
линейный монтер **82** 17
линза **100** 6
линии **79A**
линии высоковольтной передачи **80** 24
линия подачи **95** 3
лиса **68** 6
лист **61** 36a
литавра **98** 21
«Литтл Лиг» (соревнования по бейсболу для детей) **92**
лифт **45** 1; **80** 9
лифчик **22** 13
лицо **4** 1
личный состав **48B**
лоб **4** 32
ловить **96** 4
лодка **59** 18
лодочный спорт **59**
лодыжка **5** 49
ложка **29** 8
локоть **4** 8
лопата **27** 31; **82** 15
лопатка **27** 21
лосьон для загара **91** 39
лосьон после бритья **23** 21
лошади **81** 23
лошадиная упряжка **55** 33
лошадиные бега **94**
лошадь **67** 21
Луизиана **72** 18
лук **7** 31
луковица **60** 8a
Луна **74** 9
лунка **94** 8
лунное затмение **74** 6
лунный модуль **75** 7
лыжа **94** 33; **95** 17
лыжник **94** 35
лыжный ботинок **95** 15
лыжный подъемник **95** 18
лыжный склон **95C**
люстра **29** 3
лютик **60** 17
лягушка **65** 17
ляжка **4** 18
магнит **78** 27
магнитофон **100** 22
магнолия **61** 29
мазь **41** 9
май **104**
майка **20** 13; **21** 29; **22** 1
маис **60** 24
макароны **18** 10
маленький **24** 7
маленький блокнот **83** 25
малина **8** 16
малиновка **64** 9
мальчик **2** 8
маляр **85** 7
малярный ролик **37** 29
манго **8** 5
мандолина **98** 4
манекенщица **86** 5
Мариленд **72** 20
марка **46** 10
марлевые прокладки **39** 25
Марс **74** 14
март **104**
маска для подводного плавания **91** 35
маска кетчера **92** 3
масло **18** 18
Массачусетс **72** 21
мастер **84** 2; **85** 13
мастерская **36–37**
матрац **32** 17
математика **79**
материки **70**
матрос **48** 14
мать **3** 4
мачта **59** 8
машина для сушки белья **35** 24
машинист **55** 15
машинистка **83** 6
машинное масло **80** 33
машины и боевая техника **48A**
маяк **58** 14
медведи **69**
медведь-гризли **68** 23
медиатор **98** 11a
медицинская лопатка **40** 12a
медицинский спирт **39** 22
медицинское обслуживание **39**
медные инструменты **98**
медработник **42** 7
медсестра **39** 19
медуза **62** 12
между (подушками) **102** 4
междугородная автострада (-ое) шоссе **53** 1

Мексиканский залив **70** 19
мел **76** 10
меню **16** 7
менять постель **38** 13
Меркурий **74** 11
мести **38** 7
место в ложе **99** 11
место для пикника **88**
место для свидетелей **43** 18
место подачи **95** 1
месяцы **104**
метелка из перьев **35** 2
метеор **74** 5
метеоролог **86** 1
метеорологический спутник **75** 3
метка для мяча **95** 13
метла **35** 7
метро **54**
механик **84** 2
механический лобзик **36** 3
меч-рыба **65** 3
мешать **31** 1
мешетчатая крыса **66** 8
мизинец **4** 28; **5** 55
микроволновая духовка **30** 23
микроскоп **78** 30
микрофильм **47** 13
миксер **30** 12
миллиметровка **78** 11
миллион **104**
миндаль **9** 31
Миникам™ миникамера **100** 2
Миннесота **72** 23
миска **30** 24
Миссисипи **71** 58; **72** 24
Миссури **73** 25
Мичиган **72** 22
мишка **33** 3
младенец **2** 5
младший официант **16** 3
млекопитающие **66–69**
многоножка **63** 22
модельер **86** 6
мозг **5** 57
мокрая (дорога) **25** 15
мокрый **25** 15
моллюск(-и) **11D, 11** 34; **62** 3
молодой олень **67** 27
молоко **14** 5
молоток **36** 13; **43** 12
молочная ферма **81A**
молочные продукты **14** 4
моль **63** 21
монеты **13** 26
монорейльс **55** 29
Монтана **73** 26
море Бофорта **70** 15
море Лаптевых **70** 33
морж **68** 11
морковь **7** 32
мороженое в вафельном стаканчике **18** 36
мороженое с фруктами, сиропом, орехами **18** 23
морозильник **14** 3; **30** 20
морозный **25** 11
морская звезда **62** 7
морская пехота **48** 18
морские млекопитающие **68**
морские продукты **10–11, 11C**
морской вокзал **58** 29
морской конек **65** 1
морской пехотинец **48** 19
моря **70**
мотель **90** 3
моток **101** 24
мотор **52** 32
моторая лодка **59** 13
мотороллер **52** 29
мотоцикл **52** 30; **53** 19
мочалка **30** 11; **34** 7
мочевой пузырь **5** 72
муж **2** 3; **3** 12
мужская рама **52** 11
мужские трусы **22** 2
мужской костюм с жилетом **21** 40
мужчина **2** 2
музыка **99**
музыкальная комедия **99B**
музыкальные инструменты **98**
музыкальный автомат **16** 12
музыкант **99** 10
муравей **63** 12
муравьед **66** 5
мускул **5** 62
мусорная корзина **35** 31
мусоровоз **49** 6
мусорщик **49** 7
муха **63** 18
мыло **34** 15
мыльница **34** 6
мыть **26** 2
мышеловка **35** 32
мышь **66** 9
Мэн **72** 19
мягкая игрушка **33** 27
мягкое крепление **89** 22
мясник **84** 13
мясо **10–11, 10A**
мясо для тушения **10** 4
мяч **92** 10, 13, 21, 22, 26; **94** 1, 7, 19, 30
на (ковре) **102** 5, (столе) 10 (площадку) **103** 9
на борту **56**
набор инструментов для препарирования животных **78** 33
наволочка **32** 15
нагрудник **33** 20
над (черным котом) **102** 2; (водой) **103** 6
надувной плот **59** 20
надувной матрац **91** 26
наждачная бумага **37** 27
название **47** 9
наклейка **46** 21
накрывать (на стол) **17** 8
наливать **31** 4
намазывать **17** 11
наперсток **101** 21
напитки **14** 14
наполнять **26** 9
нарезать **31** 6
наручники **43** 4
насекомые **63**
насморк **40** 11
насос **52** 21
насыпь для питчера **93** 11

научная лаборатория **78**
наушники **19** 10; **100** 29
Небраска **73** 27
Невада **73** 28
невестка **3** 8
нектарин **8** 17
непромокаемая куртка **19** 5
Нептун **74** 18
несущий винт **57** 2a
нефтоочистительный завод **80** 12
нефтяная скважина **80** 1
нивелир **82** 3
Нигер **71** 61
нижнее белье **22**
нижняя рубашка **22** 9
нижняя юбка **22** 8
низкий **24** 12
Нил **71** 63
нипель **52** 27
новолуние **74** 26
новый **24** 13
нога **4** 17; **5E**
нога баранья **10** 14
нога (курицы) **11** 21
ноготок **60** 6
ноготь **4** 23; **5** 56
нож **29** 15
нож для открывания бутылок **30** 6
ножницы **101** 17
ножницы для ногтей **23** 31
ножовка (для металла) **36** 18
ноздря **4** 37
ноль **104**
номер дома **45** 24
номерной знак **50** 28
нос **4** 36; **58** 5
носилки **39** 12
носильщик **56** 5
носильщик бит **93** 18
носить **26** 16
носки **22** 17
носовая часть **57** 8
носорог **66** 16
ноты **98** 2
ночевка на открытом воздухе **89**
ночная сорочка **22** 21
ноябрь **104**
Нью-Гемпшир **73** 29
Нью-Джерси **73** 30
Нью-Йорк **73** 32
Нью-Мексико **73** 31
нырять **97** 14
Обь **71** 64
обвиняемый **43** 23
обезьяна **69** 14
обжигаться **17** 14
облачный **25** 2
оборудование **89** 27
обочина **45** 26; **53** 22
обратный адрес **46** 8
обручальное кольцо **23** 4
обслуживающий персонал **53** 12
овал **79** 18
овес **60** 23
овощи **6–7**
овощи и фрукты **14** 9
овощной гарнир **18** 16
овощной магазин **45** 28
овощной салат **18** 13
овца **67** 25; **81** 10
овчарка **69** 28
Огайо **73** 35
огнетушитель **42** 11
огнеупорное пальто пожарника **42** 13
огонь **28** 9; **42** 5
ограда **81** 9
огурец **7** 20
одежда **20–21**
одеяло **32** 20
один **104**
одинадцать **104**
однотонная (ткань) **24** 20
одноэтажный дом **27A**
ожерелье **23** 6
ожог **40** 18
озноб **40** 4
океанский лайнер **58** 27
Океаны **70**
Оклахома **73** 36
окно **27** 7; **46** 15
окно на крыше **51** 44
Окрашенная пустыня **71** 49
округ Колумбия **73** 51
окружность **79** 17
октябрь **104**
олень **67** 26
омар **11** 30; **62** 13
оператор **86** 10
операция **41** 2
описание одежды **24**
опора **52** 9
оптик **84** 9
опускной киль **59** 6
орангутан **69** 18
оранжевый **104**
орбита **74** 21
орган **98** 29
Орегон **73** 37
орел **64** 5
орех кешью **9** 27
орехи **9**
оркестр **99** 6
ороситель **27** 13; **87** 14
орудийная башня **48** 12
оружие и боеприпасы **48C**
орхидея **60** 12
оса **63** 20
осел **67** 23
осень **26**
основание **79** 7
основные готовые продукты **18**
остролист **61** 37
острый угол **79** 8
осьминог **62** 6
от (лунки) **103** 5
отбеливатель **35** 26
отбивающий **92** 7; **93** 14
отверстие для почты **46** 13
отвертка **37** 24
отвертка для винта с крестовым шлипцом **37** 25
отец **3** 5
отвесная скала **89** 21
отворот **20** 1
отец **3** 5
откидной столик **56** 22
открывать **31** 3
открытая кабина **75** 10

открытие космоса **75**
открытый **24** 15
отпечатки пальцев **43** 24
отпечаток **100** 11
официант **16** 2, 5, (-ка) 32
охладительная башня **80** 16
охотничья поисковая собака **69** 26
Охотское море **70** 35
охрана **56**
охранник **56** 9; **86** 14
очки **21** 44
очковая змея **65** 11
павлин **64** 18
падать **96** 7
падуб **61** 37
пакет **12** 8; **13** 13, 16
палатка **89** 24
палец **5** 54
палка **94** 34; **95** 14
палочки с ватой **33** 10
палуба **58** 22
пальма **61** 26
пальто **19** 20
панда **69** 20
панцирь **65** 18a
папая **8** 6
папка **83** 22
параллельные линии **79** 4
Парана **71** 60
парашют **48** 6
парикмахер **84** 3
парикмахерша **84** 10
пароварка **30** 3
паром **58** 17
партер **99** 12
партитура **98** 2
парус **59** 9
парусная лодка **59** 4
пассажир **54** 6; **55** 25; **56** 3
пассажирская машина **53** 15
пастбище **81** 6
пастух **81** 21
пастушка **81** 22
паук **63** 16
паутина **63** 15
пациент **39** 20
пачка **12** 4, 5; **13** 16
певец (-ица) **99** 24
педаль **39** 18; **52** 19
педаль газа **50** 27
педаль сцепления **50** 25
педаль тормоза **50** 26
пекарь **84** 8
пеленка **33** 13
пеленка одноразового пользования **33** 12
пеликан **64** 24
Пенсильвания **73** 38
пепельница **16** 29
первая четверть луны **74** 23
перед (камином) **102** 6
передавать **96** 5
передвижной буфет **49** 8
передние ноги **66** 3d
передние фары **51** 48
передний бампер **51** 51
передняя спинка **32** 14
переключатель сигнала поворота **50** 11
переключатель скоростей **50** 17
перекресток **44** 11
перелом кости **40** 15
пересадочный билет **54** 4
пересечение по типу «кленового листа» **53** 4
переход **44** 4
перец **7** 22
перечница **29** 9
перила **28** 11
перископ **48** 8
перо **64** 7a
перпендикулярные линии **79** 2
Персидский залив **70** 28
персик **9** 37
персональный компютер **100** 31
перчатка **94** 11
перчатки **19** 1
перчаточный ящик **50** 20
песок **91** 31
песочница **87** 13
песчаная дюна **90** 12
песчаное углубление вокруг лунки **95** 11
песчаный замок **91** 32
петлица **101** 8
петля **101** 8
петуния **60** 7
петух **64** 21
печатать на машинке **77** 10
печатное устройство **83** 4
печеная картошка **18** 20
печеные продукты **14** 11
печень **5** 65
печенье **18** 22
печь **31** 14
пешеход **44** 12
пианист(-ка) **99** 22
пиво **16** 23
пиджак **20** 2
пижама **22** 19
пикап **49** 4
пикколо **98** 12
пилильщик **62** 4
пилот **56** 15
пилочка (для ногтей) **23** 24
пилюля **41** 7
пингвин **64** 27
пинг-понг **94**
пинцет **78** 32
пипетка **78** 14
пирамида **79** 25
пирс **58** 3
писатель **86** 7
писать **77** 7
пистолет **43** 7
письменный стол **28** 14; **76** 16; **83** 13
письмо **46** 7
«питчер» **93** 12
пить **17** 2
питьевой фонтан **87** 19
пицца **18** 30
пишущая машинка **83** 10
пищевод **5** 61
плавание на плотах **89**
плавать под водой **97** 14
плавки **91** 33
плавник **65** 3b; **68** 12a
пламя **29** 26; **78** 21
план **82** 6
планер **57** 4

планеты **74**
пластинки **100** 4
платить **17** 7
платформа **54** 11
платье **20** 22
плащ **21** 38
плевательница **39** 16
плейер **100** 30
племянник **3** 13
племянница **3** 14
плечо **4** 5
плитка **13** 18
пловец **91** 28
пловчиха **91** 28
плодовое дерево **81** 2
плоскогорье **88** 1
плоскогубцы **36** 19
плот **89** 6
плотина **80** 18
плотник **85** 2
площадка **94** 13
площадка для игр **87** 15
плунжер **35** 14
Плутон **74** 19
плющ ядоносный **61** 45
пляжа **90; 91**
пляжное полотенце **90** 15
пляжный зонт **90** 21
пневматический молот **82** 22
по (мосту) **103** 8
повар **16** 1
повышенное кровяное давление **40** 10
повязка **39** 3
повязка для головы **20** 12
погремушка **33** 21
под (белым котом) **102** 3
под (маяком) **103** 1
под (письменным столом) **102** 8
подавать **17** 3; **96** 2
подбородок **4** 3
подвесная доска с крючками **36** 15
подвесная карусель с игрушками **33** 2
подвесной мотор **59** 12
подводная лодка **48** 7
подголовник **50** 35
поджелудочная железа **5** 71
подлокотник **50** 3
подметка **20** 6
подмышка **4** 10
поднимать (руку) **77** 1
подниматься (на холм) **103** 11
поднос **16** 33
подозреваемый **43** 3
подрезать **26** 8
подрубочный шов **101** 12
подсвечник **29** 28
подсобное помещение **35**
подсолнечник **60** 19
подставка **16** 27
подушечка **5** 52
подушка **32** 16
подшивка **83** 22; **101** 11
подъездная аллея **27** 1
подъем **5** 51
подъемник **82** 18
поезд **55C**
пожар **42** 5
пожар и спасение при пожаре **42**
пожарная лестница **42** 4
пожарная машина **42** 3
пожарник **42** 10
пожарный насос **42** 2
пожарный рукав, шланг **42** 8
поймать **96** 4
покупатель(-ница) **15** 17
пол **32** 29
поле американского футбола **93B**
поле бейсбола **93A**
поле гольфа **95B**
поле (пшеницы) **81** 16
поливать **26** 5
полировать **38** 3
полицейский **43** 6
полицейский участок **43A**
половина (курицы) **11** 17
половина (1/2) **79** 30
полосатый **24** 17
полочка для мела **76** 9
полка **14** 6; **47** 11, 17, 26
полнолуние **74** 24
полусредний нападающий **93** 34
полюс аккумулятора **51** 55
поля и площылки **95**
полярний медведь **69** 22
помидор(-ы) **7** 19
понедельник **104**
пони **67** 20
попугай **64** 16
порез **40** 16
пороги **89** 17
портниха(-ной) **84** 6
портфель **21** 37
посадка на Луне **75B**
посадочный талон **56** 18
последняя четверть луны **74** 25
постель **32** 21
постельное покрывало **32** 23
постельный режим **41** 1
посуда **29** 1
посудное полотенце **30** 18
посудный шкаф **29** 2
посудомоечная машина **30** 1
посылка **46** 19
посылка срочной почты **46** 23
посыльный **86** 19
посыпать песком **26** 14
потолок **28** 2
походная плитка **89** 25
початок кукурузы **6** 12
почка **5** 70
почта **44** 9; **46B, 46** 2
почта Соединенных Штатов **46**
почтальон **46** 3
почтовая открытка **46** 17
почтовая сумка **46** 4
почтовый грузовик **46** 5
почтовый индекс **46** 12
почтовый работник **46** 14
почтовый штемпель **46** 9
почтовый ящик **46** 1, 6
пояс **20** 16
пояс для чулок **22** 14
правый блокировщик **93** 29
правый полузащитник **93** 28
правый ряд **53** 6
предлоги движения **103**

предлоги описания **102**
предмет **47** 10
предметное стекло **78** 31
предметы домашнего обихода **15** 15
предохранительная загородка **33** 5
предплечье **4** 9
преступность и наказание **43**
приборная панель **50** 19
приборы **56** 14
пригородный поезд **55** 14
приемник **100** 21
призма **78** 1
приматы **69**
прилавок **16** 24
прилагательные, описывающие погоду **25**
принадлежности туалета и косметика **23B**
принимать **17** 10
принтер **83** 4
природный газ **80** 29
приспособления к пылесосу **35** 17
присяжные **43** 21
притирание **41** 9
прихватка **30** 34
прицеп (жилой) **53** 10
причал **58** 3
прищепки **35** 20
пробирка **78** 9
пробка **16** 18; **34** 10; **78** 10
пробор **4** 31
проволока **37** 35
проволочная сетка **78** 6
программист **86** 16
прогулочная коляска **45** 27
продавец **86** 12
продавец в цветочном магазине **84** 11
продавец фруктов и овощей **84** 7
проектор **76** 27
прожектор **99** 4; **100** 13
проигрыватель **100** 18
проигрыватель для компактных дисков **100** 28
производство энергии **80B**
прокурор **43** 17
пропан **80** 30
простые животные **62**
простыня **32** 19
противосолнечный щиток **50** 5
протокол **43** 15
профессии **85–86**
прохладный **25** 9
проход **14** 10; **56** 23
пруд **87** 8
пружинный матрац **32** 18
прыгать **96** 8
прыгать (в воду) **97** 14
пряжа **101** 31
пряжка **20** 17
прямая линия **79** 1
прямой угол **79** 23
прямоугольник **79** 19
прямоугольный треугольник **79** 22
птенец **64** 22
птицы **64**
пугало **81** 19
пуговица **20** 3; **101** 9
пулемет **48** 25
пульверизаторная банка **13** 24
пуля **48** 26
пустыни **71**
пустыня Атакама **71** 50
пустыня Гоби **71** 54
пустыня Мохаве **71** 48
пустыня Руб-эль-Хали **71** 52
пустыня Сахара **71** 51
пустыня Такла Макан **71** 53
пустышка **33** 22
путепровод **53** 3
путешествующий на попутных машинах, автостопом **53** 9
пушка **48** 11
пчела **63** 19
пшеница **60** 22
пылесос **35** 16
пылесосить **38** 14
пятидверный автомобиль-комби **51E**
пятка **5** 50
пятнадцать **104**
пятница **104**
пять **104**
пять центов **13** 28
пятьдесят **104**
пятьсот **104**
работа на заводе **85C**
рабочие ботинки **21** 32
рабочие перчатки **27** 26
рабочий **85** 12
радиатор **51** 56
радио **50** 18
радиус **79** 14
радужная оболочка **5** 47
разбивать **31** 7
разводной ключ **36** 12
разновес **78** 5
разносчик **85** 10
разрезать **31** 9
ракетка **75** 13
«ракетбол» **94**
ракетка **94** 2, 18, 29
ракушка **62** 1a; **91** 40
рама (для картины) **28** 4
распечатка **83** 8
расписание **55** 20
распределительный щит **83** 3
раствор для мытья окон **35** 10
растения **60–61**
растяжение связок **40** 13
расческа **32** 6
«раф» (непостриженная трава на краю поля) **95** 6
рвать (цветы) **26** 3; (бумагу) **77** 9
реактивный двигатель **57** 11
реактивный самолет **57** 18
ребенок **2** 5
ребра **10** 10
регулировщик **44** 10
редиска **7** 29
резать **31** 9
резинка **76** 21
резиновая трубка **78** 18

резиновые сапоги **19** 25
резиновый бинт **40** 13a
резиновый молоток **36** 11
резиновый пояс **22** 15
резьба **37** 42b
реки **71**
рельсы **54** 10
ремень **54** 8
ремень безопасности **50** 23
ремесла **101**
ремешок для часов **23** 11
ремонт **85A**
ремонтировать **38** 10
ремонтный мастер **84** 5
рентгеновский снимок **39** 1
рентгеновский детектор **56** 11
репа **7** 34
репортер **86** 11
ресницы **5** 46
ресторан **16A**
рефери **94** 16
рефлектор **52** 25
речные сапоги **88** 10
ринг **94** 17
Рио-Гранде **71** 57
рис **60** 21
рисовать **77** 11
рог **66** 16a; **67** 35a
рога **62** 1b
Род-Айленд **73** 39
родители **2** 6
рождественские цветы **60** 15
рожки **62** 1b
роза **60** 18
розетка **32** 26b; **36** 6
розовый **104**
роковая группа **99C**
ролик кинопленк **100** 17
ромашка **60** 5
ронжа **64** 8
рот **4** 2
рояль **98** 1
рубанок **37** 32
рубашка **21** 46
рубить **26** 11; **31** 11
рука **4B**, **4** 6
рукавица **27** 20; **30** 34; **92** 4, 12
рукавицы **19** 11
руководитель **83** 18
рукоделие **101B**
рулевая колонка **50** 13
рулетка **36** 21
рулон **12** 11
руль **50** 8; **52** 2; **59** 5
румяна **23** 32
ручей **88** 6
ручка управления **50** 24
ручная вышивка гарусом по канве **101** 26
ручная граната **48** 29
ручная пила **36** 8
ручная тележка **95** 8
ручное полотенце **34** 23
ручной багаж **56** 2
ручной мяч **94** 12
ручной тормоз **52** 24
ручной фен **34** 26
рыба (-ы) **11** 26; **65A**
рыбак **58** 2
рыболовная сеть **88** 9
рыболовное судно **58** 1
рыболовство **88**
рыбы и пресмыкающиеся **65**
рюкзак **19** 4
рюкзак с рамой **89** 28
рюмка **29** 5
ряд **81** 18
рядовой военно-воздушных сил **48** 20
с **103** (горы) 3, (площадки) 10
садовник **85** 3
садовые ножницы **27** 29
садовый совок **27** 27
сажать **26** 4
саксофон **98** 24
саламандра **65** 14
салат **6** 6
салатница **29** 25
салфетка **29** 14
самолет с винтовым двигателем **57** 7
самолеты **57**
самосвал **49** 14
санитарка **39** 8
сантехник **85** 1
сантиметр **101** 15
сапоги **19** 21
сарай **81** 5
сарай для инструментов **27** 28
Сатурн **74** 16
сахар (в бумажном пакете) **16** 13
сахарница **29** 23
сахарный тростник **60** 20
свежезамороженные продукты **14** 2
свекла **7** 33
сверло **37** 43a
сверчок **63** 5
светлый **24** 9
светлячок **63** 17
светофор **45** 21
свеча **29** 27
свидетель **43** 13
свинина **10** 6
свиные отбивные **10** 9; **18** 15
свинья **67** 30
свисток **90** 5
свитер **19** 7, (с высоким воротом) 13, 23
сгребать **26** 10, (снег) 13
север **71** 71
Северная Америка **70** 1
Северная Дакота **73** 34
Северная Каролина **73** 33
Северное море **70** 21
Северный Атлантический океан **70** 11
Северный Ледовитый океан **70** 8
Северный Тихий океан **70** 9
седло **94** 20
секретарша **83** 11
секретарь судебного заседания **43** 14
секция **79** 15
секция периодики **47** 15
сельдерей **6** 10

сельское хозяйство **81**
семнадцать **104**
семь **104**
семьдесят **104**
семья **3**
сентябрь **104**
сердце **5** 64
сердцевина **8** 2b
серый **104**
серьга **23** 16
серьги **23** 1
серьги на стержне **23** 18
сестра **3** 10
сетка **27** 19; **92** 23; **95** 2
сигарета **16** 31
сигнал заднего хода **50** 30
сигналы поворота **51** 50
«Си-Ди» (компактный диск) **100** 24
сиденье **50** 16; **52** 16; **54** 2
силос (зерновой) **81** 4
синий **104**
синтезатор **99** 21
«синька» **82** 6
синяк **40** 17
синяк под глазом **40** 5
сироп **18** 5
Скалистые горы **71** 40
скалка **30** 25
скамейка **87** 10
скамья **44** 14
скамья для команды **93** 13
скамья присяжных **43** 20
скат **65** 6
скатерть **29** 16
скафандр космонавта **75** 6
складная линейка **36** 1
складная коляска **33** 14
складной саквояж **56** 1
складывать **38** 1
скоблить **26** 15
сковорода **30** 5
скорая помощь **42** 6
скоросшиватель **76** 14
скорпион **63** 8
скрепер **36** 14
скрепки для бумаг **83** 28
скрести **26** 15
скрипка **98** 7
скунс **68** 8
слайды **100** 12
следователь **43** 2
слесарные тиски **37** 36
слесарь **85** 4
слива **9** 34
слизняк **62** 4
словарь **47** 24
слоеный торт с клубникой **18** 26
слон **66** 17
служащий **86** 13
слушать **77** 6
смазывать **38** 12
смеситель **30** 12
смотритель парка **88** 5
смычок **98** 7a
смягчитель для белья **35** 27
снаряд **48** 27
снегоочиститель **49** 5
снежный **25** 3
снимать (кожицу) **31** 5
собаки **69**
сова **64** 6
совок для мусора **35** 8
Соединенные Штаты Америки **72–73**
созвездие **74** 3
сойка **64** 8
солдат **48** 16
соленый огурец **18** 8
солист(ка) **99** 24
солнечная система **74B**
солнечное затмение **74** 10
солнечный **25** 4
солнечный элемент **80** 17
солнце **74** 7; **80** 3
соломинка **16** 10
солонка **29** 10
сорок **104**
соска для бутылки **33** 18
сосна **61** 34
сосновая шишка **61** 34b
сотейник **30** 14
«софтбол» **92**
спальный мешок **89** 26
спальня **32**
спаниель **68** 24
спаржа **6** 20
спасательная шлюпка **58** 19; **90** 10
спасатель(-ница) **90** 6
спасательный жилет **59** 1
спасательный круг **90** 9
спидометр **50** 10
спина **4** 11
спинной мозг **5** 58
спиртной напиток **16** 22
спица **52** 26
спортивная машина **53** 17
спортивные брюки **20** 10
спортивные поля **93**
спортивные соревнования между командами **92**
спортивный свитер **20** 8
спортсмен, занимающийся серфингом с парусом **59** 14
справочник адресов (на ролике) **83** 14
справочный отдел **47** 21
справочный стол **47** 22
спусковой крючок **48** 23
спутник связи **75** 2
среда **104**
Средиземное море **70** 24
средний нападающий **93** 33
средний палец **4** 26
средний ряд **53** 6
средняя разделительная баррикада **53** 18
средства массовой информации **86**
ставень **27** 8
стадо (коров) **81** 20
стакан **13** 20; (воды) **29** 6
станция метро **44** 16
станция технического обслуживания **53** 11
стартовая площадка **75** 15
стартовые ворота **95** 20
старый **24** 14
ствол **37** 43b; **48** 23; **61** 35b

стебель **60** 1a
стеганое одеяло **32** 22
стеганый жилет **19** 12
стежок **101** 19
стеклоочиститель **50** 6
стелить (постель) **38** 8
стена **28** 3
стенд для велосипеда **52** 14
стенка **28** 19
стереомагнитофон **100** 25
стереофоническая система
28 20
стержень **23** 18
стетоскоп **39** 9
стиральная машина **35** 30
стиральный порошок **35** 25
стирать **38** 16; **77** 3
сто **104**
стог сена **81** 13
стоимость проезда **55** 21
стойка **16** 24
стойка ворот **93** 35
стойка регистрации **56A**
сток **34** 9
стол **29** 7
стол для пеленания **33** 9
стол за перегородкой **16** 9
столовая **29**
столовое серебро **29** 22
стоп-сигнал **50** 29
сторона **79** 10
стоянка **45** 19
стоянка такси **55** 28
стояночные огни **51** 49
стояночный счетчик **45** 20
стояночный тормоз **50** 15
страус **64** 12
стрекоза **63** 4
стрелять **97** 16
стремянка **35** 1
строитель **82** 5
строительная площадка **82A**
строительный рабочий **82** 14
строительство **82**
струна **98** 10a
Струнные инструменты **98**
стручковая фасоль **6** 15
стручок **6** 17a
стул **29** 17
стул для машинистки **83** 17
ступень **28** 13
ступенька лестницы **82** 9
суббота **104**
суд **43B**
судебный пристав **43** 19
судейская мантия **43** 11
судейский стол **43** 17
судья **43** 10; **92** 2;
93 17, 22;
94 16
сук **61** 35a
сумах ядоносный **61** 44
сумка **21** 35; **56** 2; **66** 3c
сумка для завтрака, обеда **21** 31
сумка для клюшек **95** 7
сумка для покупок **20** 18
сумка-холодильник **91** 41
сундук для игрушек **33** 29
суспензорий **22** 4
сустав пальца **4** 22
сухое печенье **18** 27
сухой **25** 14
сушеные фрукты **9**
сушилка **30** 2
сходня **58** 20
сцена **99** 5
счет **15** 20; **16** 14; **55** 24
счетчик **55** 23
сшивание лоскутов **101** 32
сшиватель **83** 27
съедобный морской
моллюск **11** 32
сын **3** 16
сыпь **40** 1
Сьерра-Мадре **71** 42
таблетка **41** 6
табурет **78** 34
табурет у прилавка **16** 25
таймер **78** 13
«тако» **18** 24
такси **55D**, **55** 27
таксист **55** 26
талия **4** 13
тальк **33** 7
тамбурин **98** 17
танк **48** 10
танкер **58** 15
тапочки **22** 18
таракан **63** 9
тарелка (для хлеба) **29** 11, 13
тарелки **98** 18
тачка **27** 32; **82** 23
театр **99**
театральная программа **99** 17
текстовой редактор **83** 7
телевизионная антенна **27** 3
телевизор **28** 18; **100** 5
телеграфный столб **80** 26
тележка **15** 19; **56** 6
теленок **67** 31
телескоп **74** 22
телефон **32** 26; **83** 15
телефон-автомат **44** 7
телефон с наушниками **83** 2
телефонистка **83** 1; **86** 17
тело **4A**
темные очки **90** 14
темный **24** 10
температура **25** 6; **40** 2
тени **23** 33
тени для век **23** 30
Теннесси **73** 42
теннис **94**
теннисный корт **95**
тепло **80** 27
теплый **25** 8
тереть **31** 2
термит **63** 11
термометр **25** 5; **78** 22
термос **88** 14
терьер **69** 25
тесный **24** 3
тетрадь **76** 15
тетя **3** 6
Техас **73** 43
тигр **68** 2
тиски **36** 9
ткань **101** 4
ткать **101** 30
топливо для реактивных
двигателей **80** 31

тополь **61** 30
топор **36** 17; **42** 14
тормоз **52** 17
тост **18** 34
тостер **30** 16
точилка **76** 20
трава **27** 15
травы (кулинарные) **6** 9
травы и зерна **60**
трактор **81** 15
трамвай **55** 30
транспортер **56** 12
транспортировщик автомобилей **49** 17
трансформатор **80** 25
трап **58** 20
тренер **93** 21
тренировочные колеса **52** 1
треть (1/3) **79** 32
треугольник **79** 6
трехколесный велосипед **52** 6
три **104**
трибуны для зрителей **93** 10
тридцать **104**
тринадцать **104**
трогать **77** 2
тромбон **98** 23
трос **52** 23; **58** 25
тротуар **45** 25
труба **27** 9; **98** 25
трубка **16** 26; **91** 34
трусики **22** 12
трусики-бикини **22** 11
трусы **22** 3
трюм **58** 8
тряпки **35** 4
тряпочка для мытья тела **34** 22
туалет **32** 9
туалетная бумага **34** 30
туалетная щетка **34** 31
туба **98** 27
туманный **25** 12
тумбочка **32** 27
тупой угол **79** 5
туристы **88** 2
турникет **54** 12
туфли на высоких каблуках **20** 25
туфля **21** 49
тушь для ресниц **23** 28
тыква **7** 26
тысяча **104**
тюбик (зубной пасты) **13** 15
тюбик с насосом (зубной пасты, жидкого мыла) **13** 14
тюлень **68** 12
тюльпан **60** 1
тюрьма **43** 1
тягач **49** 15
у (окна) **102** 1, (телевизора) 11
убирать (посуду со стола) **17** 6
уборщик **85** 9
увеличительное стекло **78** 15
угловой столик **28** 29
угол (улицы) **44** 3
уголь **80** 7
угольная шахта **80** 6
угорь **65** 4
ударные инструменты **98**
ударять **96** 1; (ногой) **96** 3
удилище **88** 7
удлинительный шнур **36** 5
удочка **88** 7
узор **24** 21
указатель уровня бензина **50** 9
указатель уровня масла **51** 58
указательный палец **4** 25
уключина **59** 21
укол **41** 8
укус насекомого **40** 3
улитка **62** 1
улица **45** 31
уличная тележка **87** 4
уличный фонарь **45** 29
уличный указатель **44** 8
уличный торговец **87** 3
умывальная раковина **34** 19
универмаг **44** 5
унитаз **34** 29
упаковки **12–13**
упаковочная лента **46** 22
управляющий **83** 18
Урал **71** 46
Уран **74** 17
урановые стержни **80** 15
урна **44** 15; **87** 11
устрица (-ы) **11** 33; **62** 2
устройство для сигнала при пожаре **33** 15
усы **4** 40
утка **11** 25; **64** 25
утюг **35** 12
ухо **4** 34
участник «Литтл Лиг» **92** 8
учебник **76** 26
ученик **76** 19
учительница **76** 4
ушиб **40** 17
фагот **98** 14
фазан **64** 19
фазы луны **74C**
фартук **16** 6
фарш говяжий **10** 2
фасоль обыкновенная **6** 13
февраль **104**
фермер **81** 7
фестонные ножницы **101** 5
фиалка **60** 16
фигурное катание **94**
Фигуры **79C**
филе **11** 28
фильтровальная бумага **78** 16
финик **9** 23
финиш **93** 15; **95** 21
финишная прямая **95** 19
фиолетовый **104**
флаг **76** 1
флажок **82** 20; **95** 9
фламинго **64** 29
фланелевая рубашка **19** 3
флейта **98** 13
Флорида **72** 9
фонарь **35** 3; **89** 29
форель **65** 2
форма **21** 45; **92** 9
форма (для запекания мяса) **30** 17

форма для льда **30** 21
фотоаппарат **100** 8
фотограф **86** 4
фотография **100B**
фрезерный станок **37** 37
«фризби» (летающая тарелка) **90** 13
фрикадельки **18** 11
фруктовый сад **81** 1
фрукты **8–9**
фужер для вина **29** 5
фундамент **82** 11
фуникулер **55** 32
фуражка **21** 43; **92** 11
фургон **50C; 53** 26
футбол **92**
футболка **21** 29
фюзеляж **57** 14
хвост **65** 3a; **66** 3a
хвостовая часть **57** 10
хвоя **61** 34a
хлеб **14** 12
хобот **66** 17a
ходить **77** 8
ходунок **33** 23
ходьба на лыжах **94**
хоккей с шайбой **92**
холм **88** 4
холодильник **30** 19
холодный **25** 10
хор **99** 18
«хот-дог» (булочка с сосиской) **18** 2
Хуанхэ **71** 68
художник **86** 3
цвета **104**
цветная капуста (кочан) **6** 1
цветы **60**
целая (курица) **11** 16
целая рыба **11** 27
целое **79** 29
цемент **82** 10
цент **13** 27
центр **79** 13
центр площадки **95** 12
центральный нападающий **93** 27
цепочка **23** 5
цепь **52** 18
цилиндр **79** 26
цинния **60** 13
цитрусовые фрукты **8**
цифры **104**
цыпленок **64** 22
чаевые **55** 22
чай **16** 15
чайка **64** 4
чайник **29** 19; **30** 28
частные дома **27**
частный самолет **57** 3
часть выкройки **101** 6
часы **23** 10; **76** 2
чашка **13** 19; **29** 20
чашка Петри **78** 3
чек **15** 27
человек и семейные отношения **2**
человеческое тело **4–5**
челюсть **4** 38
чемодан **56** 7
червь **62** 11
червяк **62** 11
через (мост) **103** 8
черепаха **65** 12, 18
черешок **8** 2a
черника **8** 14
Черное море **70** 26
чернослив **9** 22
черные бобы **6** 14
черный **104**
черный медведь **69** 21
черта ограничения поля **93** 9
чертежная кнопка **76** 25
чеснок **7** 25
четверг **104**
четверть (курицы) **11** 18; (1/4) **78** 31
четыре **104**
четырнадцать **104**
«чипсы» (жареная хрустящая картошка) **18** 4
чистить **38** 2
чистый **24** 6
чистящее средство **35** 9
читать **77** 4
чулки **22** 5
шайба **37** 40; **92** 17
шампунь **34** 8
шапочка для душа **34** 3
шар **94** 6
шариковая ручка **76** 22
шарф **19** 19
шасси **57** 15
шахтный ствол **80** 10
швабра с губкой **35** 6
швартовная бочка **59** 19
швартовная тумба **58** 26
швейная машина **101** 1
швейцар **85** 11
шверт **59** 6
швы **39** 21
шезлонг **27** 27; **90** 20
шерсть **101** 23
шерстяная кофта **21** 26
шесть **104**
шестьдесят **104**
шестнадцать **104**
шестьсот двадцать один **104**
шея **4** 4
шимпанзе **69** 16
шина **50** 37; **52** 28
шинковать **31** 10
шип **60** 18c
ширина **79** 35
широкий **24** 4
шитье **101A**
шифр **47** 7
шкатулка для драгоценностей **32** 4
шкаф (стенной) **32** 3
шкафчик **30** 22
шланг **27** 14; **42** 8; **51** 57
шлем **21** 28; **52** 7; **82** 4; **92** 14
шлем отбивающего **92** 6
шлифовать **38** 3
шлифовальный станок **37** 26
шляпа **19** 18
шнур **32** 26a

шнур для сигнала остановки **54** 1
шнурок **20** 7
шов **101** 10
шорты **20** 14
шофер **49** 16
шпинат **6** 8
шприц **39** 27
шпулька **101** 2
штатив **78** 19; **100** 9
штатив для пробирок **78** 8
штепсельная вилка **37** 43d
штопор **16** 17
штора **33** 1
шторы **32** 12
штык **48** 24
щека **4** 35
щенок **69** 27
щетка для волос **32** 7
щеточка для ногтей **34** 20
щипцы **78** 28, 29
щипцы для удаления скобок **83** 29
щит **92** 19
щупальце **62** 12a
эвкалипт **61** 27
ЭВМ **83** 16
«эгг рол» **18** 25
экватор **71** 70
экипаж **75** 12
экономка **85** 8
экран **100** 14, 32
экскаватор **82** 26
электрик **85** 6
электрическая гитара **99** 26
электрическая дрель **37** 43
электрическая пила **27** 25
электрический генератор **80** 21
электроника **100**
электростанция **80** 20
электроэнергия **80** 32
энергия **80**
энергопродукты **80C**
энциклопедия **47** 25
эскароль (салат) **6** 7
эстрада **99** 5
эстрада для оркестра **87** 2
этикетка **46** 21
юбка **21** 36
ювелир **84** 12
ювелирные изделия **23A**
юг **71** 72
Южная Америка **70** 2
Южная Дакота **73** 41
Южная Каролина **73** 40
Южно-Китайское море **70** 39
Южный Атлантический океан **70** 12
Южный Тихий океан **70** 10
Юкон **71** 56
Юпитер **74** 15
Юта **73** 44
яблоко **8** 2
ягненок **67** 24
ягодицы **4** 15
ягоды **8**
ядерный реактор **80** 13
ядовитые растения **61**
ядро реактора **80** 14
язык **4** 41
яичница (глазунья) **18** 32
яйцо **64** 13
якорь **58** 24
ялик **59** 18
ямс **7** 24
январь **104**
Янцзы **71** 69
Японское море **70** 36
ястреб **64** 7
ящерица **65** 15
ящик для инструментов **36** 23
ящик для хранения документов **83** 21